Corporate Restructuring
and the Role of Labour Law

Corporate Restructuring and the Role of Labour Law

Bulletin of Comparative Labour Relations, 47

Editor: R. Blanpain
Guest Editors: T. Araki
               S. Ouchi

Contributors
C. Barnard
F. Gaudu
Y.H. Lee
C-P. Liou
J. Riley
S.J. Schwab
M. Shi
B. Waas
R. Yamakawa

2003
Kluwer Law International
The Hague/London/New York

Published by:
Kluwer Law International
P.O. Box 85889, 2508 CN The Hague, The Netherlands
sales@kli.wkap.nl
http://www.kluwerlaw.com

Sold and Distributed in North, Central and South America by:
Kluwer Law International
101 Philip Drive, Norwell, MA 02061, USA
kluwerlaw@wkap.com

Sold and Distributed in all other countries by:
Kluwer Law International
Distribution Centre, P.O. Box 322, 3300 AH Dordrecht, The Netherlands

A C.I.P. Catalogue record for this book is available from the Library of Congress.

Printed on acid-free paper

ISBN 90-411-1949-3

© 2003 Kluwer Law International

Kluwer Law International incorporates the imprint Martinus Nijhoff Publishers

Printed and bound in Great Britain by Antony Rowe Limited

Introduction

1. THE 6TH JIL TOKYO SEMINAR: CORPORATE RESTRUCTURING AND THE ROLE OF LABOUR LAW

This issue of the *Bulletin of Comparative Labour Relations* is a collection of papers submitted to the sixth Comparative Labour Law Seminar (JIL Tokyo Seminar)[1] on "Corporate Restructuring and the Role of Labour Law." The seminar was organised by the Japan Institute of Labour and held on 19–20 March 2002 in Tokyo, Japan.

The discussion in the two-day seminar focused on business reorganisation and the role of labour law in Europe, America and Asia (Germany, France, UK, USA, Australia, China, Korea, Japan, Taiwan). The term "corporate restructuring" as used in this seminar is broadly defined. It includes mergers, transfers of undertakings (selling of business to another person), corporate divisions, outsourcing, closing down of a department or section, and other corporate restructuring measures. The seminar discussion covered the legal frameworks regulating corporate restructuring, succession of employment contracts, collective dismissals before and after corporate restructuring, changes in terms and conditions of employment, and issues in collective labour relations such as negotiation or consultation with labour unions or other worker representatives.

All of the papers presented at the seminar basically follow the same outline.

i.   Introduction
ii. Outline of the regulations regulating corporate restructuring
     Legal framework governing corporate restructuring:
     – corporate law
     – labour law
     – special legislation concerning transfers of undertakings, etc.

---

1.   The JIL Tokyo Seminar was originally organised by Professor Sugeno (the University of Tokyo, Faculty of Law) and Professor Suwa (Hosei University, Faculty of Sociology) who were at that time senior research fellows at the JIL in 1991. Papers submitted to the third, fourth and fifth Tokyo Seminars were published in the Bulletin of Comparative Labour Relations: "Working Life and Family Life: Policies for their Harmonisation" in Bulletin of Comparative Labour Relations No. 30 (1995); "The Process of Industrialisation and the Role of Labour Law in Asian Countries" in Bulletin of Comparative Labour Relations No. 34 (1999); and "Deregulation and Labour Law" in Bulletin of Comparative Labour Relations No. 38 (2000).

R. Blanpain (ed.),
Corporate Restructuring and the Role of Labour Law, 1–14.
© 2003 *Kluwer Law International. Printed in Great Britain.*

iii. Corporate Restructuring and Succession of Employment Contracts

In the event of a merger, a transfer of business or undertakings, or other forms of corporate restructuring, are employment contracts automatically transferred?

Are there any regulations requiring the succession of employment contracts in the event of transfer of business or undertakings?

Key issues related to the implementation of EC directive 77/187 (Acquired Rights Directive) in EU Member States such as its application in the public sector and to insolvent corporations.

iv. Economic Dismissals before and after Corporate Restructuring

Issues concerning external or numerical flexibility and transfers of undertakings. For example:
- regulations related to economic dismissals in general
- economic dismissals before and after the transfer of undertakings
- role of labour unions or employee representatives such as works councils in these processes

v. Changes in Terms and Conditions of Employment

Issues concerning internal or functional flexibility to cope with corporate restructuring without resorting to dismissals. For example:
- transfer of workers
- modification of terms and conditions of employment
- changes in duties
- special issues arising in the event of transfer of undertakings

vi. Conclusion

Features of your country's labour law policy with regard to corporate restructuring.

2. SUMMARY OF NATIONAL PAPERS

The key issue of this seminar was how each country strikes a balance between two often conflicting needs: the need to increase corporate competitiveness and efficiency through restructuring, and the need to protect affected workers.

2.1. European countries: Germany, France and UK

Various approaches to this issue were reported. On the one hand, as typified by the existence of the Transfer of Undertaking Directive, there is the "EU model", in which the law intervenes to protect workers' interests in the event of corporate restructuring. Three EU Member States, the UK, France and Germany, have statutes that generally prohibit dismissals without just cause or socially justifiable reasons. The employment at will doctrine has been abandoned. In addition, the EC directive concerning transfers of undertakings

2001/23[2] provides three kinds of protections: (1) automatic transfer of the employment relations from the transferor to the transferee, which means protection and maintenance of current working conditions (Article 3); (2) protection from dismissal due exclusively to a transfer of the undertakings unless there is an economic, technical or other organisational reason (Article 4); and (3) transferor and transferee's obligation to inform and consult with the representative of employees (Article 7). The European Court of Justice interprets the scope of the EC directive broadly to cover various types of corporate restructuring including mergers, transfers of undertakings, corporate divisions and other types of corporate restructuring. Only few cases, such as those involving insolvency or bankruptcy, are exempted from the application of the law required by the EC directive (Article 5). Therefore, workers' interests in the event of corporate restructuring are highly protected under the national legislation implementing the EC directive.

However, the Directive aims to achieve partial, not complete, harmonisation and entrusts various prerequisites for the application of the Directive to the Member State's regulations. For instance, while the protection provided by the Directive presupposes that employees are protected against unjust dismissals, whether or not an individual employee is covered by a nation's protective law against unjust dismissals depends on that nation's legislation.[3] Although the Transfer of Undertaking Directive states that a "transfer of the undertaking, business or part of the undertaking or business shall not in itself constitute grounds for dismissal by the transferor or the transferee," it does not prohibit "dismissals that may take place for economic, technical or organisational reasons entailing changes in the workforce" (Article 4(1)). Therefore, dismissals for economic reasons are permitted and their regulation is again entrusted to national legislatures. Automatic transfer of employment relations from the transferor to the transferee does not freeze the terms and conditions of employment at the time of transfer. Where previous working conditions were regulated by collective agreements, those working conditions must be maintained for at least one year after the transfer (Article 3(3)). However, a new collective agreement can modify the previous working conditions, and after the lapse of the one-year period, modification through the normal legal tools becomes possible. The specific regulations concerning variation of terms and conditions of employment are also entrusted to national regulations. As a result, among EU Member States, there exists a variety of regulations and employee protections that reflect each individual nation's regulation of dismissals and methods of altering working conditions.

The German paper by Bernd Waas describes highly protective legal institutions. After analysing various regulations, inter alia, those of the Act on Business Reorganisation (Umwandlungsgesetz), Waas's paper examines

---

2.   Codifying and repealing Directive 77/187 as amended by Directive 98/50. As for the details of the EC law on transfer of undertakings, see Catherine Barnard, EC Employment Law, 446ff (Oxford, 2000).

3.   For instance, while German law provides protection against socially unjustified dismissal to employees with 6 months' service, French law requires 2 years' service in the case of economic dismissals, and UK law requires 1 year's service in the case of unfair dismissals.

3

restrictions on socially unjustified dismissals regulated by the Act on Termination Protection 1969 (Kündigungsschutzgesetz). Socially unjustified dismissals are null and void. As for economic dismissals, German law also provides highly developed protections including the works councils' involvement. With regard to transfers of undertakings, Article 613a, Civil Code prescribes special regulations that implement the EC Directive. Waas mentions the most recent amendment of Article 613a in 2002, which obliges the transferor or transferee, respectively to inform each employee individually of the imminent transfer and the consequences in terms of working conditions. After examining the important role of labour unions and especially works councils' codetermination rights in the event of alteration to the establishment (Betriebsänderung), Waas concludes that "the leading principle of German labour law is to protect the affected employees as far as possible from the detrimental consequences" of corporate restructuring, but that since such protection hampers corporate restructuring, whether employees really benefit in the long run is an open question.

The French paper by François Gaudu, after giving an overview of corporate law framework, confirms that the measures concerning corporate restructuring are basically made by the management or by the shareholders and no obligation to bargain or to allow workers' participation exists. However, a workers council (comité d'entreprise) has the right to information and consultation on all the significant matters concerning corporate restructuring. The laws of 15 May 2001 and 18 January 2002 extend the rights of works councils to include the right to be consulted before the board of directors decides to close down a department or section, to bring the disagreement to arbitration in certain cases, to request the convention of a stockholder meeting, and so forth. Art. L. 122-12 al. 2 of the French Labour Code, which has its origin in the 1928 law that was influenced by German law, requires the succession of employment contracts in the event of a transfer of business or plant. However, dismissals are possible if reasons other than the transfer exist. Once the transfer is made, the new employer can dismiss the workers following ordinary law. Under the French law, economic dismissals requires three conditions: (1) real and serious economic reasons, (2) redundancy procedures including consultation with works councils, and (3) "reestablishment" measures represented by the "employment keeping scheme" including transfer of workers, changing working conditions, transfers of workers to other companies of the holdings, outplacement, reducing working hours and so forth. As for the modification of terms and conditions of employment, Gaudu stresses that French law recognises employers' strong unilateral power. Although the modification of the employment contract such as changes in wages, working time or general definition of work, requires the agreement of the worker, the modification in working conditions such as working schedules or in the place of work can be unilaterally changed. Finally, Gaudu evaluates the French law situation relative to other nations' labour systems and concludes that it is less protective than the German or Northern European systems but more protective than the systems in the UK or USA.

The UK paper by Catherine Barnard, after reviewing the legal framework governing corporate restructuring in corporate law, examines wrongful dismissals related to violations of the notice period requirement and unfair dismissals regulated by the statutory provisions requiring fair reason for dismissals such as redundancy and the so-called SOSR ("some other substantial reason"). In the case of potentially fair reasons, the key criterion is whether the employer acted reasonably in the circumstances. The UK courts take the position that the employer is protected as long as its acts fall within a "band of reasonableness." They generally refrain from substituting the courts' judgement for that of the employer. As for the transfer of undertakings, the TUPE (Transfers of Undertaking (Protection of Employment) Regulations 1981) transposes the EU Directive into UK national law. Barnard also notes that empirical research has shown that TUPE's prohibition of variations of working conditions due to a transfer is against employees' interest "because it makes businesses harder to sell and therefore jobs hard to rescue." With regard to economic dismissals before and after the transfer of undertakings, employers must make a redundancy payment if the employee is dismissed by reason of redundancy. Among other things, whether or not a job disappears raises difficult legal issues. The UK courts have adopted the so-called "function test" and "if the job is not less but the method of doing is different or the terms are different that is not a redundancy situation and so the individual receives no redundancy pay." In the case of work reorganisation falling under the heading of SOSR, therefore, employees receive neither redundancy pay nor unfair dismissal compensation. Based upon comprehensive analyses including regulations in insolvency and in varying terms and conditions of employment, Barnard concludes that the striking feature of the UK law lies in the reinforcement of managerial prerogatives although the law provides for limited compensation and certain procedural hurdles.

2.2. United States

On the other end of the scale, there is the "American model" in which employers face few restrictions when reorganising or restructuring corporations. During corporate restructuring, workers enjoy little legal protection. As the American paper by Stewart Schwab notes, "in the United States less than 10% of the private-sector workforce is unionised. Almost all private-sector non-union workers are employed 'at will,' meaning the employer can dismiss workers at any time for any reason, without notice. To be sure, the past 30 years have seen significant erosions to the at-will doctrine... But these erosions on employment at will need not detain us here, because no American court would ever construe a dismissal because of internal business reorganisation as a wrongful discharge in violation of public policy or inconsistent with implied-contract or good-faith obligations of the employer." Anti-discrimination statutes are rarely at issue when companies merge or consolidate operations with occasional exceptions for age discrimination claims. Therefore, "the basic at-will status of American employees creates much flexibility for employers wanting to restructure operations.... Employers have complete flexibility on the number of workers they choose to dismiss or transfer to other positions. There is no regulation of transfers of workers, modifications of terms and conditions of employment, or changes in duties."

There are no special regulations requiring automatic transfer of the employment nor regulations prohibiting dismissals by reason of a transfer of undertakings. Employee protections are confined to the following. Large employers must generally give 60 days' notice of plant closings and mass terminations. Displaced workers receive unemployment benefits and protection on transferring health insurance benefits. In the unionised sector (less than 10% of the American private-sector workforce), successor firms may have to recognise and bargain with the union, and, depending on how the transaction is structured, may be bound for the remaining duration of the predecessor's collective bargaining contract. Therefore, Schwab concludes American law offers fewer legal protections of workers during corporate restructuring than the laws of most industrialised countries. The first section of Schwab's paper explains the labour law situation in the context of corporate governance prioritising shareholders' interests. The paper quotes a comparative survey in which senior managers were asked whether "shareholders' interest should be given first priority." In America, 76% of managers declared that shareholders' interests have top priority, compared to 71% in the UK, 22% in France, 17% in Germany, and 3% in Japan.[4]

2.3. Asian countries: Japan, Korea, Taiwan, China, and Australia

In Asian countries, there exists a variety of approaches to regulating corporate restructuring and employment relations. One of the common features in Asian countries is that the classic freedom of employers to dismiss is limited through legislation or case law. In this respect, Asian countries' situations differ from the American model. However, in the event of a transfer of undertakings or a corporate division, normal regulations on dismissals do not apply directly. Therefore, whether employment contracts are succeeded or not and terms and conditions of employment are maintained or not is determined through special regulations or judicial interpretation in each country. Dismissals and modification of working conditions before and after the corporate reorganisation also differ from country to country.

---

4. Allen F. & Gale D., Corporate Governance and Competition, Ch. 2 in X. Vives (ed.), Corporate Governance: Theoretical and Empirical Perspectives (Cambridge Univ. Press 2000), and is reported in Marco Pagano & Paolo Volpin, The Political Economy of Finance, 17 Oxford Review of Economic Policy 502, 507 (2001).

2.3.1. Japan

The Japanese paper by Ryuichi Yamakawa, after giving an overview of the major issues arising from merger and transfer of business undertakings, explains a new legal scheme called "division of corporation" introduced by the amendment to the Commercial Code and a new statute called the "Labour Contract Succession Law" enacted to protect workers' interests as they are affected by the division of a corporation. The main points of the Labour Contract Succession Law are as follows. As regards employees who have been engaging mainly in the work of the department to be split off and are excluded from the subject of transfer under the division plan or division contract, they have the right to file an objection to such exclusion. However, they do not have the right to exclude themselves from the transfer if they are included. On the other hand, employees who have been engaging only ancillarily in the work of the department to be split off, and yet are included under the division plan or contract in the subject of transfer, have the right to file an objection to such inclusion. Since the effect of the division of a corporation is an automatic succession of the rights and duties that constitute the business undertaking, the employment contract of an employee is succeeded by the transferee with his/her working conditions unchanged. With respect to collective labour relations, the law states that, unlike the case of a transfer of business undertakings, consultation with workers or majority unions is necessary in carrying out the division of corporation.

The validity of economic dismissal in the case of business reorganisation is determined under the case-law doctrine of abusive dismissal. In Japan, although neither the Civil Code nor the Labour Standards Law has a general provision that limits the grounds for dismissal of employees, Japanese courts have established a case-law principle called the "doctrine of abusive dismissal." The Supreme Court endorsed this as a formal doctrine holding that, "even when an employer exercises its right of dismissal, the dismissal will be void as an abuse of the right if it is not based on objectively reasonable grounds and cannot receive social approval as a proper act." Furthermore, in the context of economic dismissals, courts have introduced four requirements that an employer must satisfy in order to carry out such dismissals. An employer must establish: (1) the necessity of a reduction-in-force, (2) that it has made a good faith effort to avoid dismissals, (3) that it used a reasonable standard in selecting workers to be dismissed, and (4) that it made adequate efforts to explain and persuade the employees in order to obtain their understanding. However, Yamakawa points out that economic dismissals are less likely to happen in the case of corporate divisions. In order to utilise the corporation division scheme, the transferor and transferee are required to demonstrate that both corporations are financially competent to perform the obligations they will assume after the division.

With respect to the change of working conditions, the Japanese Supreme Court has established a unique rule, according to which workers are bound by provisions in the work rules that are unilaterally revised by their employer

7

regardless of their acceptance, if such revised work rules are "reasonable." According to the Yamakawa's analysis, when the new company (transferee) needs to unify the working conditions of those employees who come from the transferor and those who were its original employees, the necessity to change working conditions, which is one of key criteria of the reasonableness test, may be easily satisfied.

2.3.2. Korea

The Korean paper by Young Hee Lee describes the very interesting legislative changes in corporate restructuring law in the 1990s. Korea faced an urgent need for corporate restructuring, in order to get out of the financial crisis that occurred at the end of Young Sam Kim's regime. A new government, launched in February of 1998 and led by Dae Jung Kim, attempted to reform restrictions on business restructuring as part of the overall social and economic reforms. These reforms were undertaken not only to fulfill its promise to the IMF in return for its relief assistance, but also for the new phase of national development in the 21st century.

Korea's labour law regulations had been cited as important factors that hampered necessary adjustments of human resources in business and prevented flexible management. Prohibition of discharges without justifiable cause made it difficult for enterprises to carry out the adjustment of human resources, and the equal application of labour law to all types of workers, namely regular, temporary or part-time workers alike, made it difficult for employers to reduce employment costs. In addition, the underdeveloped social security system hindering reallocation of workforce, inflexible regulations on working hours and high overtime premiums, as well as industrial actions by labour unions, made restructuring or reorganisation quite difficult. Based on these criticisms by employers, the government reformed the labour law in 1997 to create a more favourable environment for business activities and corporate restructuring. The reform included the enactment of a new law regulating dispatched workers, the strengthening of Employment Insurance Act, and the revision of the Labour Standard Act which introduced a flexible working hour system and relaxation of dismissal regulations. Under the new regulations, dismissals for managerial reasons, such as redundancy discharges, were recognised as justifiable dismissals. These reforms, according to Lee's paper, have nearly eliminated labour law regulations restricting corporate restructuring.

As for corporate restructuring, there are no regulations that impose on employers any obligation to seek the opinion of employees before making changes in the business. No specific provision regulates employment status in the case of business transfer. However, until the 1997 revision, because the Labour Standard Act (Art. 30(1)) prohibited discharges without justifiable reason, employers were not able to dismiss workers on the pretext of business transfer and new employers could not expel workers by simply refusing to take over employment relations from the transferor. Therefore, workers were able to maintain their employment status, even when their work place was transferred to a new undertaking. In contrast, the 1997 revision permits discharges due to urgent managerial needs. Moreover, it added a provision prescribing that transfers, acquisitions, and mergers undertaken in order to avoid the business difficulties will be regarded as an urgent managerial need (Labour Standard Act 31(1)). Although the discharge is permissible only when its aim is to avoid a worsening business situation, since the terms *"avoiding worsening business situation"* allow for a broad interpretation, employers may now discharge employees on the grounds of business transfer with little difficulty. Thus, Lee concludes that workers are no longer guaranteed the succession of employment relations in cases of business transfers. However, under the revised law, an employer must still make every effort to avoid dismissals of workers and apply fair and rational standards to select workers to be dismissed. The employer must also provide 60-days' prior notice to a trade union, and report to the Minster of Labour in the case of large-scale dismissals.

Lee's paper then points out several other measures aimed at changing employment conditions. These include: the increase in atypical employment to curtail labour cost and to make personnel adjustment easier; the so-called "retirement in honour" which induces older workers to voluntarily resign before the retirement age with more severance benefits than usual; the changing of employment rules to introduce working conditions unfavourable to workers which is, according to case law, allowed on the condition that such modifications are deemed socially reasonable; and, finally, the changing of working conditions through concluding collective agreements.

2.3.3. Taiwan

The Taiwanese paper by Chih-Poung Liou, after introducing the current legal regulations of corporate restructuring, explains the regulatory impact of two overlapping statutes: the Labour Standard Law of 1984 and the Corporate Mergers and Acquisition Act. In the case of a transfer of undertakings or a reorganisation, both the new employer and old employer have the right to determine which employees to retain, while the employees have no right to request the transferee to retain them. Employees not retained can be discharged with advance notice and a redundancy payment. In Liou's opinion, current law does not fully consider the protection of the rights of workers employed under the old employer.

As far as the regulation of dismissals is concerned, under a Civil Law principle both parties to a labour contract have the right to terminate the labour contract at any time, but the Labour Standard Law prescribes not only procedural requirements but also substantial requirements, i.e. reasonable cause. As for economic dismissals, the Labour Standard Law permits them in four circumstances: (1) a suspension or transfer of business; (2) a business contraction or the suffering of operating losses; (3) a business suspension due to force majeure; (4) a reduction in workforce necessitated by a change in the nature of business where assigning the terminated employees to other positions would be impossible. Liou stresses that under Taiwanese law employers have no duty to explain or negotiate with either workers or unions in the case of economic dismissals. However, the "Guidelines on Protection for Labour Against Mass Dismissal," an administrative order issued in 1999, established that an enterprise has a duty to notify a union or labour representatives when it intends to retrench a large number of workers for management reasons. Furthermore "the Draft of The Protection for Labour Against Mass Dismissal Act," which contains the procedural requirements such as an announcement of the dismissal plan and negotiation with the trade union, is being discussed in the parliament.

With respect to the change of working conditions, Taiwanese courts have established a case-law rule similar to the Japanese one. According to this judicial rule, where a reasonable basis for unfavourable changes of work rules exists, the employer can implement these changes without obtaining the employees' consent.

The Taiwanese government has facilitated corporate reorganisation with the aim of increasing efficiency and competitiveness. Although legislation gives trade unions the right to collectively negotiate over unfavourable changes in terms and conditions of employment, due to the current weak position of Taiwanese labour unions, this right is not sufficient to protect workers' interests. As a result, modification of working conditions is entrusted to the above-mentioned reasonable basis requirement. This ruling, according to Liou, allows employers to adjust work conditions according to the changes in the operating environment.

2.3.4. China

The Chinese paper, by Shi Meixia, describes the Chinese legal framework governing corporate restructuring. In China business reorganisation is basically regulated by the Company Law and the Bankruptcy Law. According to the Company Law, the merger or division of a company requires the adoption of a resolution by a meeting of the company's shareholders. A merger or division of a joint stock limited company must be approved by the department authorised by the State Council or by the people's government at the provincial level. The claims and debts of the parties to a merger shall pass to the absorbing company or the newly established company. Where a company proceeds into a division, its assets shall be divided correspondingly. Where a company decides to divide itself, it shall formulate a balance sheet and a detailed inventory of assets. The debts prior to the division of a company shall be assumed by the companies that result from the division in accordance with the agreement reached between them.

As for economic dismissals, labour law imposes some procedural requirements on an employing unit that comes to the brink of bankruptcy or runs deep into difficulties in production and management. These include: 30

10

days' advance explanation of the situation to the trade union or all of its staff and workers; reporting to the labour administrative department; prioritisation of re-employment of the reduced personnel; economic compensation in accordance with the relevant provisions of the State; the right of the trade union of an employing unit to express its opinions and request for reconsideration, etc.

From Shi's paper, it is not an easy task to analyse the Chinese legal system on business reorganisation from a comparative viewpoint. The Chinese system is characterised by the socialist market and its legal situation is completely different from that in other countries. One illustration of this uniqueness is that the most serious problem to be tackled is how to handle labour relations between the "state-owned" enterprises and laid-off workers.

2.3.5. *Australia*

In the Australian paper, Joellen Riley first confirms the common-law principle that if a business is sold to a new owner, or is restructured so that the legal personality of the employer changes, the employment contracts with workers will not be transferred automatically to the new owner or entity. Australian corporate law treats each company in a corporate group as a separate legal person. Even a holding company and its subsidiaries are treated as separate legal persons. The employees of one subsidiary have no claim as of right against other subsidiaries in the group, nor against the holding company. Only in those very rare circumstances where a court is willing to "lift the corporate veil" will one corporate group member be held liable for the obligations of another. As for dismissals, under the common law, employees have very limited rights to remedies if their employment contracts are terminated wrongfully by the employer. Essentially, they have a right only to payment for a period of "reasonable notice." There is no right under the common law to reinstatement, primarily because the common law will not specifically enforce a contract for personal services.

However, the weaknesses of the common law in protecting employee interests have been addressed to some extent by statutes federal or state awards made by tribunals, collective agreements certified by the Industrial Relations Commission or individual workplace agreements called AWAs. Reinstatement is possible in cases of unlawful or unfair dismissals such as those involving discriminatory reasons. However, where reinstatement is held not to be appropriate, a tribunal or court can award compensation in lieu of reinstatement.

As for transfers of undertakings, Section 149 of the Workplace Relations Act 1996 states that "subject to any order of the Commission," an award is binding on "any successor, assignee or transmittee (whether immediate or not) to or of the business or part of the business of an employer who was a party to the industrial dispute, including a corporation that has acquired or taken over the business or part of the business of the employer." It is understood that there must be substantial identity between old and the new business. The same applies to certified collective agreements (Section 170MB). Section 170VS also provides that a successor to a business will be bound by the terms of an AWA.

To illustrate the reality of Australian law on corporate restructuring, Riley cites two very interesting cases: the "Waterfront dispute" in 1997 concerning corporate manipulation to evade employers' liability and union allegations of infringement on the freedom of association, and the BHP case concerning introduction of individual agreements and a refusal to bargain with the union. Current Australian labour law and policy encourages workplace flexibility and facilitates restructuring, but Riley suggests the policy eroding union influence might cause further disputes before the parties concerned reach a tolerable compromise.

3. CORPORATE RESTRUCTURING AND THE ROLE OF LABOUR LAW

As seen above, three regions demonstrate notably different approaches towards corporate restructuring and worker protection thereunder. In the EU Member States, the freedom of dismissal no longer exists and employers are required to demonstrate just cause. Employment protection is extended to cases of transfers of undertakings by the EC Directive and national legislation implementing the Directive. Automatic transfers of employment contracts in the event of a transfer of undertakings or another form of corporate restructuring prohibits disadvantageous changes in terms and conditions of employment by reason of these transfers. These worker-protective regulations cover three forms of corporate reorganisations: mergers, transfers of undertakings and corporate divisions. These rules modifying the classic contract law theory illustrate the remarkable role of labour law in protecting workers' interests.

However, some questions have emerged as to whether the EC Directive's stringent and highly protective regulations serve the workers' interests in the long run. Rigid restrictions on curtailing workers and lowering working conditions might decrease the chance to sell off a business that faces economic difficulties, resulting in a bankruptcy which means a total loss of employment. Such concerns were voiced in the process of adopting the 98/50/EEC Directive, which amended the original 77/187/EEC Directive. As the UK paper reports, the 98/50/EEC Directive allows the Member States a wider range of options and allows social partners to agree to derogation from the Directive in the economic interests of the undertaking concerned. The UK government notes that the underlying aim of these options is to allow Member States to promote the sale of insolvent businesses as going concerns. These issues regarding the reconsideration of the impact of worker protection and corporate restructuring in the EU and its Member States are noteworthy.

On the other end of the spectrum, in the United States, there is little labour law intervention to protect workers' interest in the course of corporate reorganisation and restructuring. Flexibility, market function, and shareholder values seem to govern this issue in the United States.

It would be not proper to categorise diversified approaches found in Asian countries by the general term of "Asian model." On the one hand, dismissal regulations in Asian countries are, generally speaking, more restrictive than in the United States. On the other hand, worker protection in the event of corporate restructuring and reorganisation is not as stringent as in the EU. Therefore, it can be said that Asian countries are located somewhere between the US and EU models. However, the extent of dismissal protection in Asian countries differs from country to country. Worker protection in the case of corporate restructuring is further diversified. Several countries have introduced partial protection for workers. For instance, Japan's Labour Contract Succession Law, which provides for automatic transfer of employment status under certain conditions, applies only to corporate division cases and does not provide protection in the event of transfer of undertakings. In Korea, until the 1997 revisions designed to facilitate corporate restructuring, the requirement of just cause for dismissals was understood to prohibit dismissals by reason of transfer of undertakings. In contrast, the Taiwan and Australian papers stress the employers' freedom to restructure. With its socialist regime, China faces unique challenges in coping with the global economy, such as redundancy in state-owned corporations.

Comparison of the degree of worker protection between countries is not at all an easy task. It is not sufficient to look at the regulation at the time of transfer of undertakings. In the EU Member States where dismissals and variation of working conditions solely by reason of a transfer of undertakings are prohibited, workers' protection before and after the transfer differs according to the national labour laws. When dismissal is severely restricted and adjustment of working conditions is difficult, corporations will inevitably lose competitiveness in the global economy. In the EU Member States, there is a general trend to decentralise collective bargaining to enable swift and flexible responses to the need to adjust working conditions. However, in Europe, flexibility can only be introduced through negotiation with representatives of workers. In this context, it is notable that Japan, Korea and Taiwan have developed case law that allows employers' unilateral changes in terms and conditions of employment through "reasonable" modification of work rules. The problem of unilateralism can be criticised but its impact is mitigated by the requirement of "reasonableness" and court adjudication thereof. In Japan, this case-law rule that introduces internal flexibility, although a subject of some debate, can be justified as a compensation for the restraint on dismissals or the lack of external flexibility.[5]

---

5.   Takashi Araki, "Accommodating Terms and Conditions of Employment to Changing Circumstances: A Comparative Analysis of Quantitative and Qualitative Flexibility in the United States, Germany and Japan", in Engels C. & Weiss M. (ed.), *Labour Law and*

In any event, the question of how to strike a good balance between protecting workers and the necessity of corporate restructuring is the key issue in every country. The role of labour law in this context is not simply to protect workers, but rather to balance protection and efficiency in the nation's economy. As the debates over the amendment of the EC Directive suggest, it is necessary for contemporary labour law not to be short-sighted, and to consider not only short-term workers' interests but also workers' long-term interests. It is possible that facilitating corporate restructuring will serve workers' interests in the long run. How and where this balance is struck will differ depending on the labour markets, industrial relations, economic circumstances and social infrastructure in respective countries. We sincerely hope the various approaches described in the following chapters will serve to prompt further discussions on the role of labour law in the age of global competition.

August 2002

Takashi Araki
Professor, University of Tokyo
Senior Research Fellow, JIL

Shinya Ouchi
Professor, Kobe University
Senior Research Fellow, JIL

Industrial Relations at the Turn of the Century, Liber Amicorum in Honour of Prof. Dr. Roger Blanpain, 509 (Kluwer Law International, 1998).

1. Australia

Joellen Riley

1. INTRODUCTION

Like most western industrial nations in recent decades, Australia is experiencing the discomforting economic pressures of global competition. Successive Australian governments have recognised a need to foster greater efficiency and productivity in Australian enterprise, and to this end have pursued programs of competition policy, corporate law and, perhaps most contentiously, industrial law reform. The current industrial law reform agenda has attempted a major paradigm shift – from a system based on extensive union involvement in the making of arbitrated industry-wide awards and agreements, to a system of individual bargaining, underpinned by a safety net of minimum working conditions.[1] This program has not always run smoothly. The new laws have been tested in the context of privatisation of government enterprises, technology-led reorganisation of the delivery of banking services, and cost-saving reorganisations in traditional industries such as mining, manufacturing and stevedoring. And we have seen some spectacular industrial disputes.

The most spectacular dispute of recent times was the Waterfront dispute of 1998.[2] Described in the media as Australia's "war on the waterfront", this dispute epitomised the conflict between the interests of capital – in running lean efficient businesses – and the interests of organised labour in securing jobs and living standards. It demonstrated most poignantly the clash of classical corporate and contract law principles with legislation protecting labour interests. Paradoxically, it was legislation passed to help break up union power that provided the crucial tool used by the Maritime Union of Australia to fight for survival in this case.[3] So it offers a particularly relevant focus for the theme of this seminar: striking a balance between the need to promote competitiveness of corporations and the need to protect affected workers.

---

1. See Stephen Deery & Richard Mitchell (eds) *Employment Relations: Individualisation and Union Exclusion An International Study*, 1999; Martin Vranken, "Demise of the Australasian Model of Labour Law in the 1990s" (1994) 16 *Comparative Labor Law Journal* 1; D Nolan (ed) *The Australasian Labour Law Reforms: Australia and New Zealand at the End of the Twentieth Century*, 1998.
2. *Patrick Stevedores Operations No 2 Pty Ltd v MUA* (1998) 153 ALR 643.
3. The Freedom of Association provisions in Part XA of the *Workplace Relations Act* 1996 (Cth).

R. Blanpain (ed.),
Corporate Restructuring and the Role of Labour Law, 15–36.
© 2003 *Kluwer Law International. Printed in Great Britain.*

There were several combatants in the battle on the waterfront. Allied on one side were the employer companies (all subsidiaries of National Stevedore Holding Pty Ltd, itself a subsidiary of listed company Lang Corporation Ltd), the National Farmers Federation (NFF), and the Coalition federal government. The members of the NFF had a particular interest because traditionally they have been heavily dependent on waterfront services in earning export income, and they had taken steps to set up their own non-union stevedoring operations. On the other side was the Maritime Union of Australia (MUA), perceived by many in the Australian community as a powerful union which had secured unusually favourable working conditions and wages for its members as a result of its willingness to exercise considerable industrial muscle. The employer companies, allegedly encouraged by the government and the NFF, took advantage of Australian corporate law principles to restructure their businesses in a way that would enable them to dismiss the entire unionised workforce. The MUA was able to stall the employers' strategy by invoking their entitlements under industrial legislation, and in particular, potent new freedom of association laws.

In order to investigate the waterfront dispute in any detail, it is necessary to understand the essential features of Australian corporate law and employment law. Understanding the Australian system involves an appreciation of the interplay of common law principles and statutory developments. This paper first sets out the relatively weak common law position of employees (in Section 2), then the statutory developments which have modified and generally improved job security and income protection for employees (in Section 3). Many of those statutory rights (for instance, the right to reinstatement for unfair dismissal) are the product of earlier Labour government law reform, often won after years of lobbying by unions. Section 4 explains the principles of Australian corporate law relevant to employee interests, and Section 5 discusses the Waterfront dispute. A final Section 6 outlines the effect of the current federal government's endeavours to encourage a return to individual contracting between employers and employees as a means of improving national productivity.

2.   THE COMMON LAW EMPLOYMENT CONTRACT

2.1.   Nature of the employment contract

Australian law conceptualises the relationship between the corporate employer and the employee as a contract. The doctrine of privity of contract means that only those parties entering into the contract will be bound by its terms. Whereas the common law will recognise the assignment of other types of commercial contracts (for instance, loan agreements), contracts for the provision of personal services are not assignable at law or in equity. If a business is sold to a new owner, or is restructured so that the legal personality of the employer changes, the employment contracts with workers will not be transferred automatically to the new owner. Instead, the contract between the original employing entity and the employee will be treated as being terminated, and a new contract will be entered into between the new employing entity and the employee. If an employee is entitled to any accrued benefits under the original employment contract, the original employer will be legally liable to pay. Any agreement to carry over liabilities to the new employing entity requires the consent of the employee. Employees who accept work with the new employer will not enjoy any legal right to a continuation of their old terms and conditions of employment unless they are entitled to the benefit of an award or industrial agreement, and the new employer is a "successor" to the old. (See Section 3 below for an explanation of awards and agreements, and the transmission of business provisions.)

2.2. Companies as parties to employment contracts

It is important to remember that Australian corporate law treats each company in a corporate group as a separate legal person.[4] Even a holding company and its subsidiaries are treated as separate legal persons. The employees of one subsidiary have no claim as of right against other subsidiaries in the group, nor against the holding company. Only in those very rare circumstances where a court is willing to "lift the corporate veil" will one corporate group member be held liable for the obligations of another.[5] After the Waterfront dispute, the Australian Labour Party (in opposition in the federal parliament) attempted on several occasions to introduce legislation which would lift the veil between companies in a group, to make parent or sibling companies liable to meet obligations to employees in certain circumstances.[6] But these proposals have never been fully debated. As the law stands, any corporate restructuring which involves the creation of new subsidiaries to employ workers, or the transfer of business assets and/or liabilities between existing members of a corporate group, will involve a change in the legal personality of the employer party to the employment contract. Such a change will mean that original employment contracts are terminated, and only the original employing entity will be liable to meet accrued entitlements of employees. If that entity is insolvent, employees will generally have no right to claim against other solvent companies in the group. In an exceptional case, employees may be able to demonstrate that a holding company exercised such control over the employer subsidiary that it should be liable to creditors of the subsidiary under insolvent trading

---

4. See *Walker v Wimborne* (1976) 137 CLR 1 at 6–7; *Industrial Equity Ltd v Blackburn* (1977) 137 CLR 567; *Pioneer Concrete Services Ltd v Yelnah* (1986) 5 NSWLR 254; *Adams v Cape Industries Plc* [1991] 1 All ER 929 at 1019.

5. For a discussion of the law applying to corporate groups see Farrar, John H "Legal Issues Involving Corporate Groups" (1998) 16 *Corporations and Securities Law Journal* 184–206.

6. Arch Bevis, ALP Federal Member for Brisbane, and an ALP Senator, Jacinta Collins, tabled identical private member's bills, both named the Employment Security Bill 1999, following the Waterfront dispute. Leader of the ALP, Kim Beazley, tabled the Corporate Responsibility and Employment Security Bill 2001 on 24 September 2001.

provisions in Part 5.8 of the *Corporations Act* 2001 (Cth), particularly Section 588V. The requirements of the insolvent trading provisions are notoriously difficult to establish, and there are statutory defences (in Section 588X).

2.3. Common law rights of employees on termination of the employment contract

Under the common law, employees have very limited rights to remedies if their employment contracts are terminated wrongfully by the employer. Essentially, they have a right only to payment for a period of "reasonable notice". There is no right under the common law to reinstatement, primarily because the common law will not specifically enforce a contract for personal services. Historically, the courts have considered that it is inappropriate to yoke together people who are antagonistic towards each other, so they are reluctant to order that employers continue to employ workers against their will, and have ordered damages instead. Damages are generally assessed as loss of remuneration for the period of notice that an employee should have been given if the employment was terminated lawfully (that is, according to the terms of the employment contract). The period of notice depends on many factors. Parties will generally be held to any agreed term of notice, but even a term agreed in writing may be held to be inapplicable when termination takes place after a long period of employment, and after substantial changes to the role and responsibilities of the employee.[7] Under the common law, the most generous "reasonable notice" period for a very senior, very long-serving employee, is unlikely to exceed one year.

There is no right under the common law to damages for loss of reputation or any particular suffering caused by the fact of termination nor the manner in which the employer terminated a contract.[8] (Loss of reputation is actionable separately under defamation laws.) In *Malik v Bank of Credit and Commerce International SA*,[9] the English House of Lords held that employees could claim damages for loss of future employment prospects caused by their employer's breach of the obligation of mutual trust and confidence inherent in the employment contract. The employer had allegedly breached this implied term by running a corrupt business. The case does not, however, create any new right for employees to claim damages for the inability to find a new job, simply because they have been dismissed or retrenched.[10]

---

7.   See for instance the case of *Quinn v Jack Chia (Australia) Ltd* [1992] 1 VR 567, where an employee originally appointed on a contract stipulating 1 month's notice, was deemed to be entitled to 12 months notice because he had been promoted to a position of greater seniority and responsibility during the course of the employment relationship.

8.   See *Addis v Grampahone Co* [1909] AC 488. This case was not overruled on this point in *Malik v Bank of Credit and Commerce International SA* [1995] 3 All ER 545.

9.   [1995] 3 All ER 545.

10. This has recently been confirmed by the British Court of Appeal in *Husain & Zafar v BCCI SA* (31 January 2002) unreported.

Generally, the rights that many Australian employees now enjoy to reinstatement or compensation if they are unfairly terminated, and to severance or redundancy pay on termination, are rights that derive from industrial awards or collective agreements, or from legislation. These rights are explained in Section 3 below.

2.4. Effect of receivership, administration or insolvency on employment contracts

Whether employment contracts are terminated on the appointment of administrators or receivers depends on the particular circumstances of the appointment. If the administrators or receivers are acting as agents of the company, and the object of the receivership or administration is to salvage the business as a going concern, then employment contracts are not automatically terminated by the appointment.[11] If administrators or receivers decide to dismiss employees the company will be obliged to meet any obligations owed to the employees under their employment contracts, or any award or agreement binding on the employer (see Section 3 below).

In liquidation, the aim of the process is to wind-up the corporate employer. In this case, employment contracts are terminated, and employees who are owed any wages or other entitlements are creditors of the company. As creditors, they have rights to vote in any creditors' meetings held by the liquidators. In a recent decision of the Federal Court, Justice Goldberg granted an application allowing unions to represent the interests of employees at the creditors' meetings for Ansett Airlines.[12] Employees as a class enjoy a statutory priority in winding up. See Section 5 below.

3.   STATUTORY RIGHTS AND OBLIGATIONS

3.1. Awards and Agreements

The weaknesses of the common law in protecting employee interests have been addressed to some extent by statute. Employees enjoy a number of rights, including rights to apply for reinstatement after unfair or unlawful dismissal, under various federal and state statutes. A full understanding of Australian industrial laws requires considerable knowledge of Australia's unique

---

11.   See *Sipad* v *Popovic* (1996) 14 ACLC 307; *International Harvester Export Company* v *International Harvester Australia Ltd* [1983] VR 539. For the position of employees in a voluntary administration, see Darvas, Paula "From the Outside Looking In: Employees and Voluntary Administration" (2001) 29 *Australian Business Law Review* 409–423; Hammond, Celia "The Relationship of Administrators to Company Employees: Issues Arising under Part 5.3A of the Corporations Law" (1999) 7 *Insolvency Law Journal* 74–85; Taylor, Terry "Employee Entitlements in Corporate Insolvency Administrations" (2000) 8 *Insolvency Law Journal* 32–42.
12.   *Rappas* v *Ansett Australia Ltd* [2001] FCA 1348 (17 September 2001).

constitutional arrangements. For the purposes of this paper, it is sufficient to note that the federal statute, the *Workplace Relations Act* 1996 (Cth), creates some general rights, and provides for the making of federal awards, collective agreements and individual Australian Workplace Agreements (AWAs). Also, most states have legislation protecting employees from unfair dismissal, and providing for the making of awards and enterprise agreements.[13] So employees may also enjoy rights under a federal or state award or collective agreement, made pursuant to a legislative scheme, and these rights will override any common law contract of employment.

3.1.1. Awards

Awards are instruments which determine industry-wide terms and conditions for the employment of certain classes of workers. Awards are made by tribunals to settle notified industrial disputes. The Australian Industrial Relations Commission's award making powers are triggered by the notification of an interstate industrial dispute, usually when a union serves a log of claims on all (or many) employers in an industry. The parties to the dispute, and other interested parties such as the state and federal government, industry peak bodies, and welfare organizations, have standing to make submissions to the Commission before an award is made. Once made, a federal award is binding on all employer respondents to the award.[14] Award terms and conditions override any common law contract terms, to the extent that the contractual terms do not meet minimum award conditions.

Since the *Termination Change and Redundancy Case*[15] in 1984, it has become common for awards to contain entitlements to severance pay on termination for redundancy. This test case awarded four weeks pay for employees with between one and two years service, rising to eight weeks pay for employees with more than four years service. This scale of redundancy benefits was awarded by the AIRC recently when previously non-unionised One-Tel Ltd employees applied for an urgent interim award when that company collapsed in June 2001.[16]

3.1.2 Collective bargaining

This system of arbitrated industry-wide awards formed the basis of Australia's unique industrial relations system for many decades. In recent times, however, the pressures of global competition and concerns to improve

---

13.   The exception is Victoria, which referred its industrial matters to the Commonwealth under s 51 xxxvii of the Constitution in 1997, while a Coalition government was in power. The present Bracks Labour government has attempted, but has not yet been successful in reintroducing, a Victorian industrial relations statute.
14.   State awards can be common awards, applying to all employers in an industry.
15.   (1984) 8 IR 34.
16.   *CPSU and One-Tel Ltd*, Print C2001/3253, 5 June 2001.

productivity have lead a move towards a more US-style system of enterprise bargaining. Federal legislation passed by both Labour[17] and Coalition governments[18] has encouraged reliance on enterprise or workplace agreements as a means of trading productivity improvements for better wages and conditions. Formerly, industry-wide awards could contain many detailed provisions setting out work practices and procedures as well as wages and benefits. Now, awards have been relegated to the role of a minimum safety net of basic wages and conditions[19].

Whereas awards are imposed on the parties by the decision of a tribunal, collective enterprise agreements require the consent of both parties. Collective agreements are generally negotiated between employers and employee representatives (unions)[20] and must be certified by an Industrial Relations Commission to enjoy statutory force. The Commission has no role in determining the content of an agreement. To ensure that agreement-making does not erode minimum award standards,[21] the federal legislation provides that a certified agreement must pass a "no-disadvantage test" before it can be certified. This means that the terms of the agreement, taken together, must not result, "on balance, in a reduction in the overall terms and conditions of employment" under relevant awards.[22] In an exceptional case, an agreement may be certified without passing this test if the AIRC considers that it is not contrary to the public interest to certify the agreement.[23]

The terms of a certified agreement are generally made to bind an employer in respect of all employees, even those who are not members of the union making the agreement. Certified agreements also commonly contain rights to redundancy pay. They also typically contain clauses obliging employers to consult with employee representatives on workplace restructuring, technological change and redundancies. Since 1997, federal awards have not been able to contain any consultancy rights, as these have been held to fall outside of the allowable award matters stipulated in Section 89A of the Act.[24]

3.1.3. Individual workplace agreements

Federal legislation introduced by the Coalition government in 1996 created a new statutory instrument enabling employers to enter into individual work-

---

17.   *The Industrial Relations Reform Act* 1993 (Cth).
18.   The *Workplace Relations and Other Legislation Amendment Act* 1996 (Cth)
19.   See *Workplace Relations Act* 1996 (Cth) section 88A(b).
20.   The *Workplace Relations Act* 1996 (Cth) also provides for non-union agreements so long as the employer is a constitutional corporation: see Part VIB, Division 2.
21.   Early drafts of the *Workplace Relations and Other Legislation Amendment Act* 1996 (Cth) sought to abandon the no-disadvantage test in favour of a set of legislated minimum conditions, however minority parties holding the balance of power in the Senate forced amendments to the legislation prior to enactment.
22.   See Section 170XA(2).
23.   Section 170LT(3).
24.   See *Re Award Simplification Decision* (1997) 75 IR 272.

place agreements (called AWAs) which would override award terms and conditions. (The Western Australian legislation already provided for individual workplace bargains.[25]) AWAs must be approved by the Employment Advocate before they have statutory force.[26] The advantage of an AWA from an employer's perspective is that it allows the parties to contract-out of the provisions of an otherwise compulsory award, so long as the AWA passes the same statutory no-disadvantage test as certified agreements. Essentially, this test ensures that the terms of an AWA must not disadvantage the employee when compared with an award in an overall sense, but there is room to reduce some benefits as a trade-off for improvements in others.

Employers have seen individual bargaining as a way of escaping award conditions, and avoiding the need to negotiate with unions. The BHP dispute in Western Australia's Pilbara region, for example, arose because BHP tried to reduce labour costs and increase workforce flexibility by offering its workforce individual agreements.[27] Unions have strenuously opposed the move to individual bargaining because they see it as weakening the industrial power of employees by restricting resort to collective action, and as a threat to their own viability. Workers on individual bargains typically see no value in maintaining their union membership. In many respects, the drive towards individualising workplace agreement making is the greatest challenge to employment security, because it atomises the workforce and destroys the collective power that Australian unions have traditionally used to secure improved wages and conditions. Individualisation has been a central feature of Coalition government industrial relations policy in Australia.[28]

3.2. Statutory termination benefits

Under the *Workplace Relations Act* 1996 (Cth), employees are entitled to minimum periods of notice if their employment is terminated except for their own misconduct. Section 170CM provides a scale of notice periods, depending on years of service and age on termination. The maximum notice period is five weeks, for employees with more than five years of continuous service who are over 45 at termination. Regulations restrict entitlement to this notice if dismissal was for any one of a number of reasons.[29] The sanction for failure to comply with Section 170CM is simply that employees may take action to

---

25. *Workplace Agreements Act* 1993 (WA) Section 10.
26. The Office of the Employment Advocate was created by the *Workplace Relations and Other Legislation Amendment Act* 1996 (Cth), to perform the functions associated with encouraging the use of AWAs, and enforcing the Freedom of Association provisions in Part XA of the Act.
27. See *Australian Workers' Union* v *BHP Iron-Ore Pty Ltd* [2001] FCA 3 (10 January 2001) Kenny J.
28. The Kennett Victorian government in 1992, the Court WA government in 1993, and the Howard federal government in 1996, have all introduced legislation encouraging individual bargaining.
29. Such as dishonesty, disobedience to lawful and reasonable instructions, or intoxication: *Workplace Relations Regulations* 1996 (Cth), Reg 30CA.

recover damages equal to pay for the notice period.[30] The periods stipulated in Section 170CM are statutory minima. If an employee has rights under common law or under an award, certified agreement or AWA to a longer period of notice, then those rights are not lost. Employees are not entitled to these minimum periods of notice (or payment in lieu of notice) if their employment is terminated as a result of a transmission of the business, and they continue to be employed by the new employer on the basis that their employment is continuous.[31]

3.3. Statutory rights to reinstatement

The *Workplace Relations Act* 1996 (Cth) , and state laws in New South Wales, Queensland,[32] South Australia,[33] Western Australia[34] and Tasmania,[35] also provide an avenue for reinstatement if employees have been terminated unlawfully or unfairly. Generally, these provisions have been based on the International Labour Organisation's Termination of Employment Convention 1982 which protects workers from dismissal "unless there is a valid reason for such termination connected with the capacity or conduct of the worker or based on the operational requirements of the undertaking".[36] Retrenchments of employees for reasons of genuine redundancy are not prohibited.

Under the federal Act, a termination will be unlawful if it has occurred without the statutory notice period. It will also be unlawful if it has been for a discriminatory reason. For instance, dismissal because a person is a member or officer of a union, or is refusing to negotiate to sign an AWA, would be unlawful.[37] The Freedom of Association provisions in Part XA of the *Workplace Relations Act* 1996 (Cth) also provide a right to reinstatement for employees who have been dismissed for reasons of their involvement, or non-involvement, in industrial associations. Dismissal because an employee "is entitled to the benefit of an industrial instrument or an order of an industrial body" is prohibited.[38] Taken together, the statutory rights against unlawful and unfair dismissal, and the freedom of association rights, have meant that employers need to establish genuine redundancy, and a fair system for selecting those who will be made redundant in a business restructure. Strategies designed

---

30.   See s 170CR(4) and (5)
31.   *Workplace Relations Regulations* 1996 (Cth) Reg 30CD.
32.   *Industrial Relations Act* 1999 (Qld) s 78.
33.   *Industrial and Employee Relations Act* 1994 (SA) s 109.
34.   *Industrial Relations Act* 1979 (WA) s 96L empowers an industrial magistrate's court to order reinstatement if an employee has been dismissed in breach of prohibitions in Section 96C, D or E against discrimination on the basis of membership (or non-membership) of a union.
35.   *Industrial Relations Act* 1984 (Tas) s 31.
36.   Article 4, reproduced in Schedule 10 of the *Workplace Relations Act* 1996 (Cth).
37.   See Section 170CK. There are many other prohibited reasons, notably discrimination on grounds of race, colour, sex, sexual preference, age, disability, pregnancy, religion etc.
38.   Section 298L(1)(h)

to exclude unions, or to avoid compliance with awards or certified agreements, risk infringing these provisions.[39]

Where reinstatement is held not to be appropriate, a tribunal or court can award compensation in lieu of reinstatement.[40] Compensation is unlimited in the case of unlawful dismissal for a breach of freedom of association provisions.[41] If the dismissal has "unlawful" or "unfair" within the terms of the Termination of Employment provisions in Part VIA, Division 3 of the Act, compensation is limited to a maximum of six months salary.[42] Reinstatement will be dependent upon the employer continuing to operate the business. In the Waterfront dispute, for instance, the High Court amended the original interim orders of North J which had obliged the administrators to reinstate employees. The High Court held administrators of an insolvent company should not be fettered in exercising their powers of administration.[43]

3.3. Special provisions for transmission of businesses

3.3.1. Awards

Since its very beginning, the traditional Australian system of conciliation and arbitration of disputes by making binding industry-wide awards has been susceptible to attempts by employers to avoid obligations by selling their businesses to newly created corporations under their own control. Early in the history of the legislation, a provision was passed to bind successors to a business to the terms of an award or agreement binding the original employer. This legislation was tested (for constitutional validity) in the case of *George Hudson Ltd* v *Australian Timber Workers' Union* (1923).[44] In that case, an employer wished to avoid being bound by the terms of an agreement struck with employees. The employer attempted to do this by winding up the business and transferring it to a new company set up for the purpose of taking over the business. (This strategy is sometimes referred to as the "phoenix phenomenon", after the mythical bird which resurrects itself from the ashes of its own funeral pyre.) When employees argued that the new employer was a successor

---

39.   See for example *Greater Dandenong City Council* v *Australian Municipal, Clerical and Services Union* [2001] FCA 349 (4 April 2001); *Patrick Stevedore Operations No 2 Pty Ltd* v *Maritime Union of Australia* (1998) 195 CLR 1 (the Waterfront case); *Australasian Meat Industry Employees Union & Ors* v *Rashad Basha Aziz & Ors* (1998) 44 AILR 3–844; *Finance Sector Union* v *Commonwealth Bank of Australia* [2000] FCA 1468. In *National Union of Workers* v *Qenos Pty Ltd* [2001] FCA 178 (6 March 2001) the employer successfully defended the claim.
40.   In fact, compensation is ordered more often than reinstatement. According to the AIRC's 2001 Annual Report, compensation was ordered in 838, and reinstatement in only 132, of the 2,715 cases proceeding to a decision by the AIRC between 31 December 1996 and 30 June 2001. See *http://www.airc.gov.au/research/annual/ar2001/AIRC0001/02a.cfm*, last visited 5 February 2002.
41.   *Workplace Relations Act* 1996 (Cth) Section 298U(c).
42.   Section 170CH(8).
43.   *Patrick Stevedores Operations No 2 Pty Ltd* v *MUA* (1998) 153 ALR 643 at 671.
44.   32 CLR 413.

to the business according to the terms of the legislative provisions, and was therefore bound to honour the agreement as to wages and conditions, the employer challenged the constitutional validity of the legislation, claiming that the federal parliament had no power to interfere with general principles of privity of contract. The High Court upheld the legislation, on the basis that it was within the scope of the federal power to encourage and maintain industrial peace in the Commonwealth. In the course of judgment the court opined that it would be "grossly unfair" to other employers who continued to be bound by the terms of an award or agreement, and to employees who had relied on the binding nature of the award or agreement. The court held that there was no injustice in binding a successor employer, because "a successor to a business could not become so without knowing the statutory obligations of his predecessor to his employees".[45]

The current formulation of the provision as far as awards are concerned is in Section 149 of the *Workplace Relations Act* 1996 (Cth) (the Act). It states that "subject to any order of the Commission", an award is binding on "any successor, assignee or transmittee (whether immediate or not) to or of the business or part of the business of an employer who was a party to the industrial dispute, including a corporation that has acquired or taken over the business or part of the business of the employer".

The meaning of this provision has been the subject of a body of case law. Although the provision has straightforward application when a business is sold as a going concern,[46] difficulties arise when businesses are substantially reorganised. Formerly, the court would apply a "substantial identity" test[47] to see if the new employer was indeed a successor to the old. This test involved a comparison of the activities of the first employer (and therefore of the nature of the work of the employees) with the activities of the new employer. This test was applied by the High Court in *Re Australian Industrial Relations Commission; Ex parte Australian Transport Officers Federation*[48] (a case involving the amalgamation of the New South Wales Department of Main Roads and the Department of Motor Transport into the Roads and Traffic Authority). This case was followed by the Federal Court in several decisions involving the out-sourcing to private enterprise of previously government activities.[49] In these cases, the Federal Court's reasons focussed on the need to maintain industrial arrangements for employees continuing to do the same work until there was conscious and consensual variation to those arrangements. "Mere changes in arrangements as to which legal entity might be the employer of an unchanged class of industrial employees" ought not to disturb

---

45. At p 435.
46. Selling some assets of a business, without transferring goodwill or negotiating continuation of employment contracts, will not constitute sale as a "going concern": see *Meat & Allied Trades Federation of Australia v Australasian Meat Industry Employees Union* (1995) 58 IR 990.
47. See *Shaw v United Felt Hats Pty Ltd* (1927) 39 CLR 533.
48. (1990) 171 CLR 216.
49. *North Western Health Care Network v Health Services Union of Australia* (1991) 164 ALR 147; *CPSU v Stellar Call Centres Pty Ltd* (1999) 92 IR 224; *Employment National Ltd v CPSU* [2000] FCA 452 (11 April 2000).

awards and agreements.[50] However, in a recent case involving a private sector reorganisation, the High Court took a different approach. In *PP Consultants Pty Ltd* v *Finance Sector Union of Australia*,[51] the St George Bank decided to close a branch, and to appoint the pharmacy operating next door to take over its commercial premises and act as its agent in offering retail banking services. The pharmacist would employ the banking staff to perform essentially the same tasks, wearing the same uniforms, and would be paid a commission on transactions by the bank. The majority judgment held that "the character of the transferred business activities in the hands of the new employer"[52] should be assessed. In this case, it was held that the pharmacy had not taken over the business of banking, because it was not earning profits from lending margins, nor accepting the risks of loan transactions. It was simply earning commissions on transactions as an agent. The business therefore had a different legal character and so did not involve succession or transmission. So the pharmacy was entitled to disregard the award. The High Court held that the old "substantial identity" test may still be relevant in cases involving government enterprise, so the earlier cases have not necessarily been overruled. Nevertheless, *PP Consultants* demonstrates that the traditional focus (expressed in the *Hudson* case) on the protective purpose of the legislative provisions has been eroded, in favour of a new regard for the legal arrangements under which businesses are structured. The case offers a clear path for private enterprises to avoid existing awards and agreements by out-sourcing business functions to labour-hire organisations.

Another important aspect of the transmission of business provision for awards is that it is subject to any order of the AIRC, which has the power under Sections 111(1)(f) and 113(1) of the Act to "set aside, revoke or vary" an award. So when a business is transmitted – through sale or restructure – to a new employing entity, it is possible for the new employing entity to apply to the AIRC to revoke or vary any awards applicable to the business. The AIRC is obliged to exercise this power according to the objects of the Act.[53] This involves finding the delicate balance between competing objects, which include promotion of both improved living standards for workers, and higher productivity and international competitiveness for business.

3.3.2.   Collective agreements

The Act also makes provision for certified agreements to continue to bind successors.[54] The same formula of words is used in Section 170MB. The test for determining whether a new employer is a successor, transmittee or assignee of

---

50.   Madgwick J., in *North Western Health Care Network* v *Health Services Union of Australia* (1991) 164 ALR 147 at 170.
51.   (2000) 176 ALR 205.
52.   (2000) 176 ALR at 209.
53.   *Workplace Relations Act* 1996(Cth) s 3.
54.   Section 170MB. Note that For constitutional reasons, any successor or assignee needs to be a "constitutional corporation" to be bound by a Division 2 certified agreement.

all or part of a business is the same as for Section 149, so the *PP Consultants* case will apply in cases of certified agreements as well.

The only difference between Section 149 and Section 170MB is that Section 170MB is not subject to any order of the Commission. This is not surprising, given the primacy given to the mutual consent of the parties in the enterprise bargaining provisions of the Act. There is nothing in the Act to prevent a successor employer from striking a new bargain with the agreement of the employees who will be bound. However, legislation has been proposed[55] (but not, at the time of writing, yet passed), to amend this provision to enable employers who are bound by Section 170MB to make an application to the AIRC to order that an employer is not bound, or is bound only to the extent specified in the order. According to this proposal, the AIRC would be required to hear submissions from any person bound by the certified agreement before making such an order. Unions would be entitled to be heard so long as they had been requested to represent the interests of at least one member who continued to be employed by the new employer. If passed, this legislation would entitle an employer to apply for a waiver of existing certified agreements in the face of employee opposition. Reasons for the proposal emphasised complaints from employer groups that the succession of certified agreements inhibited productivity and efficiency gains when businesses were restructured. The rhetoric in the Explanatory Memorandum to the Bill emphasised the needs of the new employer's business, rather than the fairness to employees which featured in the reasoning of the court's decision in the *Hudson* case, described above.

3.3.3.   AWA agreements

Presently, Section 170VS provides that a successor to a business will be bound by the terms of an AWA. Legislation proposed, but not yet passed, intends to rewrite these provisions to include a mechanism for the Employment Advocate to vary or extinguish an AWA on the application of a new employer, but not on the application of an employee.[56]

3.4.   Industrial law obligations of employers undertaking economic dismissals

Employees may acquire rights to consultation and participation in decision-making in economic dismissals under a negotiated certified agreement under

---

Division 2 agreements allow parties to make agreements without the prerequisite of demonstrating the existence of an interstate industrial dispute.

55.   Workplace Relations Amendment (Transmission of Business) Bill 2002, tabled in the House of Representatives on 21 March 2002.

56.   The latest version of this rewrite of the AWA provisions was contained in the Workplace Relations and Other Legislation Amendment (Small Business and Other Measures) Bill 2001. These provisions had not been retabled in 2002 by the time of writing.

Part VIB of the Act. Those agreements negotiated by well-organised and industrially powerful unions typically impose obligations on employers to consult with the unions over any proposals to change work practices or staffing levels. There are also some weak and indirect rights to consultation in the *Workplace Relations Act* 1996 (Cth). Section 170CL obliges employers who plan to terminate more than 15 employees for reasons of "an economic, technological, structural or similar nature", to notify commonwealth sponsored employment agencies of the number and timing of these redundancies. This must be done "as soon as practicable", and employees cannot be terminated until it has been done. Breach of this provision exposes an employer to a fine of not more than $1,000 (a small penalty) and possible orders that the employer must not terminate the employee until notification. Section 170GA gives employee representatives an indirect right to be consulted where an employer proposes to dismiss 15 or more employees for economic or technological reasons. The AIRC has powers under this section to make an order "to put employees whose employment was terminated pursuant to the decision, and each such trade union, in the same position (as nearly as can be done) as if" the employer had given the union an opportunity to consult on the retrenchments.

4.   CORPORATE LAW IN AUSTRALIA

4.1.   The position of employees

With two limited exceptions, employees do not enjoy any special status under Australian corporations law. The first exception is that unpaid employee entitlements enjoy a statutory priority under s 556 of the *Corporations Act* 2001 (Cth) in the case of a company liquidation. This means that if a company fails, employees will rank ahead of other unsecured creditors, but after secured creditors and professional administrators and liquidators, in the division of the company's assets. This priority scheme is discussed in more detail in Section 4.3 below. The second exception is that directors are prohibited from entering into any "uncommercial transaction" with the intention of avoiding obligations to pay employee entitlements.[57] If directors breach this prohibition, they will be liable to criminal and civil penalties, and they may be personally liable to pay the avoided entitlements. This legislation was enacted in 2000 in response to community concern that directors of failed companies made a practice of deliberately under-capitalising the company prior to collapse so that retrenchment payments could not be made.[58]

---

57.   *Corporations Act* 2001 (Cth) Part 5.8A "Employee Entitlements", Sections 596AA-AI.
58.   *Corporate Law Amendment (Employee Entitlements) Act* 2000 (Cth). For detailed commentary on this legislation, see David Noakes "Corporate Groups and the Duties of Directors: Protecting the Employee or the Insolvent Employer?" (2001) 29 *Australian Business Law Review* 124–148.

According to the general principles of company law, directors of a company owe a duty to act in good faith in the best interests of the company when exercising their powers and performing their responsibilities as fiduciaries. The company has been defined by case law to mean the interests of the corporators as a whole.[59] In other words, directors owe their duties principally to shareholders. Only when a company is on the verge of insolvency will directors have any obligation to regard the interests of company creditors.[60] Cases in which directors have been castigated for considering the interests of employees are notorious.[61] While legislation has been passed in other jurisdictions[62] to permit directors to consider the interests of employees in some circumstances, there has been no change to Australian law, beyond the enactment of the Employee Entitlements legislation.[63] Even in the middle of the furore of recent years over the problem of unpaid employee entitlements after corporate collapse, many commentators continued to assert the traditional view: directors owe their allegiance only to shareholders. Employees are merely unsecured creditors to the corporation. In Australia there is no established tradition of employee representation on company boards, nor is there any tradition of cooperative consultation with employee representatives through works councils.[64] On the contrary, the Australian industrial relations climate has typically been represented as antagonistic and adversarial. Any voice that employees in some industries have managed to secure has come through the exercise of industrial muscle, not legal rights. The current federal government's industrial relations policies focus on crippling, and by no means supporting or strengthening, that muscle.

4.2. Corporate restructuring and the rights of employees as unsecured creditors

Under Australian law, corporate restructuring does not require any permission from government. The only constraints on corporate restructuring arise because of the need to comply with legislated rules ensuring that shareholders and in some circumstances, creditors, are given accurate information. Employees' rights arise because they are treated as unsecured creditors of a company, to the extent that they are owed any outstanding wages, accrued leave or retrenchment entitlements under any contract or industrial instrument.

---

59.   See *Ngurli Ltd* v *McCann* (1953) 90 CLR 425.
60.   See *Kinsela* v *Russell Kinsela Pty Ltd* (1986) 4 NSWLR 722; *ANZ Executors & Trustee Co Ltd* v *Qintex Australia Ltd* [1991] 2 Qd R 360.
61.   See for instance *Hutton* v *West Cork Railway Co* (1883) 23 Ch D 654, and *Parke* v *Daily News Ltd* [1962] Ch 927.
62.   Eg, *The Companies Act* 1985 (UK) Section 309 and *The Companies Act* 1990 (Ireland) Section 52.
63.   Above note 56.
64.   But see the work of Ronald C McCallum proposing the establishment of Works Councils: McCallum "Crafting a New Collective Labour Law for Australia" (1997) 39 *JIR* 405–421.

4.2.1. The special statutory priority scheme for employees

Presently, the *Corporations Act* 2001 (Cth) Section 556 lists certain priority creditors in a winding-up. After the liquidators' various costs, comes paragraph (e) "Wages and superannuation contributions payable by the company in respect of services rendered to the company by employees before the relevant date". Next in line is (f), injury compensation payments, then (g) all amounts due, because of an industrial instrument, in respects of leave of absence.[65] Finally comes (h), retrenchment payments payable to employees of the company.[66] The section excludes any employees who are or have recently been directors of the company, and their family members, from full enjoyment of this priority.[67]

This list of priorities ranks employees after secured creditors, but before floating charge holders.[68] The main trouble with a priorities system is that first bite of nothing is still nothing. While employee entitlements continue to rank after secured creditors, and after those highly qualified and hence highly paid company liquidators, there will often be less than enough left to pay employees. The National Textiles collapse of January 2000 demonstrated the weakness of the priority scheme. The major lender to this company, the National Australia Bank, had already been repaid its loan and discharged its fixed and floating charge over the company's assets on 1 October 1999.[69] New finance was provided by Scottish Pacific Business Finance Pty Ltd (known to be a "lender of last resort") and Oldtex Pty Ltd, a company associated with National Textiles' major shareholder and director, Philip Bart. Oldtex took a fixed charge, and so was able to take assets with a book value of more than $12 million (but an estimated realisable value of just over $4 million) in exchange for a $3.8 million debt. Being secured, this ranked ahead of employee claims.

4.2.2. The government safety-net scheme

After the collapse of National Textiles in January 2000, the federal government introduced a taxpayer-funded scheme to provide a safety net for employees who risked losing wages and accrued leave and redundancy entitlements

---

65. "Leave of absence" is defined in s 9 as "long service leave, extended leave, recreation leave, annual leave, sick leave or any other form of leave of absence from employment".

66. "Retrenchment payment" is defined in Section 556(2) as an amount payable "by virtue of an industrial instrument". "Industrial instrument" is defined in Section 9 of the Act to mean a contract of employment, or a "law, award, determination or agreement relating to terms or conditions of employment".

67. Such people can claim no more than $2,000 in wages and superannuation contributions, $1,500 in leave of absence payments, and nothing in respect of retrenchment.

68. See Section 561. Before the November 2001 federal election, in the midst of the Ansett debacle, the Prime Minister, the Hon John Howard, announced in the media that the government would consider re-ranking employee entitlements, ahead of secured creditors. At the time of writing, details of this proposal had not been released.

69. Information cited here comes from the public records kept by the Australian Securities and Investment Commission, including Form 507 Report as to Affairs lodged on 29 February 2000 by V C Barilla, Joint Receiver and Manager.

because of the collapse of their employer. This scheme (the Employee Entitlements Support Scheme or EESS) was replaced by a considerably more generous scheme during the Ansett Airlines crisis. The new scheme, called the General Employee Entitlements and Redundancy Scheme (GEERS) pays up to eight weeks redundancy benefit (the level fixed by the TCR test case[70]) and benefits are capped at a salary level of $75,200 per year.[71] Many Ansett employees were owed much more than this under industrial instruments.

In both the National Textiles and Ansett cases the government also responded with specific bail-out schemes. For National Textiles employees, the government drew on its budget allocation for a Regional Assistance Program to promote regional employment growth.[72] In the case of Ansett, special legislation enabling a levy on all airline tickets (even those sold by competitors) was passed to ensure payment of some $730 million in employee entitlements.[73] But not all corporate collapses have attracted this level of generosity from the government. Indeed, the government has been criticised for these random acts of compassion. Arguably, this welfare-driven response is incompatible with the government's private enterprise orientation, and its competition policy. It represents taxpayer-funded under-writing of the losses of corporations which are inefficiently managed or, worse still, deliberately manipulated to lose employee entitlements. On the other hand, it may also demonstrate a commitment to providing a legislated, welfare-based safety net for the poor, to underpin an otherwise loosely-regulated free market.

4.3. Corporate manipulation

As the *Hudson* case described above demonstrated, unscrupulous employers have sometimes tried to take advantage of the doctrine of separate legal personality of corporations to avoid liability to meet legal obligations to employees. One way this is done is to run a business through a group of companies. Assets are held by certain subsidiaries, and it is these subsidiaries that offer security to finance creditors. The workers are employed by a separate company, which is under-capitalised. If the controllers of the group decide to shed labour, they can allow the employing subsidiary to fail.[74] The "phoenix" company is another strategy: a company controller who wants to shed labour sets up a new company, sells assets of the old company to the new company, and allows the original company to fail. In both cases, employees lose their

---

70. (1984) 8 IR 34.
71. For details of the scheme, see Abbott, Media Release dated 20 September 2001, "Even Better Arrangements to Protect Employee Entitlements", *www.dewrsb.gov.au/ministers*, last visited 3 October 2001.
72. See Chelsey Martin "New Heat Over Textiles Bail-out", *Australian Financial Review*, 19 June 2000, p 3.
73. See the *Airline Passenger Ticket Levy (Collection) Act* 2001 (Cth) and the *Air Passenger Ticket Levy (Imposition) Act* 2001, passed on 26 and 27 September 2001.
74. See for example the Steel Tank and Pipe group which failed in November 2000: Jeff Corbett, *Newcastle Herald*, 15 November 2000, p 8, available on-line at http://ptg.djnr.com/ccroot/asp/publib/story.as, last visited 3 February 2001.

jobs, and are faced with the difficult task of seeking remedies from a failed company with no assets to meet their entitlements.

With the exception of the as yet untested employee entitlements provisions,[75] Australian corporate law is not well-equipped to address the injustice of these strategies, however employees do have some protection under industrial laws, particularly under the Freedom of Association provisions enacted in 1996. The Waterfront dispute was the first case to demonstrate the potential of these provisions to protect employees from manipulative corporate strategies.

5. THE WATERFRONT DISPUTE[76]

In September 1997, National Stevedore Holdings Pty Ltd (itself a subsidiary of listed company Lang Corporation Ltd) undertook a major restructuring of its group of subsidiaries, in a strategy designed to improve productivity on the waterfront. Formerly, the group comprised several separate stevedoring companies (the "employer companies"), each owning its own assets and employing its own labour force. But in September 1997, each of the companies in the group sold its assets and its business to Patrick Stevedores Operations (No 2) Pty Ltd ("PSO"). The proceeds from these sales (some $315 million in all) was used to allow the employer companies to buy-back their own shares and reduce shareholder capital. The employer companies continued to employ waterfront workers, and they supplied labour to PSO under labour supply contracts. The labour supply contracts included a sudden death termination clause giving PSO a right to terminate in the event of any industrial action by the workers of the employer companies. In January 1998, PSO transferred its right to use one of its major docks to companies associated with the National Farmers Federation (the NFF). The NFF was known to be setting up its own non-union waterfront facilities. This politically sensitive decision triggered industrial action among the workers of the employer companies, thereby entitling PSO to terminate the labour supply contracts with the employer companies. It was alleged that PSO intended to engage the non-union NFF workforce to meet its obligations under stevedoring contracts. The employer companies were left with a workforce, but no work, and much reduced shareholder capital. Facing insolvency, the directors placed the employer companies into voluntary administration and signalled an intention to dismiss the entire workforce.

The Maritime Union of Australia (MUA) was successful in obtaining an injunction delaying the dismissal of these workers, but not because there had been any breach of any laws relating to corporate restructuring. The MUA was

---

75.   *Corporations Act* 2001 (Cth) Part 5.8A, ss 596AA-AI.
76.   For a detailed description of this event in Australian labour history, see Helen Trinca and Anne Davies *The Battle that Changed Australia: Waterfront*, 2000, Doubleday. See also David Noakes, "Dogs on the Wharves: Corporate Groups and the Waterfront Dispute" (1999) 11 *Australian Journal of Corporate Law* 27–62.

able to satisfy first the Federal Court, and ultimately the High Court of Australia, that there was a serious question to be tried as to whether PSO, the employer companies, the directors and even a government minister, had conspired to breach newly enacted freedom of association laws. The MUA alleged that the defendants had pursued this elaborate restructure with the intention of dismissing workers because they were union members, and that, if proven, would infringe Section 298K of the *Workplace Relations Act* 1996 (Cth). The Federal Court and the High Court were prepared to grant the urgent injunction. Ultimately, the threat of expensive litigation and potentially personal liability for directors drove the parties to the negotiating table. The matter was resolved without any final hearing. The case demonstrated, however, that the freedom of association provisions in the *Workplace Relations Act* potentially offered employees protection against loss of employment because of corporate manipulation.

The ALP attempted to introduce legislation which would have lifted the veil between members in a corporate group in these circumstances, so that employees' rights to reinstatement and to redundancy benefits would not be jeopardised by corporate restructures. This proposal was not pursued, however the government did ultimately introduce the *Corporate Law Amendment (Employee Entitlements) Act* 2000, which made company directors personally liable to meet employee entitlements if corporate manipulation was deliberately done to avoid payment of those entitlements. This legislation has yet to be tested.

In the meantime, more case law has tested the limits of the protection offered by the freedom of association provisions. In *Greater Dandenong City Council* v *Australian Municipal Clerical and Services Union*,[77] a majority of the full Federal Court held that a local council's decision to outsource its home and community care service to the lowest tenderer had breached these provisions. Its former employees had also tendered for this work, but were unsuccessful because their bid was based on cost estimates that assumed they would keep their original wages and conditions. The competitive bid was based on lower labour costs. Selection of the lower bidder was held to have discriminated against the former employees because they were claiming entitlement to the provisions of an industrial instrument, and was therefore in breach of the freedom of association provisions.

On the other hand, in *National Union of Workers* v *Qenos Pty Ltd*,[78] a union was unsuccessful in demonstrating that an employer's decision to "spill and fill" all positions breached these provisions. The employer was able to discharge the onus of proving that it was not motivated by a desire to rid itself of union members, even though that was in fact a substantial effect of the strategy.

---

77.   [2001] FCA 349 (4 April 2001).
78.   [2001] FCA 178 (6 March 2001).

6. WORKPLACE CHANGE WITHOUT DISMISSALS

A discussion of corporate restructuring and labour law in Australia would be incomplete without mention of an important and contentious initiative of the current federal government: the encouragement of a return to individual contracting as a method of determining wages and conditions. The present government is antipathetic to the labour movement in Australia and enacted the AWA provisions to give employers an avenue for regulating their own workplaces without negotiation with unions. Employers can however fall into traps if they pursue these strategies in the face of opposition from employees. Those traps are, firstly, that the procedures for making individual AWAs require that employees "genuinely consent" to the AWA. Section 170WG specifically prohibits the use of duress to force employees to agree to AWAs. A current employee cannot therefore be threatened with dismissal for failure to sign an AWA.[79] Nevertheless, it has been held that an employer is entitled to refuse employment to new applicants who refuse to agree to allow their working conditions to be governed by AWAs.[80]

The freedom of association provisions may also prove an obstacle to large scale moves to individual bargaining, but only if handled badly. The BHP litigation provides a useful illustration of the combined strategy of individualisation and union exclusion to bring about changes in labour costs.[81]

6.1. The BHP story

BHP Iron Ore Pty Ltd discovered the benefits of individual contracting when it investigated a proposed merger with a competitor, Hamersley Iron Pty Ltd (Hamersley). The due diligence examination of Hamersley's operations revealed that Hamersley enjoyed substantially lower labour costs than BHP, because Hamersley had, over a period of years, moved its employees to individual contracts. Hamersley had initially offered contracts with "significant monetary benefits" to employees agreeing to leave the protection of awards and collective bargains. Over the years, as staff turned over and new employees were given no choice other than individual contracts, Hamersley had been able to reduce those benefits to lower than the 1993 award. Union membership at Hamersley had been almost totally eliminated, and unions had not been successful in either bargaining collectively on behalf of employees, or representing employees as bargaining agents.

BHP decided to offer various incentives to its own employees to sign individual workplace agreements. These included pay out of accrued sick leave entitlements. A long serving employee who had taken little leave could take a

---

79.   *Shanka* v *Employment National (Administration) Pty Ltd* (2000) 166 ALR 663.
80.   *MUA* v *Burnie Port Corporation Pty Ltd* [2000] FCA 1189 (24 August 2000).
81.   *AWU* v *BHP Iron Ore Pty Ltd* [2000] FCA 39 (31 January 2000). For comment on this case see Joellen Riley "Individual Contracting and Collective Bargaining in the Balance" (2000) 13 *AJLL* 92–98.

pay out as high as $65,000. In exchange for these benefits the employees surrendered the protection of their state awards and agreements, and many resigned their union membership. The unions tried to prevent BHP from following this strategy by alleging that this conduct breached the freedom of association provisions in the *Workplace Relations Act* 1996, in particular, Sections 298K (which concerns discrimination against individuals) and Section 298M (which concerns inducement to resign from unions). Gray J granted the union's application for an urgent interim injunction, but this was varied on appeal to the Full Federal Court. In the final hearing of the matter, Kenny J found that there had been no breach of s 298K, because BHP offered the individual contracts to all employees, regardless of whether they decided to resign from the union. Also, there had been no breach of s 298M, because the union had not proved that BHP intended that employees who accepted the individual agreements should resign their union membership. BHP conceded that it intended that the unions were "to have no role in relation to operational matters within the company, including the introduction of workplace change".[82] BHP accepted that the unions could continue to play a role as representatives of workers in individual grievance disputes, but that they could play no role in collective bargaining. Kenny J agreed with counsel for BHP that the *Workplace Relations Act 1996* did not guarantee any right to collective bargaining.

This decision demonstrates the scope for substantial change to work practices in Australia, without the need to engage in the kind of manipulation that the Australian community found to be so reprehensible in the Waterfront dispute. So long as an employer does not overtly discriminate against union members, offering individual contracts to employees will not infringe the freedom of association provisions. And so long as the employer is willing to allow unions to operate as service providers to workers, the employer will be entitled to refuse to bargain collectively.

CONCLUSION

The widespread and emotive public support for the MUA during the Waterfront dispute affirmed a persistent culture of collective organisation of labour in Australia. Nevertheless, the current federal government appears committed to press on with legislative reform aimed at eroding union influence. One does not need too great a power of prophesy to foresee further industrial disruption in Australia as government, industry and unions strive to work out a tolerable compromise between the interests of internationally competitive enterprise, and equitable treatment of Australian workers.

---

82.   [2001] FCA 3 at paragraph 214.

2. Corporate Restructuring and the Role of Labour Law in China

Shi Meixia

INTRODUCTION

Since the 1980s, the economic reform in China has been accelerating to meet the requirements of the socialist market. The legislation of corporate law and labour law and other respective regulations and policies have also gone through a process of dramatic development. All of these developments are typically characterized by the reform of state-owned enterprises in urban areas. One of the obstacles that the reform has faced is how to handle the labour relationship between laid-off workers and their enterprises. So far, both the legislative organs and the government administrative departments have paid a significant amount of attention to this. Generally speaking, the result has been positive. However, the reform process will face more challenges with China's entry into the WTO.

1. HIGH RANK LEGAL FRAMEWORK GOVERNING CORPORATE RESTRUCTURING

Chinese "Company Law" is a legal document whose contents include the merger, transfer of shares, division, bankruptcy, dissolution and liquidation of companies. The term "Company" mentioned in the law refers to a limited liability company or a joint stock limited company incorporated within the territory. A "limited liability company" or "joint stock limited company" is an enterprise legal person. In the case of a limited liability company, shareholders shall assume liability towards the company to the extent of their respective capital contributions, and the company shall be liable for its debts to the extent of all its assets. In the case of a joint stock limited company, its total capital shall be divided into equal shares; shareholders shall assume liability towards the company to the extent of their respective shareholdings, and the company shall be liable for its debts to the extent of all its assets.

1.1. Merger and division under "company law"

1. *The merger or division* of a company shall require the adoption of a resolution by a meeting of the shareholders of the company. The merger

R. Blanpain (ed.),
Corporate Restructuring and the Role of Labour Law, 37–60.
© 2003 *Kluwer Law International. Printed in Great Britain.*

or division of a joint stock limited company must be approved by the department authorized by the State Council or by the people's government at the provincial level.

2. The merger of a company may take the form of merger by absorption or merger by new establishment.
3. When one company absorbs another, it is an absorption merger, and the company being absorbed shall be dissolved. When two or more companies merge to establish a new company, it is merger for new establishment, and all parties being merged shall be dissolved.
4. The claims and debts of the parties to a merger shall be taken on by the absorbing company or the newly established company when companies are merged.
5. Where a company proceeds into a *division*, its assets shall be divided correspondingly.
6. Where a company decides to divide itself, it shall formulate a balance sheet and a detailed inventory of assets.

The debts prior to the division of a company shall be assumed by the companies following the division in accordance with the agreement reached between them.

1.2. Bankruptcy, dissolution and liquidation under "company law"

1.2.1. Bankruptcy

Where a company is declared *bankrupt* according to law because it is unable to pay off its due debts, a people's court shall, in accordance with relevant laws, organize the shareholders, the relevant departments and relevant professionals to form a liquidation committee that shall conduct bankruptcy liquidation of the company.

1.2.2. Dissolution

Where one of the following circumstances occurs, a company may be dissolved:
- The term of operation as stipulated by the articles of association of the company expires or other reasons for dissolution as stipulated by the articles of association occur;
- The shareholders' meeting resolves to dissolve the company; or
- Dissolution is necessary as a result of the merger or division of the company.

1.2.3. Liquidation

After the liquidation committee has checked the company's assets and formulated the balance sheet and a detailed inventory of assets, it shall formulate a liquidation plan and shall submit such plan to the shareholders' meeting or the department in charge for confirmation.

Where the assets of the company are sufficient to pay off the company's debts, such assets shall be applied to payment of the liquidation fee, the wages and labour insurance premiums of the staff and workers of the company, due taxes and the company's debts.

The remaining assets of a company, after it has paid off all the debts and expenses as prescribed by the preceding paragraph, shall be distributed, in the case of a limited liability company, in proportion to the shareholders' capital contribution and, in the case of a joint stock limited company, in proportion to the shareholders' shareholdings.

1.3. Labour issues under "company law"

According to "Company Law", companies must also protect the lawful rights and interests of their staff and workers, and strengthen labour protection so as to achieve safety in production.

Companies shall apply various methods of strengthening professional education and extra training of their staff and workers so as to improve their quality.

1.4. "Law on enterprise bankruptcy"

1.4.1.   Coverage of the law

The law applies to state-owned enterprises (the bankruptcy of non-state-owned enterprise is covered by "Civil Procedure Law"). This law is formulated in order to suit the development of a planned socialist commodity economy and the needs of the reform of the economic structure, to promote the autonomous operation of enterprises owned by the whole people, to strengthen the system of economic responsibility and democratic management, to improve the state of operations, to increase economic efficiency and to protect the lawful rights and interests of creditors and debtors.

1.4.2.   The requirements of bankruptcy

Enterprises which, owing to poor operations and management that result in serious losses, are unable to repay debts that are due shall be declared bankrupt in accordance with the provisions of this Law.

Enterprises for which creditors file for bankruptcy shall not be declared bankrupt under any of the following circumstance:
1. If they are public utility enterprises and enterprises that have an important relationship to the national economy and people's livelihood,

for which the relevant government departments grant subsidies or adopt other measures to assist the repayment of debts;

2. If they are enterprises that have obtained guarantees for the repayment of debts within six months from the date of the application for bankruptcy;

3. With respect to an enterprise for which creditors file for bankruptcy, bankruptcy proceedings shall be suspended if the enterprise's superior departments in charge have applied for reorganization and if the enterprise and its creditors have reached a settlement agreement through consultation.

1.4.3.   Settlement and reorganization

1. With respect to an enterprise for which the creditors apply for bankruptcy, the superior departments in charge of the enterprise that is the subject of the bankruptcy application may, within three months after the people's court has accepted the case, apply to carry out reorganization of the enterprise; the period of reorganization shall not exceed two years.

2. After an application for reorganization is submitted, the enterprise shall propose a draft settlement agreement to the creditors' meeting.
    The settlement agreement shall stipulate the period in which the enterprise shall repay the debts.

3. After the enterprise and the creditors' meeting have reached a settlement agreement that has been recognized by the people's court, the people's court shall make a public announcement and suspend the bankruptcy proceedings. The settlement agreement shall have legal effect from the date of the public announcement.

4. The reorganization of the enterprise shall be supervised by its superior departments.

The reorganization plan of the enterprise shall be discussed by a congress of the staff and workers of the enterprise. The circumstances of the reorganization of the enterprise shall be reported to the congress of the staff and workers of the enterprise and its opinion shall be heeded.

The circumstances of the reorganization of the enterprise shall be periodically reported to the creditors' meeting.

1.4.4.   Bankruptcy declaration and bankruptcy liquidation

The distribution plan for the bankruptcy property shall be proposed by the liquidation team, adopted by the creditor's meeting and submitted to the people's court for judgment before implementation.

After the prior deduction of bankruptcy expenses from the bankruptcy property, repayment shall be made in the following order:

1. Wages of staff and workers and labour insurance expenses that are owed by the bankrupt enterprise;

2. Taxes that are owed by the bankrupt enterprise; and
3. Bankruptcy claims.

Where the bankruptcy property is insufficient to repay all the repayment needs within a single order of priority, it shall be distributed on a pro-rata basis.

1.4.5.   Stipulations concerning labour issues

According to Article 4 of the Law, the State should through various means arrange for the appropriate reemployment of the staff and workers of bankrupt enterprises and shall guarantee their basic living needs prior to reemployment; specific measures shall be separately stipulated by the State Council.

1.5.   "General principles of the civil law"

According to Article 45 of this law, an enterprise as legal person shall terminate for any of the following reasons:
1. if it is dissolved by law;
2. if it is disbanded;
3. if it is declared bankrupt in accordance with the law; or
4. for other reasons.

1.6.   "Civil procedure law"

1.6.1.   The respective stipulations

Chapter 19 of "Civil Procedure Law" stipulates the procedure for bankruptcy and debt repayment of legal person enterprises.
- If a legal person enterprise has suffered serious losses and is unable to repay the debts at maturity, the creditors may apply to a people's court in order to declare the debtor bankrupt for debts to be repaid; the debtor may likewise apply to a people's court in order to declare bankruptcy for debts to be repaid.
- After making an order to declare the initiation of the bankruptcy and debt repayment proceedings, the people's court shall notify the debtor and the known creditors within ten days and also make a public announcement.
    Creditors who have been notified shall, within 30 days after receiving the notice, and those who have not been notified shall, within three months after the date of the announcement, lodge their claims with the people's court. Creditors who fail to lodge their claims during the respective periods shall be deemed to have abandoned their rights.
    Creditors may organize a creditors' meeting to discuss and approve of a

formula for the disposal and distribution of bankrupt property, or for a composition agreement.

- The people's court may appoint a liquidation commission formed by relevant state organs and persons concerned. The liquidation commission shall take charge of the custody of the bankrupt property, its liquidation, assessment, disposition and distribution. The liquidation commission may also engage in necessary activities of a civil nature according to the law.

  The liquidation commission shall be responsible and report its work to the people's court.

- If the legal person enterprise and the creditors reach a composition agreement, the people's court shall, after approving the agreement, make a public announcement to this effect, and terminate the bankruptcy and debt repayment proceedings. The composition agreement shall be legally effective as of the date of the public announcement.

- With respect to the property mortgaged or otherwise used as security for bank loans or other obligations, the bank and other creditors shall have priority in the repayment of debts as regards the property mortgaged or used as security for other kinds of obligations. If the monetary value of the property mortgaged or used as security for other kinds of obligations exceeds the account of loans secured, the surplus shall go to the bankrupt property for debt repayment.

- After deduction of bankruptcy proceeding expenses from the bankrupt property, first repayment shall be made in the following order of priority:

  1. Wages and salaries of staff and workers and labour insurance expenses that are owed by the bankrupt enterprise;
  2. Taxes owed by the bankrupt enterprise; and
  3. Claims by creditors in the bankruptcy proceedings.

  Where the bankrupt property is insufficient to meet the repayment claims of the same order of priority, it shall be distributed on a pro-rata basis.

- The debt repayment of a bankrupt legal person enterprise shall be under the jurisdiction of the people's court of the place where the legal person enterprise is located.

- The provisions of the People's Republic of China on Enterprise Bankruptcy shall apply to bankruptcy and debt repayment of enterprises owned by the whole people.

  The provisions of this chapter shall not apply to non-legal person enterprises, individual businesses, lease-holding farm households or partnerships by private individuals.

1.6.2.   Comments on "civil procedure law"

The respective contents of the above provisions are similar to the provisions of "Law on Enterprise Bankruptcy". However, according to Article 206 of the Law, the coverage of the above provisions includes non-state-owned enterprises, such as collective enterprises, private enterprises, and foreign-funded enterprises. This means that the "Civil Procedure Law" is supplementary to the "Law on Enterprise Bankruptcy", which applies only to state-owned enterprises. The above stipulations were introduced because of the increasing number of cases of bankruptcy of non-state-owned legal persons.

1.7.   The respective stipulations in "labour law"

1.7.1.   Statutory consolidation and reduction of employees

According to *Article 27* of *"Labour Law"*, during the period of statutory consolidation when the employing unit comes to the brink of bankruptcy or runs deep into difficulties in production and management, and if reduction of its personnel becomes really necessary, the unit may make such reduction after it has explained the situation to the trade union or all of it staff and workers 30 days in advance, solicited opinions from them and reported to the labour administrative department.

Where the employing unit is to recruit personnel six months after the personnel reduction effected according to the stipulations of this Article, the reduced personnel shall have the priority to be reemployed.

1.7.2.   Economic compensation

According to Article 28, the employing unit shall make economic compensation in accordance with the relevant provisions of the State if it revokes it labour contracts according to the stipulations in *Article 27*.

1.7.3.   The role of the trade union

According to Article 30, the trade union of an employing unit shall have the right to air its opinions if it regards as inappropriate the revocation of a labour contract by the unit. If the employing unit violates laws, rules and regulations or labour contracts, the trade union shall have the right to request reconsideration. Where the labourer applies for arbitration or brings a lawsuit, the trade union shall render them support and assistance in accordance with the law.

1.8.   "Commercial banking law"

The commercial banks referred to in this law are bodies corporate established in accordance with "Commercial Banking Law" and "Company Law" to receive money deposits from the public, extend loans, provide settlement services and carry out other relevant functions.

According to Article 71 of this law, when a commercial bank is incapable of repaying its mature debts, it may, with the consent of the People's bank of China, be declared bankrupt by the people's court. When a commercial bank is declared bankrupt in accordance with the law, the people's court may organize the People's Bank of China and other relevant departments and personnel to form a liquidation group to conduct liquidation.

At the time of bankruptcy liquidation, a commercial bank shall give priority to paying the principal and interests of savings deposits after paying the liquidation fees and its staff wages and labour insurance fees in arrears.

2. THE RESPECTIVE POLICIES ON MERGER AND BANKRUPTCY

In addition to the above laws that are adopted by national people's congress, there are also some important policies promulgated by the State Council.

On 25 October 1994, the State Council issued "*Circular of the State Council on Some Issues of Bankruptcy in State-owned Enterprises*". This document applies to some state-owned enterprises that were on the list of 18 selected pilot cities. The main legislation grounds are "Law of the People's Republic of China on Enterprise Bankruptcy". The purpose of the Circular is to guide the work of bankruptcy in state-owned enterprises in 18 selected pilot cities.

The main principles of the Circular include the following:

1. The first measure the local authorities should take if an enterprise is to be declared bankrupt is to arrange for the appropriate reemployment of the employees of the bankrupt enterprise, to maintain social stability.

2. When an enterprise is bankrupt, the enterprise should transfer the land use right by auction or public bidding. The earnings of transfer should be used first to make arrangements for the employees. The remaining earnings and other bankruptcy property will be put into the scheme of the distribution of the bankruptcy property tighter.

3. Before the handling of the bankruptcy property, the procedure of appraisal of bankruptcy property according to law must be gone through. The property is then transferred through auction and public bidding. If the transfer earnings of the land use right are not enough to make arrangements for the employees, the shortfall should be obtained from the disposal of other bankruptcy property.

4. Some enterprises may have raised funds from their employees to maintain production operation before the bankruptcy. All of money of this kind should be regarded by the enterprise as delayed wages for the employees. Furthermore, the capital funds invested by the employees before the bankruptcy should be regarded as bankruptcy property.

5. The employees' housing supplied by the enterprise, the enterprise's school, kindergarten, hospital and other facilities in bankrupt enterprise

are not principally regarded as bankruptcy property. These kinds of assets are taken over and handled by the local government, and the employees in those units are dealt with by the local government organizations. However, if the units are unnecessary for maintaining operation or sale as a whole, the assets can be regarded as bankruptcy property.

6. Arrangements for Employees in Bankrupt Enterprises

- The various levels of government under which the bankrupt enterprises fall should make arrangements for the employees through the following means: training for work transfer, job introduction, production for their own needs, labour export and so on.
- The government encourages the employees to become self-employed. The employees can obtain re-settlement subsidy, and the right not to be classified as employees of a state-owned enterprise. The amount of re-settlement subsidy is three times the average wages in the bankrupt enterprise last year.
- The people unemployed because of the bankruptcy are entitled to unemployment insurance according to the law. After the expiration of unemployment insurance, if they are still unemployed, they can apply for social relief payment at the civil affairs department according to the respective requirements.
- The social insurance agencies at local level are responsible for the retirement pension and medical insurance of the employees from bankrupt enterprises. If the bankrupt enterprises are in the pooling system of social insurance, then the expenditure of pension and medical insurance are paid from the pooling funds. If the enterprises had not taken part in the pooling system, or if the pooling system cannot afford the pension and medical insurance expenditure, then all of the payments are paid from the earnings of the sale of the land use right. If the earnings are not enough to pay the amount, the expenses are deducted from the other bankruptcy property.
- The employees in the bankrupt enterprises who are confirmed to have totally or partially lost the ability to work due to injuries suffered at work or serious occupational diseases, or who are disabled because of work injury, should be dealt with as retired employees. If those employees' age is within five years of the retirement age, then they can enjoy retirement benefits.
- If there is a gap between the legal claim and the actual payment of dealing with employees in bankrupt enterprises, the local government should bear the remaining amount according to the relationship of administrative-subordination of the enterprises.

On 2 March 1997, the State Council issued "*Supplementary Circular of the State Council on the Issues of Merger, Bankruptcy and Reemployment in Some Enterprises in Some Cities*". The legislative bases of the document are "Law on Enterprise Bankruptcy" and "Circular of the State Council on Some Issues of Bankruptcy in State-owned Enterprises". The coverage of the

Circular is 111 state-owned enterprises. The purpose of the document is to standardize bankruptcy procedures, to promote the merger between enterprises, to carry out the Reemployment Project in state-owned enterprises and to promote industrial restructuring.

This document stresses the principle of bankruptcy, and the stipulations concerning arrangements for employees from bankrupt enterprises are similar to those in the Circular of 25 October 1994. Besides the issue of bankruptcy, this document also encourages the merger between enterprises. The State encourages the enterprises that possess dominant position to annex the enterprises that are in difficulties. The annexing enterprise bears all of debts of the annexed enterprise. The annexing enterprises can enjoy some preferential policies, such as exemption from loan interest, and enjoying benefits from writing off bad debts in pursuance of relevant state regulations.

According to the document, the annexing enterprise should make arrangements for all of the employees from the annexed enterprise. If the annexing enterprise can not allocate each employee from the annexed enterprise a working position, then the Reemployment Service Centre in the annexing enterprise can absorb the redundant employees.

There are some state-owned enterprises that do not meet the qualifications of merger and bankruptcy. The market for their products is encouraging and the internal management is sound, but they are hampered by heavy debts. The preferential policies they can enjoy include exemption from bank loan interest and the implementation of a Reemployment Project to relieve the difficulties.

The employees who are in the Reemployment Service Centre in enterprises are given basic living needs, training and reemployment.

3. ECONOMIC DISMISSAL

The Ministry of Labour issued *"Circular of the Ministry of Labour on Printing and Distributing the Provisions on Personnel Reduction due to Economic Reasons on Enterprises"* on 14 November 1994. The main contents are as follows:

3.1. The reduction of employees

According to Article 2 of this circular, an employing unit may make a reduction of its personnel when it comes to the brink of bankruptcy and is declared by a people's court to have entered the period of statutory consolidation, or runs deep into difficulties in production and management, and is up to the standards for enterprises in grave difficulties set by local governments, and if personnel reduction becomes necessary.

3.2. The procedures of personnel reduction

If personnel reduction becomes necessary, an employing unit shall conduct it according to the following procedures:

1. To explain the situation to the trade union or all of its staff and workers 30 days in advance, and provide the data concerning its production and management;
2. To put forward a plan of personnel reduction which shall contain a list of names of the reduced personnel, time of reduction, implementing measures and the measures to make economic compensations for the reduced personnel in accordance with the provisions of laws and regulations and with the agreement made in the collective contract;
3. To solicit opinions about the plan of personnel reduction from the trade union or all of its staff and workers, and to make amendments and improvements to the plan;
4. To report the plan of personnel reduction and opinions of the trade union or all of its staff and workers to local labour administrative departments, and listen to the opinions from labour administrative departments; and
5. To make public the plan of personnel reduction, deal with the formalities of revoking labour contracts with the reduced personnel, pay economic compensations to the reduced personnel according to relevant provisions and produce certificates of personnel reduction.

3.3. Employees who cannot be dismissed

An employing unit shall not reduce the following personnel:

1. Those who are confirmed to have totally or partially lost the ability to work due to occupational diseases or occupational injuries suffered at work;
2. Those who are receiving medical treatment for diseases or injuries within the prescribed period of time;
3. Female staff members or workers during pregnancy, or the post-natal or breast-feeding period; or
4. Other circumstances stipulated by laws, administrative rules and regulations.

3.4. Qualification for unemployment insurance

If the personnel who are unemployed due to reduction participate in unemployment insurance, they may register with local job-service agencies and apply for unemployment relief money.

3.5. The priority to be reemployed

Where an employing unit is to undertake new recruitment within six months from the date of its personnel reduction, the reduced personnel shall have the priority to be reemployed and the number, time and requirements of the recruitment, as well as the situation of giving priority to the reduced personnel on recruitment, shall be reported to local labour administrative departments.

3.6. The role of the government

Where an employing unit reduces its personnel in violation of laws, regulations and other relevant provisions, labour administrative departments shall order it to stop the reduction and to make corrections according to law.

3.7. The role of the trade union

An employing unit shall seriously listen to the reasonable opinions on personnel reduction from the trade union or its staff and workers.

Where an employing unit reduces its personnel in violation of the stipulations of laws and regulations or the agreement in the collective contract, the trade union shall have the power to request reconsideration.

3.8. The settlement of labour disputes

If a labour dispute takes place due to the reduction of personnel, the two parties concerned shall handle it in accordance with relevant provisions on the settlement of the labour dispute.

3.9. Economic compensation

According to *"Circular of the Ministry of Labour on Printing and Distributing the Measures of Economic Compensations for the Violation and Revocation of Labour Contracts"*, during the period of statutory consolidation when an employing unit comes to the brink of bankruptcy and if reduction of its personnel becomes necessary, the employing units shall pay the reduced personnel economic compensation according to the length of service in the unit. That is, it shall pay an equivalent of their monthly wages for each year of service.

4. REEMPLOYMENT SERVICE CENTRE IN ENTERPRISES

4.1. The causes of lay-offs in state-owned enterprises

4.1.1. Supply of labour force is more than demand of labour force

For a long time, China's large population has continued to increase. This is a pressure on employment, and is a basic cause of employment problems. At present, the annual increase in population is 14 million people.

Another cause is the high labour force participation rate. The rate in 1952 was 36.1%, and the rate in 1996 was 56.9%. The rate in urban areas is 58%. Why is the rate so high?

- Higher women's labour force participation. The figure in China at present is 45%, which is higher than many countries.
- The wage policy of "lower wages produce employment" has encouraged most of the labour force to take part in employment. Furthermore, most of the items of social insurance are connected with employment, therefore, only employment can secure benefits from the system of social insurance, such as pensions and medical insurance.
- The lack of opportunities for young people to enter universities. Many young people have to enter the labour market instead.
- The lack of natural resources and capital investment for the development of the economy. The result is a lack of working positions.

4.1.2. The planning economy

Under the system of the planning economy, the state-owned enterprises were the main channel for absorbing the labour force. The enterprises had responsibility for the arrangement of the labour force. There were also motivators for state-owned enterprises to recruit workers. The more people they recruited, the more investment they could obtain from the state. The result was that for a long time redundancy was very serious.

4.1.3. Blind investment and deficit situation

Over a long period of time, blind investment and overlapping development has resulted in the following:

- Some state-owned enterprises have a lower utilization of capacity or idle periods of time because of lack of capital and dependence on bank loans.
- Poor management and backward techniques are some of the reasons that one-third of state-owned enterprises are facing deficit and bankruptcy.
- One of the solutions to these problems is to go through the procedures of merger/bankruptcy. The consequence is lay-offs.

4.1.4. More challenges

With China's entry into the WTO, there will be an increase in the number of workers laid-off in some industries during a transitional period of time, such as in the first industry and automobile industry. Although more working position will be generated through economic development in the long term, the tense situation faced by the government at present challenges the system of employment and the system of social insurance.

4.2. Typical policies from central government

Since 1994, various measures intended to solve the problem of workers laid-off have been introduced. Government organizations and other social partners, such trade unions and women's federations, have cooperated greatly. They have achieved very positive results. Many laid-off workers have been reemployed under preferential policies.

The most typical policy document is as follows: on 9 June 1998, the State Council Issued a *Circular on Ensuring Laid-off Workers' Basic Living Needs and Strengthening the Work of Reemployment*. This document is the most important policy document concerning laid-off workers, and is a summary of various positive pilot experiences in many local areas over several years. It is a comprehensive document that stipulates the system of Reemployment Service Centres in state-owned enterprises. One of the targets of the Circular is to ensure that more than 50% of existing laid-off workers and newly laid-off workers are reemployed.

The main contents of the document are as follows:

4.2.1. Preferential polices to vulnerable groups in the labour market

If husband and wife work in the same enterprise, then only one of them can be laid-off. If they work in different enterprises, they cannot be laid-off in both enterprises at the same time.

The Circular requires enterprises to avoid laying off disabled persons and the dependents of deceased military heroes.

4.2.2. The reemployment service centre

The Reemployment Service Centre is an organization that is set up in state-owned enterprise. Its main functions are to ensure that laid-off workers' receive basic living needs and to promote their reemployment. The qualifications for employees who enter into the Centre include the following conditions: they are regular employees of the enterprise; they have a labour relationship with the enterprise; they do not find another job in other working units. Laid-off workers are allowed to remain in the Centre for up to three years. After three years, the enterprise will terminate the labour relationship with him/her. If the laid-off does not find another job, then he/she is entitled to apply for unemployment insurance benefit. The longest term of unemployment insurance is two years. After two years, if the laid-off workers still do not get employment, they can apply for social welfare benefit. From 1998 to 2000, the proportion of laid-off workers entering the Centre was more than 90%.

4.2.3.   The level of living expenses provided by the centre

Generally speaking, the level of living expenses provided by the Centre for laid-off workers is higher than the benefit of unemployment insurance. The capital source of the living expenses and the social insurance fees paid by the enterprise are from three channels: one-third from the enterprises themselves; one-third from society (unemployment insurance fund); one-third from the government.

4.2.4.   To promote reemployment through diversified channels

The issue of employment in China is a challenge for the long term. The fundamental solution to this challenge is to maintain the increase of economic development and to explore new employment fields. The options that are encouraged by the government include:

- To cultivate new economic increasing point, to strengthen the construction of basic industries and facilities, to develop the labour-intensive industry. Tertiary industry, such as commercial industry, the tourist industry, the catering trade and the community service field, is especially encouraged by the government, because these kinds of jobs do not have very high requirements in terms of capital and technical knowledge.
- To promote the development of non-state-owned enterprises, including collective enterprises, self-employment and private enterprises. If laid-off workers apply to run self-employment businesses, small private enterprises or domestic handicraft industries, the commercial and industrial registration agency and the agency of urban construction management should handle the approval procedure without delay. In the first year of running a business, laid-off workers can enjoy exemption from normal commercial and industrial fees. If laid-off workers run community service businesses, then the registration procedures should be simplified, and laid-off workers should enjoy exemption from business tax, individual income tax and some administrative fees for three years.

4.2.5. To speed up the system of social security

The new system of social security in China has been designed to adapt to the needs of the socialist market economy and of modern enterprise. The coverage of pensions, medical insurance and unemployment insurance will be widened to include all kinds of enterprises, including state-owned enterprises, private enterprises, foreign-funded enterprises, and other non-stated-owned enterprises. The system of social security should meet the needs of the rational allocation of human resources.

4.2.6. To strengthen reemployment training

According to the Circular, the job-introduction agency has an obligation to provide a free service for laid-off workers. The working units are encouraged to recruit laid-off workers, especially female laid-off workers. All kinds of channels should be involved in the training of laid-off workers, such as training financed by the government, by the enterprises and by other social organizations, and even by the workers studying themselves. The organizations that provide training for laid-off workers are entitled to some subsidies.

4.3. Another important document on the issue of lay-offs

- In addition to the document whose main contents are introduced above, another important document is *"Circular on Strengthening the Management of Laid-off Workers in State-owned Enterprises and Construction of Reemployment Service Centre"*. This document is a regulation that was promulgated by the Ministry of Labour and Social Security, the National Commission of Economic Trade, the Ministry of Finance, the Ministry of Education, the State Statistic Bureau, and the All China Federation of Trade Union, in 1998. The regulation aims at the implementation of the document that is discussed above. Therefore, the contents are more concrete. In terms of the procedures of personnel reduction, it is similar to "The Provisions on Personnel Reduction due to Economic Reason in Enterprises". The contents relating to labour contracts are as follows.
- On the Modification of Labour Contracts. If a laid-off worker enters the Reemployment Service Centre, his/her original labour contract will be replaced by an "agreement of ensuring basic living and reemployment". The agreement of reemployment is concluded between the internal Reemployment Service Centre and the laid-off worker. The term of the agreement is three years. The agreement should stipulate the rights and obligations of both parties and their responsibilities. The issues of arrears of wages and medical fees, the sum of raised fund, should be included in the agreement. The debt relationship between enterprises and laid-off workers

should not end because of the lay-off situation and the modification of the labour contract.

- On the Termination of Labour Contracts. If agreement cannot be reached on the modification of the labour contract and the laid-off worker does not want to enter the Reemployment Service Centre, then the labour relationship between the enterprise and laid-off worker can be revoked.

If the laid-off worker who enters the Reemployment Service Centre is employed by another employer or becomes self-employed, then the enterprise can revoke the agreement and labour contract with the newly recruited laid-off worker. The new employer should pay the continuous contributions of social insurance for the newly recruited laid-off worker. The laid-off worker who becomes self-employed can pay the contributions of social insurance for himself according to the stipulations of the local agency of social insurance.

The working conditions of laid-off workers who are recruited to work in other working units are under the supervision of the labour department according to the laws and regulations on labour supervision.

5.   THE PHENOMENON OF HIDDEN EMPLOYMENT

5.1.   General situation

The phenomenon of hidden employment is very popular among laid-off workers. This phenomenon is defined as a situation under which a laid-off worker has a job in another unit, but still has legal labour relationship with the original enterprise. According to the sample survey conducted by the research workers of the Ministry of Labour and Social Security in 2000, more than 50% of laid-off workers actually have another job. In some places and enterprises, the rate reached 60% to 80%. There were 3.5 million laid-off workers who had hidden employment in 2000. Generally speaking, the rate of hidden employment in large- and medium-sized cities and in coastal areas is higher than in medium- and small-sized cities and in inland cities.

5.2.   Forms of hidden employment

1.   The laid-off worker who has not terminated the labour relationship with the former enterprise has agreed a labour contract with a new employer. That means that he/she has a double labour relationship with two employers at the same time.
2.   Although the laid-off worker has worked in another unit, there is no written labour contract. This kind of relationship is called "fact labour relationship" in China. Some of them reached a temporary agrrement with the new employer.

3. Some laid-off workers who already have an individual business licence retain the labour relationship with the former enterprises. These kind of laid-off workers are characterized by the related skill and capital, and also have some knowledge of management.
4. Some laid-off workers who do not have regular working units or working position, or run temporary business without a business licence work as pedlars or temporary employees.

The first three kinds of hidden employment are called stable employment, the last one is called unstable hidden employment.

Regarding the phenomenon of hidden employment, there are different opinions. Some people think this phenomenon is abnormal from the standardized labour relationship point of view. The later employer enjoys benefits from the respective lower labour cost. They do not need to pay the social insurance fee and minimum wages for the laid-off workers. Other people think that this phenomenon is understandable. This is a balance mechanism by which laid-off workers have another channel to obtain income and to relieve their present living difficulties, and to help to maintain social stability.

However, regardless of the argument on the advantages or disadvantages of hidden employment, this is only a phenomenon in the transitional period of economic reform. It will disappear gradually along with the standardization of labour relationships.

5.3. The causes of the phenomenon of hidden employment

The main cause is that laid-off workers do not want to terminate the relationship with their enterprises. The consequence is that it is very difficult for state-owned enterprises to revoke labour contracts with laid-off workers. The barriers include:

- Lack of ability for enterprises to pay lump-sum compensations for revocation of labour contracts because of economic dismissal. Normally, the employees involved in economic dismissal in an enterprise are not a minority. It is an unaffordable load for many state-owned enterprises at present. If enterprises pay all of the economic compensations to laid-off workers, then the enterprises would be bankrupt, and the situation would be worse.

    Besides the compensations, the debts owed by enterprises to laid-off workers are another barriers for the termination of labour contracts. The debts include arrears in wages, social insurance contributions from employers, the raised funds borrowed from employees in the past and the contribution of the housing public funds owed by enterprises. Laid-off workers are worried that if they leave the enterprises, all of these debts would not be returned.

- The linkage of the relationship of social insurance is a problem. As a laid-off worker, the issue he/she is most concerned with is pensions and medical insurance. In recent years, the non-stated-owned enterprises are becoming main channels for absorbing employment. Many of these enterprises are unwilling to take part in the system of social insurance. They try to escape from the contributions obligation. According to the existing Chinese system of social insurance, if the employers do not pay the contribution, the employees are not entitled to social insurance benefits. Of course, the existing laws and regulations require that all kinds of enterprises should take part in the system of social insurance.

- Lack of ability to obtain reemployment. Many of the laid-off workers are middle-aged people, with a lack of employment skills and a poor educational background. They are at a disadvantage in the labour market. It is not easy for them to leave the original enterprises. To many people, to leave enterprises means to lose everything because in the past the state-owned enterprise guaranteed employees everything.

The tendency in a lay-off is to separate laid-off workers from the enterprises through law and regulations, and through policies. There are some preferential policies for laid-off workers, especially for middle-aged and old employees, and female employees. However, the critical solution is to generate more working positions. The government has focused on the field of community services.

6.   THE TRANSFER OF REEMPLOYMENT SERVICE CENTRE TO UNEMPLOYMENT INSURANCE

In 1998, the State Council issued a famous document named by *"Circular on the Work of Ensuring the Laid-off Workers' Basic Living Standards and Promoting Reemployment"*. After that, Reemployment Service Centres were set up in state-owned enterprises in many places. From 1998 to 2000, there were 21 million laid-off workers who entered into internal Reemployment Service Centres, of which 13 million laid-off workers had been reemployed. There were 95% of laid-off workers who received basic living benefits. The practice has proved that the system of guaranteeing basic living needs in state-owned enterprises is an effective transitional measure. It has played an active role in stabilizing society. The reason for the implementation of the system of a basic living needs guarantee is there was a lack of a social security system and market mechanism. Therefore, it is only a transitional measure. In terms of reform, the system of basic living needs guarantee cannot adapt to the requirements of the system of modern enterprises. Besides, the setting up and the operation of Reemployment Service Centres are thought to be a high-cost measure. The input is bigger than the output. It is impossible for the government bear the financial burden of it forever, and a system that is independent from the enterprises is needed. Therefore, the merger of the system of basic living needs with the system of unemployment insurance is necessary. The target of the merger is to relieve the enterprises' burden and to standardize the system of social security.

The pilot plan for the social security system in Lining Province was carried out by the State Counciland started in 2001. The system of a basic living guarantee for laid-off workers in state-owned enterprises has been transferred into the unemployment system. That means that from January 2001, laid-off workers in state-owned enterprises have gone directly into the unemployment system instead of entering into the internal Reemployment Service Centre first.

The policies are as follows:

6.1. The role of "regulation on unemployment insurance"

The implementation of "Regulation on Unemployment Insurance" should be strengthened. The coverage of unemployment insurance should be extended to enterprises and institutional organizations and their employees in urban areas. The fund management of collection and expenditure and the basic management work should be strengthened. The purpose is to ensure unemployed people's basic living standards and to promote reemployment.

6.2. The reemployment service centres are no longer set up

From January 2001 on, state-owned enterprises have not set up the internal Reemployment Service Centre. The newly laid-off workers have not entered into Service Centres. The enterprises can terminate the labour contracts with laid-off workers according to laws and regulations. If the enterprises have paid the full amount of unemployment insurance stipulated by the regulations, then their laid-off workers are entitled to enjoy unemployment insurance benefits. The central government requires local governments to complete the work of merging the reemployment service centre system with the system of unemployment insurance.

6.3. The termination of labour relationship

Laid-off workers who had already entered into the Reemployment Service Centre can retain the benefits stipulated in the original agreements between them and the Reemployment Service Centre. The term of this kind of agreement is three years. After three years, if the laid-off worker is still not reemployed, then the enterprise can terminate the labour contract with the worker. The worker then applies for the benefit of unemployment insurance or the benefit of minimum living standards guarantee.

6.4. The handling of debts owned by enterprises

There is a need to carry out the principle of separating the termination of labour relationship from the relationship of credit and debt. In many state-owned enterprises, one of the obstacles for laid-off workers wishing to leave enterprises is that enterprises owe them some economic compensation, such as the delayed payment of wages. Operational measures can differ at local levels.

6.5. Preferential policies

If the length of employee's actual service is more than 30 years, or if the employee will reach retirement age in less than five years, the employees who are at a disadvantage in the labour market can retire from the enterprise, with their basic living expenses fundedby the enterprise. During this time, the enterprise remains responsible for paying the social insurance premiums for the employee. When the employee meets the requirements of retirement age, he/she can officially enjoy retirement payment.

6.6. The housing issue

Apartments in which laid-off workers have lived, and which are owned by the enterprises, can be purchased by the laid-off workers according to the reformed housing policies at local levels.

7. ON THE AMENDMENT OF "LAW ON ENTERPRISE BANKRUPTCY"

The original "Law on Enterprise Bankruptcy" was adopted on 2 December 1986, and came into force on 1 November 1988. The Law had not adapted to the changes of the reform. Therefore, the revised work of amendment started in 1994. Now the new bankruptcy law could well be adopted in the near future. The original law focused on the issues of bankruptcy in state-owned enterprises and on social stability. Along with the development of the market economy, the issue of bankruptcy of non-state-owned companies, foreign-funded enterprises and partnership needs to be stipulated. The issue especially will be more obvious after China's entry into the WTO.

    The former bankruptcy law was characterized by the planning economy to some extent. For instance, according to Article 24 of the Law, the members of the liquidation team shall be designated by the people's court from among the superior departments in charge, government finance departments, and other relevant departments and professional personnel, instead of the independent and professional organization composed of experts. This means the administrative departments can interfere in the procedure of bankruptcy. The new draft of the law accepts some international expert opinion.

    Some main discussions of the draft are as follows:

1. The issue of state-owned enterprises will mainly follow the special stipulations by the State Council, although the issue has a important status in the draft law.

2. The coverage of the draft includes six kinds of enterprises, such as company, partnership, individual enterprise, and foreign-funded enterprise.
3. The role of the government in the procedure of bankruptcy will be weakened gradually. The independent intermediary organizations and professional persons will play an increasingly more and more important role.
4. The new draft law accepts the approach taken by other countries. This is the system of bankruptcy reorganization. Liquidation is not the only solution: the enterprise that has potential to be saved should be given an opportunity to be reorganized.

CONCLUSION

Regarding the issues of merger, division, bankruptcy and labour protection for employees in China, there exist laws, regulations and policies. To non-stated-owned enterprises, the issue of merger, division and bankruptcy is less difficult. What they need to do is to follow the general laws and regulations. Of course, some employers try to use legal loopholes to escape from legal responsibility. However, to state-owned enterprises, the problem is very often complicated. The most problem that causes most headaches is how to make arrangements for laid-off workers. The government needs continued economic reforms while at the same time maintaining social stability. Therefore, to handle these issues in state-owned entities needs some specific policies. Considering the situation in which there will be an increasing number of merger, division and bankruptcy cases during the transitional period following China's entry into the WTO, it is useful to compare the Chinese situation with the experiences in other countries, to try to find out more possible options for China.

REFERENCES

1 *"Company Law of the People's Republic of China":* Adopted at the Fifth Meeting of the Standing Committee of the Eighth National People's Congress on December 29, 1993 and promulgated by Order No. 16 of the President of the People's Republic of China on December 29, 1993, and effective as of July 1, 1994.
2 *"Law of the People's Republic of China on Enterprise Bankruptcy":* Adopted at the 18th Meeting of the Standing Committee of the Sixth National People's Congress and Promulgated by Order No. 45 of the President of the People's Republic of China on December 2, 1986, for trial implementation three full months after the Law on Industrial Enterprises with Ownership by the Whole People comes into effect.
3 *"General Principles of the Civil Law of the People's Republic of China":* Adopted at the Fourth Session of the Sixth National People's Congress, promulgated by Order No. 37 of the President of the People's Republic of China on April 12, 1986, and effective as of January 1, 1987.

4 *"Labour Law of the People's Republic of China"*: Adopted at the Eighth Meeting of the Standing Committee of the Eighth National People's Congress on July 5, 1994, promulgated by Order No. 28 of the President of the People's Republic of China, and effective as of January 1, 1995.

5 *"Commercial Banking Law of the People's Republic of China"*: Adopted at the 13th Session of the Standing Committee of the Eighth National People's Congress on May 10, 1995.

6 *"Circular of the State Council on Some Issues of Bankruptcy in State-owned Enterprises"*, 1994, the State Council issued on October 25.

7 *"Supplementary Circular of the State Council on the Issues of Merger, Bankruptcy and Reemployment in Some Enterprises in Some Cities"*, the State Council issued on March 2, 1997.

8 *"Circular of the Ministry of Labour on Printing and Distributing the Provisions on Personnel Reduction due to Economic Reasons on Enterprises"* (LMI [1994] No. 447 issued by the Ministry of Labour on Nov. 14, 1994).

9 *"Circular of the Ministry of Labour on Printing and Distributing the Measures of Economic Compensations for the Violation and Revocation of Labour Contracts"*, issued by the Ministry of Labour on December 3, 1994.

10 *"Circular on Ensuring Laid-off Workers' Basic Living Needs and Strengthening the Work of Reemployment"*, issued by the State Council on June 9, 1998.

11 *"Circular on Strengthening the Management of Laid-off Workers in State-owned Enterprises and Construction of Reemployment Service Centre"*. This document is a regulation that was promulgated by Ministry of Labour and Social Security, National Commission of Economic Trade, Ministry of Finance, Ministry of Education, State Statistic Bureau, All China Federation of Trade Union together in 1998.

12 *"Civil Procedure Law of the People's Republic of China"*, adopted at the Fourth Session of the Seventh National People's Congress on April 9, 1991, promulgated by Order No. 44 of the President of the People's Republic of China on April 9, 1991, and effective as of the date of promulgation.

13 Li Shuguang, Ge Ming and Li Qi (1996), "Bankruptcy and Reorganization of Chinese Enterprises", the Publishing House of People's Daily, Pages from 40–50, and Pages from 147–161.

14 Mo Rong (1999), "Background and Causes of Laid-off Workers in State-owned Enterprises", from 'The Most Critical Task—Guideline of the System of Basic Living Guarantee and Reemployment in State-owned Enterprises', the Publishing House of Economic Science, Pages from 36–39.

15 Yu Faming (chief editor), "Perspective of Labour Relationship of Laid-off Workers", Pages from 13 to 20, the Publishing House of Economic and Science.

3. France

François Gaudu

1. INTRODUCTION

Labour law interferes with corporate restructuring in two ways:
- Workers' rights sometimes depend on collective relationship regulations, such as the right to strike, fair bargaining duty or workers' participation in decisions inside the company.
- Workers' rights also depend on statutory regulations of the individual labour contract, such as dismissal regulations, lay-offs, redundancy, or transfer of labour contracts when a business is transferred.

In France, statutory regulation of the individual labour contract is much more developed than collective relationship regulations, especially collective bargaining. For an ordinary worker, a lot of things – minimum wages, retirement, Social security, etc. – are conferred by statutory law. And this also applies to corporate restructuring: the duties of employers and employees are not only defined by the sole content of the offer and the acceptance, as in classic civil law (and also in common law). Contracting sets off a series of statutory regulations. Collective agreements complete the statutory regulations and fulfil the same role (in France, collective agreements most frequently cover a whole industrial sector, like metallurgy, textiles, etc.).

Contracting is not only saying yes: contracting is like "clicking" to install software. The statutory and collectively bargained regulations are in fact imperative. It is therefore not possible for the individual labour contract to set this statute aside.

However, I must also point out that dismissal regulations were adopted by consensus of all (or most of) the parties concerned. For example, the duty to give notice or to pay a dismissal allowance to the dismissed worker in proportion to his seniority first appears in collective agreements before World War II. France went through very serious social crises, for example in 1936 and 1968, but this employment regulation was not an issue of those crises.

Why this (relative) consensus? Employment stability perhaps led to the French version of "fordism". It must also be taken into account that France, for more than 50 years – from 1920 to 1974 at least – needed manpower.

The same remark applies to the regulation of the transfer of labour contracts when a business is transferred, a measure wanted by bosses of the steel industry, as I shall mention later.

R. Blanpain (ed.),
Corporate Restructuring and the Role of Labour Law, 61–78.
© 2003 *Kluwer Law International. Printed in Great Britain.*

Since 1973–74, France has gone through an uninterrupted period of business restructuring. Social and human consequences have been considerable. The modernisation of the French economy has been accomplished at great cost.

French law denotes a contradictory situation:
- The level of unionisation is very weak (less than 10% in the private sector).
- But public opinion has great expectations regarding labour and employment law, and looks very favourably on a high level of protection for workers.

The combination of public expectations and the weakness of the unions has led Parliament to develop a legislative process based on discussion, which in reality has little effect. What is really wanted by the Government or the Parliamentarians, as a matter of fact, is to have something to advertise. The two new statutes of 15 May 2001 and 18 January 2002, of which I will speak later, illustrate this criticism, in my opinion.

During the last two decades, the economic power of the State has certainly decreased. Nevertheless, the State still plays an important role (at least, as tax collector, and through the Social Security system, the State is often the greatest creditor, when a business runs into difficulties). French bosses are often ex-members of the high civil service, if they are not ex-students of a prestige military school (École polytechnique). This creates connections.

2.   OUTLINE OF THE REGULATIONS REGULATING CORPORATE RESTRUCTURING

2.1.   Corporate law (and commercial law)

French corporate law ignores the question of outsourcing and plant closure (with a new exception, dealt with below).

Corporate law however considers, of course, merger (a), takeover, holding and transfer of the holding of a majority of shares or stocks (b). Bankruptcy and insolvency law also contains regulations concerning business restructuring (c).

2.1.1.   Merger

Merger is regulated by a EC directive (n° 78/855, 20 October 78), transposed in French law in 1988 (L. 5 January 88, Art. L. 236-1 ssq. Com. Code). Merger by absorption of one company into another and merger that creates a new company are covered. Scission (partial transfer of the estate) is also regulated.

Both EC directive and French law considers that merger and scission realises the transfer of the whole estate, assets, credit and liabilities. Many contracts are transferred to the absorbent company or to the new company (except those concluded *intuitu personae*). The individual labour contract (or employment contract) is transferred, following EC directive of 1978 and Art. L. 122-12 Lab. Code in the French law.

Merger implies exchange of shares to other shares. Once the exchange rate has been calculated, the Boards of Directors fix the content of the merger's scheme. Then, the shareholders (or stockholders) must vote on the scheme at an extraordinary assembly (special quorum and majority rules).

The company's works council (see below) must be consulted before the assembly. Furthermore, in public companies, two delegates take part in the Board of Directors' meetings. However, corporate law doesn't make void decisions that violate statutes outside corporate law...

2.1.2. Takeover, holding and transfer of the holding of a majority of shares or stocks

The Commercial Code gives definitions for subsidiary companies (>50%) and participation (between 10% and 50%). Issues relate to accountancy, labour law, and some commercial or corporate regulations, which become more flexible. Reciprocal shareholding is prohibited (Com. Code, L 233-29) as soon as one company owns more than 10% of another. Self-holding, since 1989, is useless, because the stocks are then deprived of the right to vote.

Regarding corporate law, the regulation chiefly concerns the companies quoted on the stock exchange. Crossing of certain levels of participation (5%, 10%, 20%, 33% and 50%) must be notified to the company concerned and to a public authority ("Conseil des Marchés Financiers"). Omission of such notification deprives the stocks exceeding the regarded level of notification of the right to vote for two years, a penalty which a Court can extend.

When participation exists, the company's works council can ask for the creation of a holding's works council. The answer depends on several standards, all of which show the strength of links between the two companies. Criteria other than financial participation are used to complete the evidence of the holding: same leadership, long-term contracts shaping a lasting pattern.

Specific regulations of long-term contracts exist, but generally speaking the effects of "contract based holding" are underestimated.

For fiscal reasons, the transfer of the holding of a majority of shares or stocks is often used instead of transfer of the estate. Some companies have internal regulations of shares or stocks transfers (like agreement clauses). But statutory law concerns mainly the takeover on the stock exchange.

Beyond 33% of shares, a buyer can't increase his participation without recourse to a public takeover (Fin. Mark. Code, L. 433-3-I). Indirect holding, in particular by subsidiary companies, must be taken into account. Of course, the assailant can also make his offer when he is still below 33%.

The purchase offer must concern all of the stocks. The offer is precisely regulated – the content of the offer, informing the market on the projects of assailant ... – and must respect the principle of equality between the stockholders. Purchases outside the public market are then prohibited. On the other hand, the management of the company that is being bought up must protect the interests of the stockholders, despite its own interests. To preserve the operation on the stock exchange, the offer must not exceed 3 months.

The new law of 18 January 2002 gives new rights to the works council in the case of a public takeover: extended information rights, the right to convoke the assailant to hear him (or his agent). If the assailant doesn't answer this invitation, his rights to vote cannot be used, until the works council has heard him. Commercial lawyers still dispute the meaning of this last rule, because the voidness, in corporate law, is very strictly limited (the new rule belongs to Labour Code, and not to corporate law). On the other hand, public takeover makes any help useful: the management sometimes uses the workers as allies to resist the assailant (squire of the white knight...). Conversely, the assailant – following the content of his project – can sometimes find an advantage in talking with eventual opponents, such as workers who are sometimes also small stockholders.

2.1.3.   Insolvency

The question depends on the law of 25 January 1985.

The insolvency procedure has three purposes:
– Preservation of the business and continuation of the activity;
– Preservation of jobs;
– Liquidation of liabilities.

Obviously, those purposes are at least partially contradictory. To fulfil and conciliate them, the procedure begins with an observation period, after the declaration of insolvency. Judges nominate a judicial agent, both to manage the business and to prepare economic proposals to the tribunal (usually a commercial one). During the observation period, dismissals are prohibited except in the case of emergencies. Eventual purchasers of the business can make offers, which require details concerning the price, the economic scheme and the level of maintained employment. The management also works to propose solutions. Finally, the observation period ends and the tribunal makes a decision.

The tribunal's choice is between either a reinvigorating scheme for the business or its liquidation.

If the liquidation is chosen, the whole estate is sold to pay the creditors. But the purchase of a plant or a complete production entity at a global price is also possible (see below).

If the tribunal decides to reinvigorate the business, it has two different technical choices:
– Continuation, which means that the previous organisation will manage the business. However, the need for fresh money often brings the need for new shareholders, and the transfer of the holding is not rare.
– Business transfer. The tribunal accepts in this case the offer previously made by a purchaser.

In both cases, the tribunal must define a scheme whose purpose is the reinvigoration of the business. This scheme has the same authority as a judgement, and verification measures occur following the judgement.

In this procedure, the works council has the same (theoretical) access to the judges as the debtor. The representative of the works council must be heard before all important decisions. If this hearing does not take place, the judgement is void.

Nevertheless, commercial judges are elected by businessmen, and the way the commercial tribunal operates is particularly opaque.

2.2. Labour law

Except in the case of insolvency, where the judges decide, decisions concerning corporate restructuring are basically made by the management or by the shareholders. No bargaining duty applies, nor measures to allow workers' participation.

However, the workers' representatives composing the company's works council (the "comité d'entreprise", below works council) have an extended right to information and consultation, which the laws of 15 May 2001 and 18 January 2002 were intended to improve.

The works council's chairman is the employer, but the latter can't vote when he consults the council as representative of the workers. The council is made up of elected workers of all categories. Perhaps 80% of these are members of Unions (during the first vote round, only "representative Unions" can introduce candidates, and there is no second round if the majority or workers express a vote). The council has what we call "civil personality" (in French law, an entity which is not a human being cannot be entitled to any right nor action if it is not recognised as a "person"), and it receives from the employer 0.2% of all the wages to finance its activities. Thus, it can afford lawyers, as well as experts. Furthermore, it can often call on an accountant charged to the company. The violation of the works council's rights is a criminal offence ("délit d'entrave").

The general principle is that the works council must be informed and consulted on all the significant matters concerning corporate restructuring. EC law doesn't ignore the question, but generally speaking, French law requires more.

In addition to this general principle, the law specifies that the works council must be *informed* during the month after the elections of its members on:
- The legal shape of the business;
- The eventual ownership of the company in a holding;
- Anything the management knows about the distribution of the interests between stockholders who own more than 10%.

The council has the right to the same information and the same copies as the stockholders, at the same time and in the same conditions, plus the right to convoke the company's auditor in order to receive explanations. Certain colleagues commercial lawyers aim to write: information given to workers' representatives is more comprehensive than information given to stockholders.

Anything the management knows about the existence of an eventual takeover must also be notified.

The works council must be *consulted* on events like:
– Economical or juridical corporate restructuring (merger, transfer, important changes in the organisation of production, acquisition or transfer of a subsidiary company, new participation taken in the company or by the company in another one...).
– Any significant schemes to introduce new technologies.
– A declaration of insolvency and measures decided during the insolvency procedure.

Each year, in order to examine the accounts presented to the stockholders, and in extraordinary circumstances such as mass redundancy and insolvency, the council can have recourse to an accountant. This accountant is selected by the council, but paid by the company; the judge resolves disputes.

The frequent use of these rights has created a small market: several accounting firms work only for unions. Possibility also exists to initiate an alert procedure. Like the minority of stockholders, the works council can finally ask the commercial judge to nominate an expert, to examine certain risky management decisions.

The effect is that the social consequences of decisions must be, if not exactly taken into account, at least publicly examined.

On the other hand, the members of the works council have no real power. Elaborating an alternative strategy is therefore a frustrating activity. Most works councils, for this reason, protest more than they propose. In France, consulting the workers' representative is frequently regarded by the director, at best as a communication operation, at worse as an unpleasant waste of time.

In the case of major difficulties, however, the situation changes and the works council has a certain degree of recourse to commercial and corporate law, as previously mentioned.

The new law of 15 May 2001 and 18 January 2002 improves these rights. Apart from the issues of redundancy (see below) and takeover (above), the more noticeable changes are:
– The closure of a department or section must be decided by the Board of Directors, after consultation with the works council about the planned decision, and before consultation regarding mass redundancy (Art. 97, L. 2002).
– The social and local impact of certain decisions, such as closure, or a "scheme of strategic development likely to affect working and employment conditions" (*a* very vague notion) must be studied in a special written report by the management (Art. 97 and 98, L. 2002).

- When the closure of a department or section is forecasted, an "important disagreement" between the management and the works council can occur. When such a divergence occurs, and if the consequence would be that at least 100 employees are laid off, each party is allowed to bring the question before a mediator. The duration of the mediator's commission cannot exceed one month, and in the end the Board of Directors decides. Let us point out here the influence of the German *Interessenausgleich*.

In my opinion, these provisions, in the French context, may have a dilatory effect without producing any substantial improvement of the workers' situation.

Other changes may be of greater importance:
- The works council can call on an auditor, paid for by the company, in the case of a merger, and has the right to be heard by the "Conseil de la concurrence", the jurisdiction in charge of antitrust legislation (L. 2001).
- The works council can ask for the convening of a stockholders' assembly. Use of this facility requires designation by the judge of a mandatory. Previously, this option was reserved for minority stockholders. A precedent in the use of such a facility by a works council already exists (Marseille, Trib. Com., 7 November 2001, CE Gemplus c/ SA Gemplus, BRDA n° 22/ 01, p. 4).
- The representative of the works council can assist in any stockholders assembly. He can ask for a decision scheme to be included on the meeting's agenda. He can be heard in certain cases.

Many of these provisions are obscure, but they nevertheless open new fields of activity to the works council.

2.3. Business transfer

The EC directive of 1977 is the product of a long-term cooperation between German and French law.

In 1928, France adopted the text of Art. Form L. 122-12 Lab. Code (former Art 23, al. 7). This 1928 law is explicitly borrowed from German law (several provisions contained in BGB, HGB and GmbHG; *cf.* Hueck and Nipperdey, "Lehrbuch des Arbeitsrecht", t. 1, Mannheim/Berlin/Leipzig, 1931, p. 290 ssq.). During the process of harmonisation between French law and the law of the former German territories recovered by France in 1918, many wished to the keep German legislation regarding business transfer, not only Unions, but bosses of the iron industry as well. Then, the 1928 law obtained the agreement of the two sides of the Parliament.

Later, Germany reformed its law and adopted the present regulation. It is rumored – at least in France – that French jurisprudence was then (1972) taken into account. Whatever the case, a few years later, the EC directive of 1977 was introduced. This very ambitious text was pretty easily accepted, because French and German legislation were very close (and Italian legislation too, with the notion of *azienda* contained in the Italian civil code; thus, the three biggest countries among the six founders of the EC had similar regulations).

Why did Germany introduce this legislation before France? The reason – this is a hypothesis that I would like to submit – is that the German economy was very concentrated, with famous huge holdings (*Konzern*), a long time before the French economy. Concentration of capital and of the economy had given birth to a "market" in which holdings sell and buy plants. Whenever this kind of business-transfer market occurs, a regulation to resolve labour questions when a business is purchased becomes necessary, to simplify operations.

Eighty years after Germany, the EC tried to establish an open market – an open market for business transfer as well. This may be the reason that the 1977 directive was adopted without difficulty.

3. CORPORATE RESTRUCTURING AND SUCCESSION OF EMPLOYMENT CONTRACTS (OR INDIVIDUAL LABOUR CONTRACTS)

3.1. Notion of business transfer

Art. L 122-12, al. 2 of the French Labour Code requires the continuation of individual labour contracts (referred to as labour contracts below) when a business or a plant is transferred.

Since 1934, the definition of the application conditions of the law has not changed. The traditional definition used to be "application in all cases in which the same business continues with a new management" (Soc. 19 January 1966, Bull. civ. IV, n° 67; Soc. 19 February 81, Bull. civ. V n° 102).

Following the EC Court of Justice, the "Cour de cassation" has adopted a new definition, whose meaning is not considerably different: application to "all transfers of an economic entity that keeps its identity and whose activity is continued or started up again" (AP 16 March 1990, Bull. civ. n° 4). This definition includes at least two conditions: the continuation of the activity (a) and the transfer of an economic entity (b).

3.1.1. The continuation of the activity

This notion concerns both the preservation of the destination and the habitual use of the means of production, and the preservation of employment opportunities.

Originally, the criterion of continuation of the activity was used to justify an application of L 122-12, al. 2 in the case of a partial transfer of assets or means of production. A company sells a single plant. The labour contracts must be continued with the purchaser, because the means of production keep their destination and the employment opportunities still exist. There is no need for the company's whole estate to be transferred, as long as the continuation of activity is possible.

The notion of continuation of the activity is then used to distinguish the simple selling of an object from a business transfer, in the case of a partial transfer of an estate.

For example, if a company buys a truck, it is not usually required to employ the former driver. However, if the purchase of the trucks allows a transfer of a clientele, another situation may occur. If a company acquires the trucks along with the clientele of a previous transportation company, the drivers' labour contracts must be continued (Soc. 7 March 1989, Bull. civ. V, n° 179).

In certain cases, activity becomes impossible, for instance as a result of mistakes made by management. Let us assume that a plant was poorly managed after being rented by its owner, and no further activity was reasonably possible. The end of the lease transfers the remaining means of production back to the owner, who is however not required to continue the labour contracts.

It can happen that a business stops its activities for a short while before starting up again. For instance, a company is in state of insolvency, and the tribunal decides that it must be liquidated. All the workers are dismissed. But a few weeks later, a businessman asks to buy some production units – a plant or several plants. The purchase of organised elements with which activity seems to be starting up again implies application of L 122-12.

The continuation of the activity is a condition of application of Art. L 122-12. But this condition is not sufficient. The continuation of the activity must be the consequence of the transfer of means of production.

3.1.2.   The transfer of an economic entity

Primarily, business transfer was seen in a very concrete way. Business was viewed as a factory. France used to be a rural country, and the application of the law transposed onto business relationships the pattern of the farming estate, with land and buildings, tools and stock.

Fairly quickly, however, the incorporeal part of the assets had to be taken into account: patents, trademarks, the whole incorporeal estate. In France, the sale of business and stock generally includes transfer of the lease, because a "right-to-the-lease" guarantees a stable situation to the shopkeeper. The long-term lease contract has become a sort of means of production, the transfer of which is taken into account, as soon as it allows the transfer of a clientele. Concession contracts are also considered as means of production, as well as agency for a trademark.

Art. L 122-12 specifically applies to merger. Regarding insolvency, as long as a whole production unit (corresponding to the notion of "economic entity keeping its identity... ") is sold, the text applies likewise.

Application in the public sector is possible, if the public entity considered is allowed to hire workers with private labour contracts. Companies held (or partially held) by the State are then submitted to L. 122-12 (Renault, France Telecom...), but administrative entities, cities, public universities and schools, and, indeed, the State itself, are not. If the State takes back an activity that it had previously conceded to a private company, that previous economic entity legally disappears, because recruitment in the civil service requires employees to pass a competitive examination.

3.1.3. No legal relationship between the two successive employers is required

Before 1985, the "Cour de cassation" decided that the law applies, even if the new employer has no legal relationship with his predecessor. The first case concerns the succession of two private electric companies that used the same means of production and supply as successive concessionaires of the same city. When the first contract ended, the city decided to contract with a new concessionaire. Thus, the two successive companies were not partners, but competitors. Nevertheless, the company concluding the second contract became the employer of all the workers of the first company (Civ. 27 February 1934, D.H. 34.252).

During a short period (1986–90), the jurisprudence changed. The previous solution reappeared afterwards. The most important reason for this new reversal was the jurisprudence of the EC Court of Justice, concerning the implementation of EC directive 77/187. The EC Court adopted the former French position, "no legal relationship required...". Following the EC treaty, the national courts must interpret their national statutes in such way that their law finally complies with an interpretation of the directive given by the EC Court.

3.1.4. Key issues regarding EC directive 77/187

The application criteria of L 122-12 and of EC 1977 directive are very similar. However, the EC Court added a new criterion to those previously used by the French "Cour de cassation": when an employer hires a significant part of the manpower of a previous economic entity, this can show that the economic entity has be transferred to the said employer. In fields of activity like business cleaning, maintenance or security, "an organised mass of workers specifically and permanently assigned to a shared job, in the absence of means of production, corresponds to an economic entity" (CJCE 10 December 98, *Hernandez Vidal*, Rev. Jur. Soc. 99.186). The "Cour de cassation" accepts this criterion as a complementary one, but has never yet used it as sole evidence.

Another issue concerns the transfer of activities generally outsourced, like business cleaning or security.

During a short period (1978–85), the "Cour de cassation" applied L 122-12 when a company lost a business cleaning, maintenance or security contract that another company took over. The reasons were many – analogy with transfer of concession, reaction to abusive outsourcing – but no clear theory of the question has been elaborated.

In 1985, the present solution was adopted: the sole loss of a contract does not prove the transfer of an economic entity.

Nevertheless, the question remains obscure. In the *Schmidt* case (14 Avr. 1994, Dr. Soc. 94.936), the EC Court decided that the outsourcing of a business cleaning operation requires application of EC directive 77/187. But in another case, *Ayre Süzen*, the Court decided that to change a business cleaning company, without transferring any means of production, does not imply that the second company becomes the employer of the workers of the first one. The two decisions are not easy to accommodate, because it is difficult to admit that outsourcing a function and transferring this function from one company to another are such different operations.

3.2. Effects of art. L. 122-12

The text contains two rules: the new employer must continue to employ the same workers (a) and the labour contracts must be transferred (b).

3.2.1. *The new employer must continue to employ the workers*

This means that the first employer – often the seller – cannot dismiss his workers in order to sell more easily. The dismissal by the first employer is possible if:
– Other reasons than the transfer exist (disciplinary reasons, for instance);
– The company is in the process of an insolvency procedure. When the tribunal decides on a scheme to reinvigorate the business, it must determine the level of employment that will have to be maintained. In application of this decision, dismissal can arise before the transfer.

The second meaning of the rule (a) is that the new employer must take the previous workers back, even when the former employer irregularly dismissed them before the transfer. The new employer is bound by all the individual contracts, despite the previous dismissals.

Violation of rule (a) has the following consequences:
– Regarding the first employer, the irregular dismissal before the transfer is regarded as "without real and serious cause". The worker, if two years of seniority, receives at least six months of wages in damages.
– The irregular dismissal by the first employer is also void. But in comparison to classic voidness, this has only very incomplete effects: the worker is not reinstated. But he can sue the new employer, in spite of the fact that the previous dismissal was by the first employer, even if there is no collusion

between the two successive employers. In practice, the damages for dismissal without real and serious cause are often asked of the new employer, because he is more solvent.

Once the transfer is made, the new employer can use all the rights of any employer. He can dismiss the worker, following ordinary law.

3.2.2.   The individual labour contracts are transferred

In France, workers' rights have many sources: statutory labour law is very developed, and business transfer obviously has no effect on statutory law. Social insurance, retirement plans, minimum wages, etc. are generally speaking not affected by the business transfer. Other rights of the workers are defined either by individual contract or by collective agreements.

The fact that the individual contract is transferred means that the new employer is bound by the clauses of the contract. Nevertheless, like all employers, he can propose a modification of the contract for economic reasons (see below). If the worker refuses, the employer has no other choice than to give up or to dismiss the worker, with, in the latter case, the implied costs. The seniority of the workers is also calculated by adding all the working periods accomplished for successive employers during the same contract.

Many collective agreements in France (as in Germany) concern a whole business or profession. In these instances, the transfer has no consequence, because the new employer and the previous one often belong to the same profession.

Company collective agreements also exist. These agreements are not transferred. However, they survive for one year, during which the new employer has a duty to bargain. If the bargaining fails, the workers keep the individual acquired rights (which correspond to a situation already completed, such as seniority bonuses). But collective rights (for instance, collective working time regulation), or individual expectations arising from the previous collective agreements, disappear.

This mechanism creates a very strong link between all the individual labour contracts and the business, regarded as an estate, a property. If you purchase the business, you "acquire" the individual labour contracts. Of course, both parties can dismiss and also offer a change of labour contracts. The survival, for one year, of employment terms and conditions, relates in France to clauses of collective agreements and not clauses of individual contracts. But if the new employer dismisses, he is then obliged to suffer all the costs implies by common dismissal and redundancy regulations. The law creates an incentive to keep the workers. Furthermore, the worker has no choice: if he refuses the change of employer, he is treated as if he resigned.

Now, in a new economy, the value of the business may be nothing more than the value of the organised manpower. Selling a consulting activity and selling a farming estate are very different matters. As lawyers, we frequently consider situations in which a claim arises. But in many cases, especially when manpower is needed, employers are very happy to be able to buy the labour contracts with the business.

4. ECONOMIC DISMISSALS

I must first point out that in France, suing an employer and claiming compensation before the labour judges is very common for the individual worker. The labour jurisdiction – called "Conseil des Prud'hommes" – is both cheap and easily accessible. The judges are elected by employers and employees. No lawyer is required to plead – a union representative can represent the worker – and I would say that the ordinary cost of a dispute, for the worker, is between one hundred and two hundred dollars. This jurisdiction is confined to individual disputes arising from the labour contract (the individual labour contract, for French lawyers). Arbitration clauses are prohibited in French labour law, so the workers, especially in small business and companies without unions, know very well how to use this tribunal.

Thus, the individual rights of workers are not simply theoretical, especially in case of dismissal or redundancy. The labour judges may work slowly, but eventually the company must pay if it has broken the law.

When he dismisses an employee, the employer must always give notice and pay a dismissal allowance (except in the case of certain offences committed by the worker), the level of which depends on the employee's seniority. Furthermore, economic dismissal must fulfil three types of conditions:
–   First, the economic reason to dismiss must be real and serious.
–   The dismissal is subject to a specific procedure. If the dismissal of more than 10 employees in a month is foreseen, the consultation of the works council will be the key element of the procedure (redundancy procedure).
–   The employer bears a duty to try to reemploy the dismissed workers.

1. The economic reason to dismiss must be real and serious. Economic reason, in a nutshell, means job suppression or dismissal as consequence of the worker's refusal to change his labour contract, when the motive of this change is economic.

But a real economic motive doesn't necessarily mean a serious one. The Courts use of the principle of proportionality to assess this question (without nevertheless distinguishing the question of reality and the question of seriousness). For example, the dismissal of an employee whose wages are too expensive, in a company whose profits are considerable, has no real and serious economic reason (Soc. 24 April 1990, Bull. civ. V, n° 183). Thus, the damage sustained by the worker in consequence of the dismissal must not be out of proportion with the advantage gained by the company with the dismissal.

The Parliament tried to induce a more restrictive definition of economic dismissal in the law of 18 January 2002, but the "Conseil constitutionnel" declared this new definition incompatible with the principle of free enterprise contained in the Constitution. Therefore, the definition of a dismissal for economic motives remains as the consequence of economic difficulties, technologic changes or business reorganisation, required to maintain competitiveness.

If the economic reason to dismiss is not "real and serious", the worker receives significant damages (six months of wages at least, if two years of seniority).

2. Key role of the works council. The council is consulted several times on the same questions. It can make suggestions, and must receive answers: the procedure is very close to a bargaining procedure.

The first consultation of the council allows the employer to seize the labour administration, which must verify the regularity of the procedure. In the end, the management decides. But, if reestablishment measures are insufficient with regards to the financial means of the company, the procedure is void and the workers must be reinstated in their former jobs.

The consultation concerns:
- The economic reasons for dismissal and the employer's plans.
- The quantity of job losses and the categories of workers affected (but not their names).
- The criteria used to choose the dismissed workers (such as "last in, first out"). The employer must take into account certain criteria fixed by the law, such as seniority, family situation, etc. Since L. 18 January 2002, professional efficiency is no longer a criterion fixed by the law. Nevertheless, compared with other developed countries, these criteria are not very strict.
- The measures taken to indemnify or reestablish the workers whose jobs have disappeared (former "plan social", "plan de sauvegarde de l'emploi", "employment-keeping scheme", since L. 18 January 2002, if the loss of more than 10 jobs in one month is planned).

The administrative authority ("Directeur départemental du travail") verifies:
- The regularity of the works council consultation.
- The compliance of the "employment-keeping scheme" with the law's requirements.

If the administrative authority discovers an irregularity, he writes to the employer, and this letter is communicated to the workers' representatives. This is not an injunction, but an element of evidence that the works council can use in a judicial procedure.

Beyond this verification function, the administrative authority negotiates agreements with the employer, according to the terms of which the State may give money to pay the partial costs of reestablishment or compensation measures (such as early retirement). Important public funds are dedicated to this purpose, and this gives a certain bargaining power to the representative of the State.

3. The content of reestablishment measures (employment-keeping scheme) must be proportional to the economic situation of the business. In

case of insolvency, the level of these measures can be low, but when the company is prosperous, judges expect substantial proposals.

If the "employment keeping scheme" seems insufficient, the works council can sue, as can the Union and the individual worker. The insufficiency of the scheme nullifies the whole procedure, and as a consequence the dismissals (if any) are void, and the workers must be reinstated.

It is desirable that the "employment-keeping scheme" should contain proposals to transfer workers, or to change the terms and conditions of employment, to transfer workers to other companies of the holding (the reestablishment duty concerns the whole holding), outplacement, training measures etc. Since L. 2002, reducing working time to 35 hours per week is required.

In fact, early retirement and cash bonuses are very often used.

However, the requirement for an "employment keeping scheme" concerns only 15% of all economic dismissals. Nevertheless, the duty to reestablish the workers concerns all the economic dismissals. It means that, before they are able to dismiss, employers must try to find other solutions. If the employer neglects this duty to try to reestablish the dismissed worker, the dismissal is considered without real and serious cause, and the worker receives the appropriate damages.

5.   CHANGES IN TERMS AND CONDITIONS OF EMPLOYMENT

Issues regarding changes in terms and conditions of employment are closely linked to dismissal regulations.

In France, the unilateral power of management, in terms of the power to give orders, is relatively strong. French unionists are very surprised when they heard that the choice of foremen, or details of working conditions, are bargained for elsewhere. Statutory protection is very well developed, but beyond that, management decides.

Thus, changes in the workers' duties are fairly easy for the employer to decide, as long as he respects the individual labour contract. Jurisprudence distinguishes the modification in working conditions and the modification of the labour contract:
–   If the employer wants to modify the labour contract, the worker can refuse the change. But the economic necessity to bring about the change frequently gives the employer a real and serious reason to dismiss.
–   If the employer wants to change the working conditions, but stays within the limits of the contract, the worker must obey. If he refuses, the employer may carry out a dismissal without notice or allowance.

A modification of the wages, the working time or the general definition of the worker's functions, generally means modification of the labour contract. Change in the working schedule or in the place of work is, within certain limits, considered a simple change in the working conditions that does not modify the contract. But this question could inspire a whole symposium. . .

A specific clause can of course be introduced in the labour contract: for instance, a mobility clause, or on the contrary, a clause which protects the workers against changes in duties (for example, no work on a specific day of the week).

However, real wages are often fixed by a collective agreement. In this case, a new collective agreement can lower the wages, because the labour contract does not include the content of any collective agreement. The preservation of individual acquired rights does not apply when one collective agreement replaces another. But many agreements contained a negotiated clause which preserves the acquired rights.

If an employer wants to change the terms and conditions of a labour contract for economic reasons, a specific procedure must be followed (L. 20 December 1993, Art. L 321-1-2 Lab. Code):

- The employer must send a written offer by registered letter to the worker. This letter must inform the worker that he has one month to consider the offer.
- If the worker does not answer within one month, his silence is considered equivalent to acceptance.

This procedure deviates from the principle of civil law, according to which silence doesn't mean acceptance. However, in the case of mass redundancy, this procedure is not applicable, because the timing of the "employment-keeping scheme" needs more than a single month.

6. CONCLUSION

Despite this very complex regulation, workers sometimes learn in the morning that the employer will announce a closure to the newspapers in the afternoon. The reason is the weakness of Unions, but also the structure of the works council rights: very extended rights to information and consultation, but no power at all. It seems to me that the German equivalent (*Betriebsrat*) is more efficient, because many questions must be co-decided.

Finally, I would point out the matter of the violence of conflicts relating to corporate restructuring.

Foreign visitors can observe a lot of strikes in France, but those strikes are of a very short duration, and concern mainly the public sector (museums, railway, etc.). In the private economy, there are very few strikes, statistically less than in Germany, the United Kingdom or the United States. Why? Again, it is down to union weakness, and the fact that statutory law provides a good basic protection.

But corporate restructuring leads to very intense labour conflicts. Frequently, workers take possession of the plant to prevent relocation elsewhere. In the last two years, on several occasions, workers whose plant was closing down threatened its destruction, with huge environmental impact. In one instance, the workers actually began to carry out their threat. I don't know if it is appropriate to call it "neo-Luddism".

The reasons for this violence are too numerous to explain here. Suffice it to mention that France used to be a rural country, which has an immemorial tradition of collective use of the land (of which the anarcho-syndicalism tradition of French unions is itself, at least partially, a consequence). When an owner uses his property in a way which goes against the interests of the whole community, this property is frequently trespassed, even if the trespass breaks the law. Besides this, a plant closing down often leads to a decline in the whole area, so that everybody more or less admits to this kind of trespass.

Finally, the intensity of conflicts ends up reinforcing the power of the State as arbitrator.

How can we evaluate the incidence of corporate restructuring regulation? Following French employers, it is easier to dismiss in France than in Germany or elsewhere in Northern Europe. However, it is much more complicated than in Great Britain or in the United States (except maybe in very unionised industries).

4. Germany

Bernd Waas

1. INTRODUCTION

Corporate restructuring has played a major role over recent years in Germany. Large numbers of companies have changed their external boundaries and their internal structures. From the viewpoint of the German legal doctrine these processes have essentially taken two forms, namely the transfer of assets (*Einzelrechtsnachfolge*) on the one hand and the universal succession by means of corporate law (*Gesamtrechtsnachfolge*) on the other.[1] In the former case a person disposes of his or her assets by making use of the usual contractual tools such as sales contract or lease. In the latter case the succession is regarded in Germany to be effectuated by operation of the law and not strictly by contract. When dealing with the issue of corporate restructuring, both ways must be considered: the acquisition of assets which may or may not have consequences in terms of labour law, and the universal succession;[2] the latter will be referred to in the following as corporate restructuring under corporate law.

2. LEGAL FRAMEWORK GOVERNING CORPORATE RESTRUCTURING

2.1. Corporate law

A couple of years ago a fundamental reform of the law on mergers and reorganisations took place in Germany with the so-called Act on Business Reorganisations (*Umwandlungsgesetz*),[3] which came into effect on 1 January 1995. Prior to the reform the law on reorganisations was a bit of a "hodgepodge" because this area of the law had been dealt with in no less

---

1. See *Beinert*, Corporate Acquisitions and Mergers in Germany, 3d ed., The Hague a. o., 2000.
2. See on the role of labour law in business reorganisations recently *Deinert*, Arbeitsrechtliche Rahmenbedingungen und Folgen nationaler und transnationaler Umstrukturierungen von Betrieben und Unternehmen in Deutschland, in: Recht der Arbeit (RdA) 2001, 368.
3. Umwandlungsgesetz (UmwG) – the literal translation being Conversion or Transformation Act – of 28 October 1994 (BGBl. I, 3210, ber. 1995, 428) as lastly amended by the Act of 23 July 2001 (BGBl. I, 1852); see for a bilingual version of the Act *Benkert/Buerkle*, Law of Reorganisations/Reorganisation Tax Law – Umwandlungsgesetz/Umwandlungssteuergesetz, Koeln, 1996.

R. Blanpain (ed.),
Corporate Restructuring and the Role of Labour Law, 79–102.
© 2003 *Kluwer Law International. Printed in Great Britain.*

than five different statutes. The Act on Business Reorganisations eliminates the earlier shortcomings by providing for the first time a comprehensive codification of this part of the law. At the same time the Act addresses problems which previously arose from the inconsistency of the old regulation and tries to fill some lacunas where the former statutes proved to be incomplete.

The Act on Business Reorganisations provides for four types of transformation, which, however, are not available to all types of entities (civil law partnership, general partnership, limited partnership, limited liability company, stock corporation, etc.).[4] First, there is the so-called change of legal form (*Formwechsel*), in which case a transformation of the legal form of an entity to a different legal form takes place. Second, there is the so-called merger or consolidation (*Verschmelzung*), where business entities may be amalgamated by either transferring the assets and liabilities of one or more entities as a whole to an entity that is already in existence (merger, *Verschmelzung durch Aufnahme*), or by transferring the assets and liabilities of one or more entities as a whole to an entity that is newly established (consolidation, *Verschmelzung durch Neugruendung*). Third, there is the so-called splitting (*Spaltung*), by which the assets and liabilities of one entity can be separated and then allocated to different entities.[5] Fourth, there is the so-called transfer of assets (*Vermoegensuebertragung*), which enables an entity either to transfer its assets and liabilities as a whole to an entity already existing and then dissolve (as in a merger) or to transfer its assets and liabilities as a whole to two or more entities already existing and then dissolve (as in a split-up) or to only partially transfer its assets and liabilities to one or more entities (as in a split-off or a spin-off). Unlike in the case of merger or splitting, in the case of transfer of assets the compensation for the transferred assets and liabilities may not consist of interests in the acquiring entity but has to take a different form, for instance cash.[6]

In general, a business reorganisation consists of three basic steps. To start with, the participating entities have to conclude an agreement or, in the case that only one entity participates in the reorganisation, such entity has to establish a plan of reorganisation. In the case that only one entity participates, such entity has to establish a plan of reorganisation.[7] The stakeholders of the participating entities have then to be informed by written reports about the

---

4. See for a more detailed discussion of the provisions of the Umwandlungsgesetz from a labour law perspective, Willemsen (ed.), Umstrukturierung und Übertragung von Unternehmen: arbeitsrechtliches Handbuch, 1999, 36 ff.

5. In a so-called split-up (Aufspaltung) the entity splitting up transfers its assets and liabilities as a whole to two or more already existing or newly established entities. In a split-off (Abspaltung) the entity splitting off transfers only parts of its assets and liabilities to one or more already existing or newly established entities. In a spin-off (Ausgliederung), as in a split-off, the entity spinning off transfers part of its assets and liabilities to one or more already existing or newly established entities (which become subsidiaries of the transferring entity), but retains some of its assets and liabilities.

6. For further details, Begg (ed.), Corporate Acquisitions and Mergers – Germany, The Hague a. o., loose-leaf, 64 ff.

7. The Act provides in great detail for the minimum contents of such an agreement or plan.

details of the proposed reorganisation. On the basis of this information the owners decide by resolution on the reorganisation. Finally, the reorganisation has to be registered in the commercial register. Dissenting shareholders, employees and creditors that are affected by a business reorganisation enjoy special legal protection, in particular by tender options and liability provisions. The review of reorganisations by the courts, however, is limited to compliance with formal requirements. The reorganisation cannot be legally challenged on the grounds that either the underlying business rationale or the compensation for the interests affected has been improperly determined.

2.2. Labour law

2.2.1. Individual labour law

In Germany contracts of employment can be terminated by either party by giving notice of termination.[8] If no applicable collective bargaining agreement provides otherwise, the statutory notice periods have to be observed. Presently, the uniform notice period for all employees is fours weeks ending on the fifteenth day of a calendar month or at the end of a calendar month (Section 622, par. 1 of the Civil Code, *Buergerliches Gesetzbuch*). The statutory notice period applicable to a unilateral termination by the employer increases with the length of service of the employee to be discharged (from one month after two years of service to seven months after 20 years of service[9]). Statutory notice periods are mandatory and cannot be contracted out (Section 622, par. 5).[10] However, regulations diverging from the statutory period of notice, even to the disadvantage of the employee, may be adopted by a collective bargaining agreement (Section 622, par. 4). No notice periods need to be observed in the rather rare case that there is a serious cause for dismissal justifying notice with immediate effect (*fristlose Kuendigung aus wichtigem Grund*[11], Section 626 of the Civil Code). Business-related reasons, however, normally do not qualify for dismissal with immediate effect and do not enable the employer to deviate from applicable notice periods in any other way. As this even applies to mass redundancies, the situation may arise that notice periods for different employees do not coincide with each other or with the coming into effect of the underlying measure causing the dismissals.

Termination by the employer is unlawful if, first, it contravenes either

---

8. See Weiss/Schmidt, Labour Law and Industrial Relations in Germany, The Hague a. o., 2000, 102 ff.
9. See Section 622, par. 2 of the Civil Code.
10. Note the exceptions as laid down in Section 622, par. 5 of the Civil Code.
11. Meaning that because of the circumstances of the individual case, and on balancing of the interests of both parties concerned, the party terminating the employment relationship cannot reasonably be expected to continue the employment until the end of the notice period (Section 626, par. 1).

one of the statutory regulations of protection against dismissal[12] or a contractual restriction of the right to terminate. The general legal protection against termination of the employment relationship is embodied in the so-called Act on Termination Protection 1969 (*Kuendigungsschutzgesetz*).[13] This law is by far the most important statute in the field of individual employment law. As for its area of application, essentially the following two requirements exist. First, according to Section 1, par. 1 of the Act, continuity of employment in one and the same establishment (*Betrieb*) or company of at least six months is required. And second, according to Section 23, par. 1 of the Act, there is an additional requirement that the employer in the ordinary course of business employs more than 5 employees (with part-timers being counted on a percentage basis). Section 1 forms the key provision of the Act on Termination Protection 1969. According to Section 1, par. 1 the employer is not allowed to terminate the employment relationship, unless the dismissal is "socially justified" (*sozial gerechtfertigt*) under the Act.[14] If the dismissal is not "socially justified" it is invalid, that is null and void. For a termination to be "socially justified" within the meaning of Section 1, the employer must be able to show that his or her decision to terminate can be based either on a reason inherent in the employee (*personenbedingte Kuendigung*, for example because of permanent illness etc.) or on the employee's conduct (*verhaltensbedingte Kuendigung*, for instance because of poor performance or breach of other contractual duties) or on immediate business-related reasons (*betriebsbedingte Kuendigung*) preventing continued employment (Section 1, par. 2).

2.2.2. Collective labour law

a. Collective bargaining

In Germany, freedom of association, the so-called *Koalitionsfreiheit*, is of crucial importance in the field of collective labour law. *Koalitionsfreiheit* is the right of employers, employers' associations and trade unions to regulate terms and conditions of employment on their own authority and independently of any influence exercised by authorities of the state (but within the general conditions set by the Constitution and by legislation). The most important element of this is the right to create an appropriate system of regulation of working and economic conditions (*Arbeits- und Wirtschaftsbedingungen*) through the conclusion of collective agreements (right to free collective bargaining, *Tarifautonomie*). The freedom of association and the autonomy to bargain collectively, being two of its essential parts, are protected by Art. 9,

---

12.   It must be stressed, however, that according to Sections 4 and 7 of the Act on Termination Protection 1969 there is an assumption of the validity of dismissal where a complaint against unfair dismissal has not been presented within three weeks after the dismissal.

13.   Kuendigungsschutzgesetz (KSchG) of 25 August 1969 (BGBl. I, 1317), as lastly amended by the Act of 23 July 2001 (BGBl. I, 1852).

14.   See for a more detailed discussion of the concept of social justification *Weiss/Schmidt*, Labour Law and Industrial Relations in Germany, The Hague a. o., 2000, 106 ff.

par. 3 of the German Constitution, the so-called Basic Law (*Grundgesetz*),[15] and therefore have the legal quality of a fundamental right.

The most important piece of legislation in the field of collective bargaining is the so-called Act on Collective Bargaining Agreements of 1949 (*Tarifvertragsgesetz*).[16] Because collective bargaining agreements[17] according to Section 4, par. 1 of the Act are directly binding and therefore mandatory upon the parties of an individual employment contract it can be said that the parties to such agreements act as quasi-legislators. Collective agreements are negotiated and entered into between individual trade unions on one side[18] and either employers' associations (leading to so-called association-level agreements, *Verbandstarifvertraege*) or individual employers on the other (the latter resulting in company agreements, *Firmentarifvertraege*). Single-employer bargaining, however, is relatively rare, and covers only some 6% of the labour force.[19] The main level of bargaining is the sector level (so-called general collective agreements, *Flaechentarifvertraege*).[20]

In the first place collective bargaining agreements cover matters of remuneration (pay agreements, *Entgelttarifvertraege*), but typically also contain provisions as to other basic terms of employment (such agreements called framework agreements on employment conditions, *Rahmentarifvertraege*). Legally speaking, collective bargaining agreements are only binding on the members of the trade union and the members of the employers' association who have concluded the relevant agreement (Section 3, par. 1 of the Act on Collective Bargaining Agreements).[21] In practice, however, they constitute almost general minimum standards. Since employers are reluctant to provide premiums on trade union membership, in practice collective agreements are widely extended by virtue of the individual contract of employment to all employees of the industry to which the contracting parties belong (so-called *individualvertragliche Inbezugnahme*[22]). Apart from that, the applicability of an existing collective agreement can be extended by state authorities to include

---

15.   Grundgesetz fuer die Bundesrepublik Deutschland of 23 May 1949 (BGBl. I, 1), as lastly amended by the Act of 19 December 2000 (BGBl. I, 1755).

16.   Tarifvertragsgesetz (TVG) of 25 August 1969 (BGBl. I. 1323), as lastly amended by the Act of 29 October 1974.

17.   Collective agreements are highly important in the area of industrial relations. Some 5,000–7,000 collective agreements are concluded annually, although the majority of them only amend, follow or supplement previous ones.

18.   Groups of employees, which do not enjoy the legal status of trade unions, cannot be parties to such agreements.

19.   Although it should be noted that, because of the relatively high degree of rigidity of the German collective bargaining system, such agreements are increasingly popular among employers.

20.   General collective agreements that fix wages and salaries are usually negotiated on an annual basis. Most collective agreements are regional. But because trade unions and employers' associations in practice are highly centralised, minimum pay rates vary relatively little from region to region.

21.   In the case of a company-level agreement the employer is simply bound in his capacity of party to the agreement.

22.   See for more details on the German position in this regard *Waas*, Zur Rechtsnatur der Bezugnahme auf einen Tarifvertrag nach deutschem Recht, in: Zeitschrift für Tarif-, Arbeits- und Sozialrecht des oeffentlichen Dienstes (ZTR) 1999, 540.

employees and employers formerly not bound by the agreement by means of an official procedure which is called declaration of general binding (*Allgemein-verbindlicherklaerung*).[23] Collective agreements entered into by employers and trade unions take precedence over other forms of industrial accord, such as works agreements (*Betriebsvereinbarungen*) or individual contracts, unless the latter are more favourable to employees (Section 4, par. 3 of the Act on Collective Bargaining Agreements of 1949).

b. Co-determination

From a historical point of view the concept of worker participation in management is carried out on two completely different levels in Germany: first, at the level of the establishment (so-called works constitution, *Betriebsverfassung*); and second, at the level of the company (so-called co-determination at board level, *Unternehmensmitbestimmung*). In addition to that, there is the fairly recent feature of European Works Councils (*Europaeische Betriebsraete*), whose field of action, however, is not the individual establishment but the enterprise. The legal basis of European Works Councils is the Act on European Works Councils (*Europaeisches Betriebsraete-Gesetz*),[24] implementing the relevant Directive at the European level.[25]

(1) Shop-floor-level co-determination

The works constitution (*Betriebsverfassung*) forms the basis for the institution of employee representation bodies within establishments. It is governed by the Works Constitution Act (*Betriebsverfassungsgesetz*),[26] which is sometimes also referred to as the Labour-Management Relations Act. The principal active organ of the works constitution is the works council (*Betriebsrat*).

a. The works constitution

The works constitution applies to all establishments located in the Federal Republic which are established under private law[27] (Section 130 of the Works Constitution Act). The interests of executive staff, however, are protected not by the works council but by a separate representative body for executive staff,

---

23.   A generally applicable agreement has the same direct and imperative effect for the concerned employees and employers as such agreement produces for the employment relationship that is subjected to it by virtue of membership of the parties concerned (Section 5, par. 4).

24.   Gesetz ueber Europaeische Betriebsraete (Europaeisches Betriebsraete-Gesetz – EBRG) of 28 October 1996 (BGBl. I, 1548, ber. 2022), as lastly amended by the Act of 21 December 2000 (BGBl. I, 1983).

25.   Council Directive 94/45/EC of 22 September 1994 on the establishment of a European Works Council or a procedure in Community-scale undertakings and Community-scale groups of undertakings for the purposes of informing and consulting employees, Official Journal L 254 of 30 September 1994, 64.

26.   Betriebsverfassungsgesetz (BetrVG) of 25 September 2001 (BGBl. I, 2518), originally being Betriebsverfassungsgesetz of 15 January 1972 (BGBl. I, 13).

27.   In the public service, however, the system of co-determination on the basis of the so-called Public Service Staff Representation Act (Personalvertretungsgesetz) through other organs of staff representation is modelled very much along the same lines as in the private sector.

the so-called "Spokespersons Committee" (*Sprecherausschuss*).[28] According to Section 1 of the Works Constitution Act employees at an establishment with five or more permanent employees are entitled to elect a works council. The works council enjoys a wide range of participatory rights, including the right to be informed, to make suggestions, to be heard, to be consulted, and above all, the right of co-determination (*Mitbestimmung*).[29] The latter right means that the employer may not take decisions without the approval of the works council. However, it must be noted that co-determination rights refer to "social" matters only,[30] not, for instance, to economic decisions. The works council, according to Section 77 of the Act, has the power to enter into works agreements for the establishment (*Betriebsvereinbarungen*), and is authorised to institute legal action if its rights are disregarded.[31] The relationship between the works council and the workforce is governed by the duty of the former to conduct its business impartially, without regard to race, religion and creed, nationality, origin, political or union activity, sex, or age (obligation to neutrality and equal treatment according to Section 75 of the Act). The employer bears the costs of the works council's activities and in principle is also liable for the works council's actions (Section 40). In companies where several works councils exist, an additional company-wide works council (*Gesamtbetriebsrat*) must be formed (Section 47). In addition to this, in a group of companies, a group works council (*Konzernbetriebsrat*) has to be established, if the company works councils of the member companies so decide (Section 54).

The Act requires the works council and the employer to work together on a basis of co-operation in good faith (*Gebot der vertrauensvollen Zusammenarbeit*) and with due regard to rules contained in statutes and collective agreements (Sections 2 and 74). This, however, does not place the works council in a position of direct subordination to the trade unions as representative bodies. Rather, within individual establishments the unions perform a supportive and monitoring role without, on the other hand, reducing the powers that arise from their role as "natural" representatives of workers' interests.

In companies normally employing at least 100 employees an additional organ called an economic committee (*Wirtschaftsausschuss*) must be established (Section 106, par. 1). Depending on the size of company, this committee consists of at least 3–7 members, at least one of whom must belong to a works council (Section 107, par. 1). The committee members are appointed by the works council or company-wide works council, respectively. The committee's function is to consult with the employer on economic matters and to communicate such matters to the works council or company works council (Sections 108 and 109). Its area of responsibility includes the company's economic and financial

---

28. See Gesetz ueber Sprecherausschuesse der leitenden Angestellten (Sprecherausschussgesetz – SprAuG) of 20 December 1988 (BGBl. I, 2312), as amended by the Act of 21 December 2000 (BGBl. I, 1983).
29. Apart form that, the Act provides for some participating rights that are vested in the members of the workforce themselves.
30. See Section 87 of the Works Constitution Act.
31. See, for instance, Section 98, par. 5 of the Act which provides for special enforcement of certain participatory rights by court order.

position, its production and marketing situation, production and investment programmes, and plans for rationalisation or any other substantial alteration to the establishment (Section 106, par. 3). The employer is under a legal duty to provide the committee with prompt and comprehensive information on these matters, including any necessary documents, provided that such disclosure does not endanger business or trade secrets (Section 106, par. 2). The functions of the economic committee may also be transferred to a works council's executive committee (consisting of its chairperson, vice-chairperson and a number of additional members), which may not be larger than the size specified for an economic committee (Section 107, par. 3).

Works councils are legally distinct institutions and thus separated from the trade unions. At the same time works councils are legally empowered to conclude so-called work agreements (*Betriebsvereinbarungen*) which, according to Section 77, paras 2–6 of the Works Constitution Act, have the same legal effect as collective bargaining agreements. Out of this situation arises the necessity to harmonise these two possible sources of agreements, since unrestricted power of works councils to enter into collective agreements and a full range competition between works councils and trade unions could harm the bargaining structure. In order to prevent this, under German law work agreements which deal with remuneration or other working conditions are not admissible if the same matter is usually governed by or even actually dealt with in a collective agreement (Section 77, par. 3). In other words, works councils are in principle prevented from engaging in bargaining for higher wages.[32]

b. European works councils

In companies which operate branch establishments or subsidiaries in various EC Member States, special "works councils" must be set up for the purpose of representing the cross border-interests of employees in all of the employer's establishments throughout the Community. These bodies, however, have neither institutional backing comparable to that of the German-style works councils, nor corresponding rights. In particular, though the European Directive provides for compulsory information and consultation of workers in companies with a European dimension, it does not provide for any co-determination rights.

(2) Board-level co-determination

As for co-determination at board level it must be noted that this is essentially based on the structure of the stock corporation, although the most important law in this field,[33] the so-called Co-Determination Act of 1976

32.   Apart from that, it is stated in Section 87, par. 1 of the Works Constitution Act that work agreements may not relate so social matters within the meaning of this provision that are usually subject to co-determination if the subject matter to be dealt with is prescribed by a collective bargaining agreement applied in the establishment. The works council, in other words, has no right of co-determination where such a matter is provided for by the provisions of an applicable collective agreement.
33.   In this area the Co-Determination Act of 1976 the Works Constitution Act (Betriebsverfassungsgesetz) of 11 October 1952 (BGBl. I, 681), as lastly amended by the

(*Mitbestimmungsgesetz*),[34] according to Section 1, par. 1 of the Act, is also applicable to, inter alia, partnerships limited by shares and limited liability companies as long as they regularly employ more than 2,000 employees. Under the Act the supervisory board of such companies must consist of an equal number of shareholders and labour representatives (Section 7). In public limited companies and private limited companies that are subject to co-determination, there must also be a so-called "labour director" with specific responsibilities for social and labour matters (Section 33). The "labour director" is to be appointed by the supervisory board either as a full member of the management board (enjoying equal rights) or, in the absence of a management board, as one of the managers.

It must be noted, however, that the influence accorded by co-determination to employees is not as far-reaching as might appear at first sight. The main reason for this is that supervisory boards decide by majority vote and, though employees enjoy the right to equal representation, the chairman (who is always appointed by the shareholders), is given the casting vote in case of a tie (Section 27, par. 2 of the Act, so-called non-parity co-determination, *nichtparitaetische Mitbestimmung*). Moreover, the influence accorded to employees is rather indirect because the function of the supervisory board consists primarily of the appointment and supervision of the managerial board. The supervisory board itself does not enjoy any managerial rights. The "labour director", on the other hand, must not be perceived to be an employee representative, but does enjoy a position equivalent to that of the other directors. Nevertheless, it goes without saying that the mere fact of having representation of the labour side does have a considerable impact on the decision process of the management board and therefore should by no means be underestimated.

As regards the form of co-determination to be applied in the European Company (*Societas Europae*, or SE), which was designed to facilitate cross-border mergers, three variants will be available under the law.[35] The first is modelled closely on the practice in Germany and the Netherlands. The second variant corresponds more to the French system. The third provides minimum conditions for co-determination. In this case the form of co-determination can be agreed between management and employees as they think fit, but employees' representatives must be informed of the company's business situation and

---

Act of 23 July 2001 (BGBl. I, 1852), and the Coal, Iron, Steel Co-determination Act (Gesetz ueber die Mitbestimmung der Arbeitnehmer in den Aufsichtsraeten und Vorstaenden der Unternehmen des Bergbaus und der Eisen und Stahl erzeugenden Industrie, Montan-Mitbestimmungsgesetz) of 21 May 1951, BGBl. I, 347, as lastly amended by the Act of 23 July 2001 (BGBl. I, 1852), must also be taken into account.

34. Gesetz ueber die Mitbestimmung der Arbeitnehmer (Mitbestimmungsgesetz – MitbestG) of 4 May 1976 (BGBl. I, 1153), as lastly amended by Act of 23 July 2001 (BGBl. I, 1852).

35. See Council Regulation (EC) No. 2157/2001 of 8 October 2001 on the Statute for a European company (SE), Official Journal L 294 of 10 November 2001, 1 and Council Directive 2001/86/EC of 8 October 2001 supplementing the Statute for a European company with regard to the involvement of employees, Official Journal L 294 of 10 November 2001, 22 both of which, however, will only become effective on 8 October 2004 and therefore have not been implemented yet in Germany.

consulted in this regard at least every calendar quarter. As a general principle the nature of co-determination shall, however, be governed by the provisions on the matter in the Member State in which the SE is located.

2.3. Special legislation concerning transfer of undertaking

Share transactions do not immediately affect the employment relationship, as the company in these cases always remains the employer. With asset sales, however, it is different. In this case there can be a change in the identity of the employer. According to Section 613a, par. 1 of the German Civil Code, which implements Council Directive 77/187/EEC[36] to the same effect, all rights and obligations of employees that belong to the transferred undertaking insofar as they arise from the employment relationship will be transferred to the buyer.

As for the key requirement of "business transfer"[37] it should be noted that it is not necessary that each and every asset of a business or part of a business be transferred in order to make Section 613a of the Civil Code applicable. A transfer of an essential part of the assets is sufficient. According to the European Court of Justice the decisive criterion is whether the business in question retains its identity. The retention of that identity is indicated inter alia by the actual continuation or resumption by the new employer of the same or similar activities. In order to determine whether there is a transfer of an undertaking as a "going concern", it is, according to the Court, necessary to consider all the facts characterising the transaction. This includes the type of establishment or business; whether or not the business's tangible assets, such as buildings and moveable property, are transferred; the value of its intangible assets at the time of the transfer; whether or not its customers are transferred; the degree of similarity between the activities carried on before and after the transfer; and lastly, the period, if any, for which these activities were suspended. Relatively recently the Court has added to this list another criterion by stating that it can constitute a transfer within the meaning of the Directive if a majority of the employees are transferred from one employer to another.[38] From a German perspective this aspect is a new one, as the Federal Labour Court previously stressed that the transfer of employees was only the legal consequence and not a prerequisite of a transfer.[39]

Although the transfer of the employment relationship takes place by operation of the law and therefore automatically, the individual employee who

---

36. See Council Directive 98/50/EC of 29 June 1998 amending Directive 77/187/EEC on the approximation of the laws of the Member States relating to the safeguarding of employees' rights in the event of transfers of undertakings, businesses or parts of businesses; Official Journal L 201 of 17 July 1998, 88.

37. Such transfer can also take place in the public sector, especially in the context of the privatising of former state institutions.

38. *ECJ*, Judgment of 11 March 1997, Suezen/Zehnacker Gebaeudereinigung Krankenhaus-service (C-13/95), Rec. 1997, I-1259.

39. See for further details *Waas*, Zur Konsolidierung des Betriebsbegriffs in der Rechtspre-chung von EuGH und BAG zum Betriebsuebergang, in: Zeitschrift fuer Arbeitsrecht (ZfA) 2001, 377.

would be affected by the transfer enjoys a legal right to object (*Widerspruchsrecht*). This right, which was "invented" by the German Federal Labour Court,[40] is part and parcel of the employee's freedom of contract (*Vertragsfreiheit*), which for its part is guaranteed by Art. 2 and 12 of the German Constitution.[41] If the employee makes use of this right, the contract of employment remains in force with the transferor. The transferor, however, may be entitled to terminate the employment relationship if the labour court can be convinced that there are valid grounds for dismissal (non-existence of a suitable job for the objecting employee). In any event, since it can be crucial for the purchaser of a business to acquire key personnel, it should be clear whether the particular employees concerned give their consent to the transfer.

In accordance with Article 3, par. 1 of the Directive, the transferor's rights and obligations arising from a contract of employment existing on the date of a transfer are, by reason of such transfer, transferred to the transferee under German law. However, according to Section 613a, par. 2 of the Civil Code, after the date of transfer the transferor continues to be liable, along with the transferee, in respect of obligations arising from the employment relationship as far as these arose before the transfer and become valid within the period of one year after this date. If such obligations become valid after the date of transfer, the former employer is liable for them only on a pro-rata basis, which means that part of the assessment period that had expired at the time of the transfer.

Continuity in the event of a change of ownership is also guaranteed in collective labour law. The works council remains in office, provided that the organisation of the establishment has not been changed in such a way (by a merger, for instance) as to make this impossible. If in other words the business transferred preserves its autonomy, i.e. continues to exist as a separate operating unit rather than being absorbed by a more complex structure, the status and function of the representatives or representation of the employees affected by the transfer must be preserved. A co-determination right exists in the event of a transfer of ownership, but only if it is connected with a substantial alteration to the establishment (Section 111 of the Works Constitution Act).[42]

In principle, Section 613a of the Civil Code is also applicable to transfers taking place in the context of insolvency proceedings. However, according to a ruling of the Federal Labour Court, the provision is not to be applied insofar as it stipulates that the new transferee is liable for claims which had already arisen at the time of the institution of insolvency proceedings. In this case the

---

40. See, for instance, *Federal Labour Court* of 6 February 1980, Arbeitsrechtliche Praxis Nr. 21 zu § 613a BGB.
41. This position of the Federal Labour Court is consistent with European law; see in this regard *ECJ* Judgment of 5 May 1988 Berg/Besselsen (C-114/87), Rec. 1988, 2559; *ECJ*, Judgment of 25 July 1991, D'Urso and others/Marelli (C-362/89), Rec. 1991, I-4105; *ECJ*, Judgment of 16/12/1992, Katsikas and others/Konstantinidis and others (C-132/91), Rec. 1992, I-6577.
42. See for a more detailed discussion infra (D V).

principles of distribution within the framework of the insolvency proceedings have priority.[43]

Section 613a of the Civil Code constitutes mandatory law. An employee cannot waive the rights conferred upon him, nor can these rights be restricted. The latter is also true when the employee has given his consent and the disadvantages resulting from his waiver are offset by such benefits that, taking the matter as a whole, he is not placed in a worse position.

The most recent development in this field comes with a recent Act amending Section 613a, which passed the second chamber of the German parliament on 1 March 2002 and is intended to implement respective EC-law.[44] One of the major features of the new Act, which presumably will come into effect on 1 April 2002, is the obligation of the transferor or transferee, respectively, to inform each employee individually about the imminent transfer and the consequences in terms of working conditions. This duty is not designed to discharge the employer from his obligation to inform the works council, but places him under an additional burden.

3. CORPORATE RESTRUCTURING AND SUCCESSION OF EMPLOYMENT CONTRACTS

3.1. Transfer of undertakings

As already indicated earlier, in the case of an asset sale the new owner takes over the rights and obligations arising from the employment relationship as it exists at the time of the transfer. This essentially means that the transferee must pay the same wages, including all fringe benefits, to which the employee was entitled before the transfer.

Perhaps the most important but in any event the most difficult question arising in this context concerns the legal fate of collective bargaining agreements and works agreements.[45] Section 613a, par. 1, sentence 2 of the Civil Code states that all provisions which are the result of collective bargaining continue to apply to the new employer. This covers not only provisions of a collective bargaining agreement concluded by a trade union and an employers' association or an individual employer, respectively, but also provisions of a so-called works agreement. According to Section 613, par. 1, sentence 3 of the Civil Code collective bargaining agreements and works agreements do not lose their legal relevance, unless both the employee and the

---

43.   See Section 128 of the Insolvency Act in particular.
44.   But goes considerably further than what would be required by it.
45.   This is particularly true for cases in which the restructuring of the business leads to a situation where conflicting collective bargaining agreement apply to a single establishment or even to a single contract; see in this regard *Waas*, Tarifkonkurrenz und Tarifpluralitaet, Baden-Baden, 1999.

new employer[46] are already bound by one or the other collective bargaining agreement. This provision is designed to ensure that employees continue to enjoy the rights that derive from a collective bargaining agreement, at least for a certain period of time. In order to achieve this, the provisions of collective agreements are transformed into provisions of the individual contract of employment by way of a legal fiction (*individualrechtliche Weitergeltung*) and at the same time declared mandatory for a period of one year. After the lapse of this period the transferee is free to make use of the normal legal instruments in order to vary the employment contract. Only if the new employer and the employee are bound by another collective bargaining agreement[47] does the legal fiction outlined above not come into play. Apart from that, it must be noted that the employer in two exceptional cases is not subjected to the (limited) mandatory effect of (formerly) collective bargaining provisions. First, if the collective bargaining agreement expires before the lapse of the period of one year, the rights and duties arising from such agreement can be changed within the general legal boundaries. And the same applies if neither the (new) employer or the employee are members of an employers' association or trade union, respectively, and both parties reach an agreement after the transfer on making their individual contract subject to the provisions of any collective bargaining agreement.[48]

3.2. Corporate restructuring

According to Section 613a of the Civil Code all employment relationships are automatically transferred to the new owner in the case of an asset sale. For a long time it was far from clear whether this would apply equally to other cases of business reorganisation. According to Section 324 of the Act on Business Reorganisations Section 613a, paras 1 and 4 of the Civil Code relating to the transfer of the employment relationship upon a transfer of a business unit remain "unaffected" by a merger, splitting or transfer of assets. Although the formulation has been subject to criticism this provision is now widely considered to mean that all employment relationships are transferred in the case of a business reorganisation under the Act.

In the case of a splitting, however, the problem arises of how to determine in a particular case exactly which employment relationships are transferred to which company. Principally speaking, the employer enjoys far-reaching freedom to decide upon the employment relationship he does or does not want to have transferred to another business entity. If, however, the requirements of Section 613a of the Civil Code are fulfilled in a given business

---

46.   According to the Federal Labour Court it is not sufficient that only the employer is bound to such agreement; see Federal Labour Court of 21 February 2001, in: Betriebs-Berater (BB) 2001, S. 1853 with annotation by *Waas*.
47.   In the case that the employer has concluded such agreement individually before or after the transfer, or that he belongs to another employers' association that is a party to a collective agreement.
48.   For further reading see *Waas*, Tarifvertrag und Betriebsuebergang, Baden-Baden, 1999.

reorganisation, no such freedom exists. In these cases it has to be determined according to objective criteria whether a particular employment relationship "belongs" to a certain part of the business. In other words, the employer is not allowed to "separate" an employment relationship from a certain entity by simply providing in the reorganisation plan or reorganisation agreement that the former will be transferred to company A whereas the latter will be transferred to company B.

Another (and by far more difficult) problem concerns the legal position with regard to collective agreements. From the start a differentiation must be made between collective bargaining agreements concluded by employers' associations (or an individual employer) and trade unions on the one hand, and works agreements, entered into by employers and works councils on the other. As for the former, it is safe to say that a universal successor, for instance a newly established company to which assets and liabilities of another company were transferred, becomes bound by such agreement if it is a member of the relevant employers' association. However, as membership is strictly personal and thus not easily transferable, it is equally clear that one cannot claim that the universal successor *as a rule* is bound by a collective agreement in the same way as the predecessor. Since the Act on Business Reorganisations itself does not expressly address the question, the solution to it is far from clear. Only if the relevant collective bargaining agreement has been declared generally binding is it beyond any doubt that the successor is as bound by the agreement as the predecessor. Apart from that it is argued that one should, by drawing an analogy to certain provisions in the Act on Collective Bargaining Agreements, hold the successor bound to the collective agreement which was in effect before the universal succession. Whether (and to what extent) this solution on the so-called collective (*kollektivrechtlich*) level is convincing, is open to discussion.[49] In any event the successor in these cases is bound on an individual (*individualrechtlich*) level. Because Section 613a of the Civil Code is applicable not only to asset sales but also to universal successions (Section 324 of the Act on Business Reorganisations), employees enjoy identical protection when it comes to the preservation of their legal status as far as it arises from collective agreements.

As for works agreements the situation is different. Again, however, it must be noted from the start that Section 613a of the Civil Code may lead to the protection of the rights of an employee based on such agreements. It may even be that, depending on the circumstances of the individual case, the works agreement itself can be maintained. According to legal doctrine in Germany, a works agreement is regarded as the "law of the establishment" which, inter alia, means that it "survives" a universal transfer as long as the establishment itself retains its identity.[50] If, in other words, the establishment transferred continues to exist as a separate operating unit rather than being absorbed by a

---

49. See in this regard for instance *Schaub*, Arbeitsrechts-Handbuch, 9dn ed., 2000, 1179ff. with additional references.
50. See *Schaub*, Arbeitsrechts-Handbuch, 9dn ed., 2000, 1181 with references to respective rulings of the Federal Labour Court.

more complex structure, the works agreement remains fully in force. If, on the other hand, the establishment itself is split or merged with another pre-existing establishment of the new employer, the result is a loss of the identity of the establishment, with the relevant works agreements ceasing to have effect.

4. ECONOMIC DISMISSALS

4.1. Economic dismissals regulations in general

4.1.1. Act on termination protection 1969 (kuendigungsschutzgesetz)

As indicated earlier, the Act on Termination Protection 1969 (Kuendigungsschutzgesetz) restricts the power of the employer to terminate the employment relationship for business-related reasons. A couple of legal requirements must be fulfilled in order to render a dismissal lawful.[51] First, the employment opportunities for the individual employee must have been lost or, in all likelihood, will be lost in the foreseeable future. Second, the employer must have complied with the selection criteria as laid down in the Act. And third, the employee cannot be employed in another vacant position in the same establishment or in any other establishment of the employer.

a. Loss of employment opportunities
As for the loss of employment opportunities, it has to be stressed that developments such as declining sales or the loss of an important customer as such do not constitute sufficient reasons for a dismissal. In order to be admissible, the employer must be able to show that he has taken a concrete "entrepreneurial" decision whose implementation has the effect of ceasing employment opportunities. The burden of proof is fully on the employer. But though it is true that the "entrepreneurial" decision is subject to the labour court's scrutiny, the power of the court is a relatively narrow one. The court is obliged to examine whether, first, the employer's decision is reasonable, and, second, whether his decision necessarily leads to a loss of employment opportunities. What the labour court is not allowed to do is to substitute the business judgement of the employer. On the other hand, as termination is regarded as a means of last resort (so-called principle of *ultima ratio*), an employer is always required to show that all attempts to avoid terminations (reduction of overtime, implementation of part-time work) have failed. The relevant time for evaluating the decision of the employer is the end of the period of notice. This means that even if by the end of this period the economic circumstances of the employer have improved, this will in principle have no effect on the justification of the dismissal.[52]

---

51.   See *Weiss/Schmidt*, Labour Law and Industrial Relations in Germany, The Hague a. o., 2000, 107 ff.
52.   Only under exceptional circumstances may the employee have the right to be reinstated (Wiedereinstellungsanspruch).

b. Selection of the individual employee
An employee who is affected by a dismissal can, under certain circumstances, claim that this particular termination (as applied to that employee, as opposed to others) would not be justified. An employer, when terminating the employment relationship, always has to take into account the "social aspects" (*soziale Gesichtspunkte*) of his decision to select a certain employee for dismissal. The procedure that has to be followed by the employer essentially contains two steps. First, it must be determined on the basis of the individual establishment (not the entire business) which employees, having regard to both their actual work and their qualifications, can be classified together for the purpose of establishing their "social priority" (so-called concept of "comparability"). And second, the relevant "social aspects", such as seniority, age, the number of persons who are dependent on and have to be supported by the employee, must be assessed by the employer.

c. Lack of other employment opportunities
Finally, unilateral termination of an employment relationship is not legitimate if the employer's company has other vacant job positions. Although the law on protection against dismissals principally focuses on the individual plant or establishment, the duty of the employer to ascertain whether there are open positions extends to other establishments within the company.[53]

4.2. Works council participation

In establishments where a works council exists, the protection against dismissal as provided under individual labour law is supplemented by collective-law provisions.[54] According to Section 102 of the Works Constitution Act, the employer is obliged prior to a dismissal to inform the works council (as a body, not only its chairperson) of the proposed dismissal, indicating the type of dismissal (ordinary or extraordinary dismissal), specifying the reasons for discharge, and offer the works council an opportunity of stating its position on the matter. If the employer pronounces a dismissal before the works council has responded or before a set period has elapsed,[55] the dismissal is invalid irrespective of whether or not it is lawful in other respects (Section 102, par. 1, sentence 3). The works council has the right to object to a dismissal if the employer has not sufficiently considered the relevant "social aspects" when choosing the employee to be dismissed, if the unilateral termination contravenes one of the agreed company guidelines on personnel policy, if the employee could be further employed in a vacant job in the same establishment or another establishment of the same company, or if re-training or further

---

53.   *Federal Labour Court* of 17 May 1984, Collection of the Decisions of the Federal Labour Court (BAGE) 46, 191.
54.   See *Weiss/Schmidt*, Labour Law and Industrial Relations in Germany, The Hague a. o., 2000, 108 ff.
55.   The relevant period being one week in the case of ordinary dismissals with notice and three days in the case of summary dismissals

education which the employer could reasonably be expected to provide, or an alteration of the conditions of the contract of employment (subject to the consent of the employee concerned), would make continued employment possible (Section 102, par. 3). An objection by the works council, which in any event has to be sufficiently precise, has no bearing on to the effectiveness of a dismissal. However, if a dismissed employee then makes an application to the courts for protection against dismissal, an objection issued by the works council, if deemed by the court to be justified, in principle means that without any further assessment of the interests involved, the court rules the dismissal to be unfair (so-called "absolute Sozialwidrigkeit"[56]). An objection also secures for the employee the right to continued employment during dismissal proceedings (*Verpflichtung zur Weiterbeschaeftigung*, Section 102, par. 5).

4.3. Specific requirements for mass redundancies

In the case of a mass redundancy, the employer, apart from the normal requirements, must satisfy additional specific qualifications.[57] Essentially, the employer is under a duty to give written notice to the works council in the event that the employer wants to dismiss more than five employees in an operation which in the ordinary course employs more than 20 and less than 60 employees; if the employer wants to dismiss more than 25 employees (or 10% of those employed) in an operation that in the ordinary course employs at least 60 and fewer than 500 employees; or if at least 30 employees are likely to be dismissed within a reference period of 30 calendar days and the operation in question has more than 500 employees (Section 17, par. 1 of the Act on Termination Protection 1969).

   In this context the employer has to provide workers' representatives with all relevant information and, in any event, has to provide the following information in writing: the reasons for the intended dismissals; the period over which redundancies are to be effected; the number and categories of employees normally employed; the number and categories of employees to be made redundant; the criteria proposed for the selection of those workers to be made redundant; the method used for calculating any severance payments (Section 17, par. 2). The legal rationale behind these requirements is the expectation of the legislator that the employer and the works council will have an opportunity to enter into discussions about efforts to reduce the number of terminations and to minimise their disruptive effect.

   Apart from the obligation towards works councils the employer is under an obligation to notify the competent public authority in writing of any projected collective redundancies. This notification must contain all the relevant information concerning the projected redundancies and consultations held, except for the method used to calculate compensation. Principally, layoffs

---

56.   See Section 1, par. 2 of the Act on Termination Protection.
57.   See *Weiss/Schmidt*, Labour Law and Industrial Relations in Germany, The Hague a. o., 2000, 113 ff.

do not take effect until this notice has been at the competent authority for at least one month, and after the legal period of notice has expired (Section 18, par. 1). On the other hand, it must be noted that the competent public authority has no power to approve or disapprove of the terminations apart from a review of the legal formalities.

4.4. Economic dismissals before and after the transfer of undertakings/ corporate restructuring

According to Section 613a, par. 4 of the Civil Code the transfer of an undertaking, business or part of a business does not in itself constitute a good reason for dismissal by the transferor or the transferee. However, this provision renders a dismissal ineffective only if the transfer was the only or at least the predominant reason for terminating the employment contract. Section 613a, par. 4 of the Civil Code, in other words, does not stand in the way of unilateral terminations that may take place for economic, technical or organisational reasons entailing changes in the workforce.

4.5. Role of labour unions or employees' representatives in these processes

As a rule, a transfer of a business or part of a business must be reported to the relevant economic committee (Section 106, paras 2 and 3 of the Works Constitution Act). The transferor has to inform its own committee and the transferee has to inform its committee where the target company is to be integrated into an existing business. Information has to be given in timely manner before the transfer is effected. The transfer of a business as such is not subject to any co-determination rights of the works council. But in many cases the transfer will constitute a so-called operational change (*Betriebsaenderung*) under Section 111 of the Works Constitution Act.

The legal concept of operational change or substantial alteration to the establishment (*Betriebsaenderung*), which forms the basis of participation of the works council, is laid down in Sections 111 and 112 of the Works Constitution Act. It covers major decisions on cut-backs or closures of establishments; reductions of operations or relocations of the establishment (or of important parts of it); mergers with other establishments; fundamental alterations to the establishment's organisation, the purpose of the establish- ment or its facilities; and the introduction of fundamentally different work methods and production processes. Rationalisation programmes and the introduction of new working methods or production processes also fall under this heading. The assumption is, for the cases listed, that the changes may result in serious disadvantages for the workforce or for large sections of it. Consequently, in establishments regularly employing more than 20 employees, who are allowed to participate in works council elections, the works council must be given prompt and full information on any such proposed changes (Section 110, par. 2). In practice, substantial alterations to the establishment constitute the main area of use of the participation rights of the works council in economic matters, and, in principle, entitle the works council to both a so-called "reconcilement of interests" and a so-called "social (compensation) plan".

4.5.1.   The so-called reconciliation of interests

The reconciliation of interests (*Interessenausgleich*) as laid down in Sections 111 and 112 of the Works Constitution Act (*Betriebsverfassungsgesetz*) is a procedure aimed at reconciling the viewpoints of the employer and the workforce in the event of a proposed substantial alteration to the establishment. The procedure involves weighing the respective interests against each other and agreeing, for example, on whether the major change envisaged should be carried out at all, and if so on the extent, timing and nature of the change. Detailed arrangements for the subsequent implementation of the changes are then subject to the co-determination rights of the works council. If employer and works council fail to agree on such a reconcilement of interests, they may call on the Director of the labour office to mediate (Section 112, par. 2). Should they not wish to do so, or should mediation prove not to be successful, they can refer the matter to arbitration, although this will not be binding on them.

If the employer fails to follow the procedure outlined above, the employer is obliged to make severance payments up to a maximum of 18 months' pay, depending on age and continuity of employment, if notice is given before the required procedures are exhausted (Section 113 of the Works Constitution Act and Section 10 of the Act on Termination Protection 1969, so-called *Nachteilsausgleich*). In addition, the employer must compensate the employee for any other economic detriments he or she may have suffered in the course of the year after termination of the employment contract (Section 113, par. 2 of the Works Constitution Act).

4.5.2.   The so-called social (compensation) plan

The social (compensation) plan, on the other hand, is a programme drawn up in the form of a special works agreement to compensate for or reduce economic disadvantages for employees in the event of a substantial alteration to the establishment. It resembles a special form of redundancy programme and gives the employer and the works council a discretionary power to decide on both the nature of the disadvantage to be compensated for and the amount of such compensation. If the employer and the works council fail to agree on a "social plan", again they may call on the labour office to mediate. Should they choose not to do so, or should mediation prove unsuccessful, they may refer the matter to arbitration, whose decision this time has binding effect and substitutes for an agreement between employer and works council (Section 112, par. 4). In arriving at its decision, the committee must among other things be guided by the actual disadvantages caused and the labour market prospects for the employees affected. However, in fixing the total sum to be made available under the plan, it must not place an unreasonable financial burden on the employer (Section 112, par. 5). If the committee incorrectly exercises its discretionary powers, the employer and the works council may apply to the courts to have the plan ruled invalid (Section 76, par. 5). There is no obligation to draw up a "social plan" provided that the proposed alteration to the establishment consists only of dismissals, and that certain maximum limits in terms of a percentage of the total workforce are not exceeded (Section 112a, par. 1). Nor is there an obligation to agree on a "social plan" when the case involves a newly formed enterprise (Section 112a, par. 2). However, a reconciliation of interests must be arranged in any event. Any termination of employment initiated by the employer due to operational change that is based on a severance agreement qualifies as a dismissal. In cases of insolvency, employees suffering dismissal receive compensation for job loss, up to a maximum of two and a half months' pay, which is given preferential settlement in the bankruptcy proceedings (Section 123, par. 1 of the Insolvency Act, *Insolvenzordnung*[58]). A "social (compensation) plan" can be drawn up regardless of whether or not a reconciliation of interests has been sought.

From the perspective of the enterprise, the obligation to establish a social plan conflicts both with the human resource objectives of flexibility and adaptability to changing environments and with the general objectives of profitability. This reduces the opportunities for the employer to find the optimal size and structure of the workforce. In contrast, trade unions and works councils regard the increased costs that are associated with social plans as a means of limiting the excessive use of dismissals. In other words, the high costs of reducing the workforce can be a tool to force management to search for alternatives other than dismissing employees.

4.5.3. Specific aspects of business reorganisations

As for business reorganisations under the Act on Business Reorganisations, apart from the participation rights arising under the Works Constitution Act, the interests of employees receive protection in that employers are under a far-reaching duty of disclosure. This obligation encompasses both the measures planned by management and the consequences of the reorganisation for the employees. There is a duty to notify the works council by supplying the agreement or draft thereof or, respectively, the draft of the conversion resolution (Sections 5 and 126, paras 3 and 3 of the Act on Business Reorganisation). On the basis of this information the works council can examine whether the duty of disclosure was properly complied with and demand

---

58.   Insolvenzordnung (InsO) of 5 October 1994 (BGBl. I, 2866), as recenty amended by Act of
       26 October 2001 (BGBl. I, 2710).

a reconciliation of interests from the employer. If a splitting of a business unit takes place, the works council remains in office and carries on the affairs until a new works council is elected (Section 321, par. 1 of the Act). With respect to the merger of business units or partial business units, the works council of the largest business unit should make use of this transitional mandate (Section 322, par. 1 of the Act). And as far as co-determination at board level is concerned, the Act on Business Reorganisations also tries to ensure that the existing set-up shall be maintained as far as possible (Section 325, par. 1 and 203 of the Act).

5.   CHANGES IN TERMS AND CONDITIONS OF EMPLOYMENT

5.1.   Transfer of workers

The assignment of an employee to a different area of work by the employer is admissible only under certain circumstances under German law. Under individual labour law, the precondition for a legally valid transfer is that the possibility of transfer is (expressly or implicitly) reserved under the contract of employment, so that the employee can fairly and reasonably be expected to accept unilateral designation of the nature or location of the work performance. In a case where the employer is prevented from a unilateral transfer, a dismissal for variation of contract must take place.

In any event, however, a transfer is subject to co-determination if, first, more than 20 employees entitled to vote are employed in the establishment,[59] and, second, the new job is expected to last for more than one month or involves a significant change of employment conditions.[60] According to Section 99 of the Act, a transfer[61] shall be ineffective for the employee if it takes place without the works council's consent.[62] This means that as long as there is no such consent, the employee is under no duty to comply with the assignment. It should, however, be noted that the works council is only allowed to object to the assignment by invoking the grounds that are expressly (and exclusively) mentioned in Section 99, par. 2 of the Act.

5.2.   Modification of terms and conditions of employment

Under German labour law the employer enjoys the so-called right to issue instructions (*Direktionsrecht*). Since in the contract of employment the duty to work normally is indicated only in relatively general terms, the employer has the right to put this obligation into definite terms and assign particular work

---

59.   See Section 99, par. 1 of the Works Constitution Act.
60.   See for the latter the legal definition as provided in Section 95, par. 3 of the Act.
61.   This transfer may consist of the assignment to a different task or a change in the employee's work location or a transfer to another establishment or any other substantial change in working conditions.
62.   In this case, according to Section 99, par. 4 of the Act, the employer has to file with the labour court, whose decision can substitute in the absence of the works council's consent.

tasks to the employee. The employee, on the other hand, is principally under an obligation to obey orders given by the employer.

This right to issue instructions, however, only goes so far and does not amount to a power to vary the employment relationship unilaterally. An employer who wishes to alter the terms and conditions has to pronounce a so-called dismissal for variation of contract (*Aenderungskuendigung*).[63] Such a dismissal contains two elements: first, an offer from the employer to the employee to continue the employment relationship under altered terms and conditions; and second, a declaration of the intention to finish the employment relationship if the employee rejects this offer. Given its latter element it is subject to legal protection against dismissal (Section 2 of the Act on Termination Protection) which, therefore, protects not only the stability but also the actual terms of the employment contract. There are three possible ways in which employees can respond to a dismissal for variation of contract. First, they can accept the offer incorporating variation without stating any reservation. Alternatively, they can accept the offer incorporating variation subject to the reservation[64] that the variation of the terms and conditions of employment is socially unjustified. Lastly, they can reject the offer incorporating variation. In this case, since no action is brought before the labour court, dismissal for variation of contract ends the employment relationship.

5.3. Special issues in the event of transfer of undertakings

As already mentioned, in the case of an asset sale the relevant contracts of employment are automatically transferred from the seller of the business to the purchaser. This means that in principle, employees' rights arising from their employment contract may not be altered even if, for instance, the overall amount of their wages remains unchanged. However, insofar as national law makes it possible to amend an employment relationship, such changes are not entirely ruled out merely because the undertaking has in the meantime been transferred. The rights and obligations arising from an employment contract may in other words be changed vis-à-vis the transferee, subject to the same restrictions as could have been applied to the transferor, assuming that the transfer in itself is not the reason for this change.

6. CONCLUDING REMARKS

When it comes to corporate restructuring, the leading principle of German labour law is to protect the affected employees as far as possible from the

---

63. See *Weiss/Schmidt*, Labour Law and Industrial Relations in Germany, The Hague a. o., 2000, 117 ff.
64. In this case, however, they must, according to Section 2 of the Act, invoke the reservation within three weeks by making an application for protection against dismissal.

detrimental consequences which are often attached to these processes. The legal position of the employee is maintained whether it derives from the individual employment relationship or from collective agreements. From an employee's perspective this stance of German labour law undoubtedly looks fortunate. But because it certainly hampers restructuring, it is open to discussion whether employees really profit by it in the long run.

5. Japan*

Ryuichi Yamakawa

1. INTRODUCTION

In recent years, restructuring of corporations has taken place frequently in Japan. This is mainly because Japanese corporations have been struggling to become more efficient in the competitive global market. In addition to the closing of less profitable departments, many Japanese companies have carried out business reorganisation. Traditional methods of such reorganisation are mergers and transfer of business undertakings. Furthermore, in May 2000, the Commercial Code of Japan was amended to introduce a new reorganisation scheme called the "division of corporation." At the same time, since the division of a corporation may affect the workers of the corporation to be divided, a new statute called the "Labour Contract Succession Law"[1] was enacted to protect workers' interests.

This chapter examines some of the major issues arising under Japanese labour law with respect to corporate restructuring, with an emphasis on business reorganisation. Part II briefly discusses issues arising from merger and transfer of business undertakings. Next, Part III introduces the "division of corporation" scheme under the amended Commercial Code and explores how the Labour Contract Succession Law protects workers' interests when "division of corporation" is carried out. Then, Parts IV and V respectively discuss the protection of workers from economic dismissals and the issue of the changes in working conditions in the context of business reorganisation. Finally, Part VI concludes with a few comments on the features of Japanese labour law in respect of business reorganisation.

---

*   The author would like to thank Professor Vai Io Lo for her valuable comments on the manuscript of this article.
1.   The formal name of this new statute is "Kaisha no Bunkatsu ni Tomonau Rodo Keiyaku no Shokei tou ni kansuru Houritsu" (Law Relating to Succession of Labour Contract and Other Matters in the Event of Division of Corporation), Law no. 103 of 2000.

R. Blanpain (ed.),
Corporate Restructuring and the Role of Labour Law, 103–122.

2. MERGER AND TRANSFER OF BUSINESS UNDERTAKINGS

2.1. Merger and labour law

In the event of a merger, a corporation as a subject of merger (merged corporation) disappears in the legal sense, and its rights and duties are automatically transferred as a whole to another already existing or newly established corporation that acquires the merged corporation. Employment contracts of the employees of the merged corporation are also taken over by the other corporation, whether the employees give consent or not.[2] This is also true with a collective bargaining agreement.

Sometimes redundancy may arise from organisational restructuring as a result of merger. However, the employer may not freely discharge redundant employees. The Japanese employer's right to discharge its employees is generally restricted under the abuse of right doctrine developed in case law.[3] In addition, it is often necessary for the new employer to change the contents of the employment contracts of the inherited employees in order to adjust them to the new environment or to unify their working conditions with those of incumbent employees. In such a case, the employer may modify working conditions through the exercise of its personnel management rights, such as transfers or the unilateral change of work rules under certain conditions.[4] These issues are further discussed in Parts IV and V.

2.2. Transfer of business undertakings and labour law

Transfer of business undertakings ("Eigyo-Joto") is a contractual measure to assign rights and duties that constitute a business undertaking to another entity.[5] Unlike merger, the assignment of rights and duties in this case does not automatically take place, but is carried out as the performance of a transfer contract. Also, the transferor does not always cease to exist, especially in the event of partial transfer.

One of the legal issues arising from transfer of business undertakings is whether an employee of the transferor has the right to refuse to become a subject of transfer, that is to say, to refuse to become the transferee's employee. This issue has been debated, especially in cases involving partial transfer. In recent years, many courts have answered this question affirmatively, relying on

2.   Kazuo Sugeno, Japanese Labour Law 393 (Leo Kanowitz trans. 1992).
3.   *See infra* notes 36–39 and accompanying text.
4.   *See infra* notes 55–56 and accompanying text.
5.   In this sense, the transfer of business undertaking does not include a situation where there is no contractual relationship between the two companies. For example, when company A dissolves itself, discharges all the workers, and sells most of the assets to company B, and then company C buys these assets and hires some of the discharged workers, it is difficult to find the transfer of a business undertaking. If there is substantial identity between company A and company B, however, courts may hold that company C cannot refuse the succession to the employment contracts of other workers. *See infra* note 6 and accompanying text.

Article 625 of the Civil Code.[6] This article provides that the employer may not transfer its rights under the employment contract to another employer without the employee's consent.

Another issue is whether the transferor and transferee may exclude some of the employees from the subject of transfer. This issue will become particularly important if the transferor is to be dissolved as a result of the transfer, and the remaining employees are to be discharged. In EU countries, the so-called "acquired rights" directive[7] provides that the rights and duties of the transferor under an employment contract are automatically and mandatorily assigned to the transferee. In Japan, however, there is no such statute. Thus, a number of lower court decisions have held that it is up to the parties to the transfer contract (i.e. transferor and transferee corporations) to decide whether employment relationship is to be included as a subject of transfer.[8]

Nevertheless, in cases where there is substantial identity between the transferor and transferee, some courts have held that the transferee may not refuse the succession of employment relationship.[9] In effect, these rulings have relied on the doctrine of piercing the corporate veil. Also, in cases where the contract of the transfer of a business undertaking does not contain a clear provision that includes employment relationship as a subject of transfer, courts have sometimes found an implied agreement to that effect.[10] Furthermore, when the parties to the agreement explicitly or implicitly stipulate that a part of the workforce will be excluded from the transfer for such impermissible reasons as sex, race and union membership, such provision is illegal and void as a violation of public policy.[11] As a result, the excluded employees shall be transferred to the transferee.

When the Labour Contract Succession Law was enacted (see below) in respect of the division of corporations, discussion took place as to whether a new legislation was necessary for the protection of workers in the event of merger and transfer of business undertakings. The Ministry of Labour (currently the Ministry of Health, Labour and Welfare) took the view that such legislation was not necessary because, as stated above, case law can provide substantial protection in the case of transfer.[12] Still, when the Diet passed the Law, relevant Committees in the Upper and Lower Houses made a resolution that further research and examination should be conducted regarding the necessity for the protection of workers in the course of transfer of

---

6.   E.g. *Umemura* v *Maruko K.K.*, 881 Hanrei Taimuzu 151 (Nara Dist.Ct. Katsuragi Branch, 18 June 1992).
7.   Council Directive 77/187.
8.   E.g. *Ito* v *Ibaraki Shohisha Kurabu*, 628 Rodo Hanrei 12 (Osaka Dist.Ct., 22 March 1993). This case also concerns the succession to a collective bargaining agreement.
9.   E.g. *Matsuyama Seikatsu Kyodo Kumiai* v *Nakagawa*, 18 Rodo Kankei Minji Saiban Reishu 890 (Takamatsu High Ct., 6 September 1967).
10.   E.g. *Yamaguchi* v *Shin Kansai Tsushin Shisutemuzu K.K.*, 668 Rodo Hanrei 48 (Osaka Dist. Ct. 5 August 1992).
11.   *See* Ryuichi Yamakawa, Koyo Kankei Ho (Employment Relations Law) 241 (1999).
12.   This view is based on the report of the Study Group that recommended the enactment of the Labour Contract Succession Law. *See infra* note 20.

undertakings.[13] At present, a study group established by the Ministry is conducting research based on this resolution.[14]

As in the case of merger, issues relating to economic dismissals and changes in working conditions may often arise before or after the transfer of business undertakings. Again, these issues are discussed later in Parts IV and V.

3.   DIVISION OF CORPORATION AND LABOUR CONTRACT SUCCESSION LAW

3.1.   Division of corporation under the commercial code

As stated before, the amendment to the Commercial Code in May 2000 introduced a new scheme of business reorganisation called the "division of corporation."[15] Under this scheme, a corporation (transferor) divides itself into business undertakings and automatically assigns them to another corporation (transferee). For example, a corporation that has a hotel department and a railroad department may divide itself and transfer the hotel department to another corporation. The transferee may be a new corporation that is established through a resolution at a meeting of the transferor's shareholders (Chart 5.1), or an already existing corporation (Chart 5.2). In the former case, the division of corporation is carried out according to a division plan, which is to be adopted in the shareholders' meeting. In the latter case, the division is carried out according to a division contract between the transferor and transferee, which is also to be adopted at shareholders' meetings of both corporations.

In both cases, the rights and duties that constitute the business undertaking to be divided are assigned to the transferee as a result of the adoption of the division plan or contract at the shareholders' meeting.[16] The division plan or division contract determines which rights and duties are to be assigned to the transferee. Like merger, this assignment takes effect automatically, i.e. without any contractual arrangement to assign rights and duties. Although the debtors may change as a result of such assignment, the consent of the transferor's creditors is not necessary. Instead, the transferor corporation shall disclose the contents of the division plan or contract and take certain procedures to protect its creditors, such as giving them an opportunity to file an objection or providing payments or collaterals to those who have filed the objection.[17] The assignment takes effect when, after such procedures are completed, the fact of the division is registered.

---

13.   *See* Rodo Keiyaku Shokei Ho (Labour Contract Succession Law) 101, 110 (Ministry of Labour ed. 2000).
14.   *http://www.mhlw.go.jp/topics/0102/tp0226–2.html* (last visited 11 April 2002).
15.   *See generally* Masahiro Maeda, *Kaisha Bunkatsu ni Kakaru Shoho To no Ichibu Kaisei ni Tsuite* (Partial Amendment of the Commercial Code regarding Division of Corporation), 1182 Jurisuto 2 (2000).
16.   Articles 374–10 and 374–26 of the Commercial Code.
17.   Articles 374–4 and 374–20 of the Commercial Code.

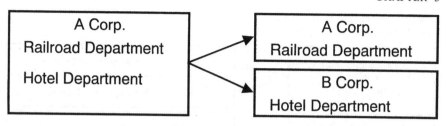

Chart 5.1: Division of Corporation to Establish a New Corporation (B)

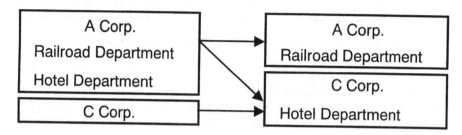

Chart 5.2: Division of Corporation to Assign to Existing Corporation (C)

When the Diet discussed the bill to amend the Commercial Code, one criticism was that the division of corporation would be used to discard an unprofitable department and the employer could easily discharge employees working therein.[18] Thus, the amended Commercial Code requires the transferor and transferee to demonstrate to their stockholders and creditors that both corporations are financially competent to perform the obligations they will assume after the division.[19] This presupposes that each corporation will not fall into a state of insolvency as a result of the division. To this extent, the amendment provides for a safety valve, i.e. to prevent a corporation from discarding an unprofitable department.

3.2. Labour contract succession law

3.2.1. Necessity of legislation

Under the amended Commercial Code, the transferor corporation, with the agreement of the transferee corporation (if the transferee already exists), may freely determine through the division plan or contract which rights and duties are to be taken over by the transferee, so long as the subject of transfer qualifies as a business undertaking. Since the Code does not exclude employment relationship from the coverage of this scheme, the transferor employer can determine freely which employees are to be assigned to the transferee.

18.   *See* Rodo Keiyaku Shokei Ho, *supra* note 13, at 76.
19.   Articles 374–2(1)2 and 374–18(1)3 of the Commercial Code.

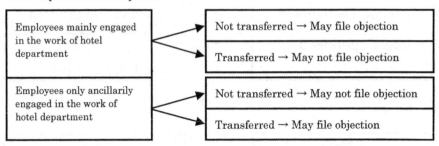

Employees engaged in the work of
hotel department to be split off

Chart 5.3: Employee's Right to File Objection in Division of Corporation

Moreover, since Article 625 of the Civil Code, which requires the employer to obtain the consent of its employees in the event of transfer of employment contract, does not necessarily apply to such automatic succession as merger and division of corporation, an employee whom the transferor has determined will transfer does not have a right to refuse the transfer.

Thus, under the amended Commercial Code alone, an employee of the transferor who has been engaging in the work of the department to be split off will not be able to move to the transferee even if he/she wants to, if the division plan or contract excludes him/her as a subject of transfer. The disadvantage of being excluded from the transfer will become serious if such an employee has been working mainly in the department to be split off. On the other hand, an employee who has been working in such a department will be forced to move to the transferee if the division plan or contract includes him/her as a subject of transfer. The disadvantage resulting from a compulsory transfer will become serious if such employee has been working in the department only ancillarily, e.g. only one day a week in the department, while working in another department for the rest of the working week.

In this sense, the amended Commercial Code will cause problems in terms of the protection of workers. This is one of the main reasons that the Labour Contract Succession Law was enacted at the same time as the amendment of the Commercial Code. This legislation was mostly based on the proposal in the report prepared by the Study Group on Labour Relations Law Relating to Business Reorganisation.[20] This group was established by the Ministry of Labour as an advisory board and headed by Professor Kazuo Sugeno of the University of Tokyo.

---

20.   Kigyo Soshiki Henko ni Kakaru Rodo Kankei Hosei to Kenkyuu Kai Hokoku (2000),
        cited in Rodo Keiyaku Shokei Ho, *supra* note 13, at 380.

3.2.2.   Succession of individual employment contract

In order to avoid serious disadvantages to employees involved in the division of corporation, the Labour Contract Succession Law has several provisions regarding the employee's rights to request the transfer of employment contract and to refuse forced transfer. The contents of these rights are as follows (Chart 5.3):

(1)   Inclusion in the transfer (article 4)

As regards employees who have been engaging mainly in the work of the department to be split off and who are excluded under the division plan or contract from the subject of transfer, they have the right to file an objection to such exclusion. If this objection is filed in a timely manner, their employment contract shall be automatically and mandatorily assigned to the transferee. On the other hand, such employees do not have the right to exclude themselves from the transfer (Article 3).

This treatment is based on the idea that the disadvantage to employees who have been engaging mainly in the work of the department to be split off is particularly serious when they are excluded from the transfer, since they will be separated from the work in which they have been mainly engaged. On the other hand, the disadvantage to such employees as a result of automatic transfer is not so serious, since they can continue to work in a substantially similar organisation and the contents of their employment contracts remain unchanged after the transfer.[21]

(2)   Exclusion from the transfer (article 5)

As regards employees who have been engaging only ancillarily in the work of the department to be split off and yet are included under the division plan or contract in the subject of transfer, they have the right to file an objection to such inclusion. If this objection is filed in a timely manner, their employment contracts shall be automatically and mandatorily excluded from the transfer, and they continue to belong to the transferor. The Law empowers employees who have been engaging only ancillarily in the work of the department to be split off to file such an objection because the disadvantage to such employees is quite serious if they are separated from the work in which they have been mainly engaged.

It should be noted that employees who have not been engaging at all in the work of the department to be split off shall not be subject to the scheme of division of corporation. Thus, the division plan or contract may not provide for the transfer of such employees, and the consent of such employees is

---

21.   As stated below, the working conditions of such employees may be changed unilaterally by their new employer after the division through the revision of work rules. *See infra* notes 55–56 and accompanying text. However, such unilateral change may take place regardless of the division of corporation, and there are certain restrictions on such revision based on the reasonableness doctrine established by case law.

necessary under Article 625 of the Civil Code, if the transferor wants them to be moved to the transferee.[22]

(3)   Advance notice to employees

In order to provide employees who may be affected by the division with an opportunity to consider the matter and file an objection, it is necessary to notify them of whether they are included in or excluded from the subject of transfer in the division plan or contract. Therefore, the Labour Contract Succession Law requires the transferor to give notice to its employees regarding their treatment at least two weeks before the shareholders' meeting that will determine the adoption of the division plan or contract (Article 2).

(4)   Criteria to determine the scope of automatic transfer

Several issues remain unaddressed by the Law itself. Among them, the most important one is how to determine whether an employee has been engaging "mainly" or "only ancillarily" in the work of the department to be split off. In December 2000, the Ministry of Labour promulgated a set of guidelines regarding the enforcement of the Labour Contract Succession Law.[23] While this set of guidelines contains a number of items, such as the working conditions that must be maintained after the transfer, the criterion for distinguishing between "mainly" and "only ancillarily" is as follows:[24]

Whether an employee has been engaging in the work of the department to be split off mainly or only ancillarily shall be determined at the time of the making of the division plan or contract. However, even when an employee is mainly engaging in the work of the department to be split off at that time, such employee shall not be deemed to be working mainly in such department, if his/her work is only temporary (e.g. training) and it is clear that the employee at issue will not be engaging in the work of such department when his/her work is completed. Also, even when an employee is not working mainly in the department to be divided at the time of the making of the division plan or contract, such employee shall still be deemed to be working mainly in such department, if it is clear that such employee will be engaging in the work of such department and is working in another department only temporarily.

In the event that an employee is engaging in the work of the department to be split off as well as in the work of other departments, whether the employee is engaging in the work of the former department mainly or only ancillarily is determined in light of the totality of circumstances, including how much time the employee has spent on the work of the department to be split off, the role that the employee has been playing in respective departments, and so forth.

---

22.   Takashi Araki, *Gappei, Eigyo Joto, Kaisha Bunkatsu to Rodo Kankei* (Merger, Transfer of Undertakings, and Division of Corporation in the Context of Labour Relations), 1182 Jurisuto 16 (2000).

23.   Rodo Sho Kokuji, No. 127, 27 December 2000 (hereinafter "Guidelines"), *cited in* Rodo Keiyaku Shokei Ho, *supra* note 13, at 253.

24.   Section 2(3) of Part 2 of the Guidelines.

With respect to an employee who is working in an administrative department in charge of general affairs, human resource management, accounting, and financial management in banking, if such employee is exclusively working for the department to be split off, he/she shall be deemed to be engaging mainly in the work of that department. When such employee is also working for another department at the same time, his/her status shall be determined according to the totality of circumstances as stated above. When it cannot be determined under the totality of circumstances whether such an employee is engaging in the work of the department to be split off mainly or only ancillarily, he/she shall be deemed to be engaging mainly in the work of that department, if the majority of the transferor's employees (except for the employees at issue) are to be transferred to the transferee, unless extraordinary circumstances apply.

Finally, if the transferor changes, before making the division plan, the job or workplace of the employee who is clearly supposed to be transferred or not to be transferred to the transferee in the light of his/her past job history, with an intention to exclude such employee from the transferee or transferor, the determination shall be made on the basis of his/her past job history.

(5) Effect of transfer

Since the division of corporation is a scheme to carry out automatic succession as in the case of merger, the transferee succeeds to the rights and duties that constitute the business undertaking as a subject of transfer with their contents unchanged. Therefore, when the employment contract of an employee is succeeded by the transferee, his/her working conditions under the contract should remain intact. The Guidelines of the Ministry of Labour clarify this by stating that both the transferor and transferee shall not unilaterally and adversely change the working conditions because of the division of corporation.[25] The change of working conditions before or after the division for reasons other than the division itself shall be regulated under the basic principles of the law of employment contract or collective labour relations. Thus, although the consent of individual employees or trade unions is basically necessary for such change, there may be certain exceptions under the case law doctrine of reasonable modification of work rules.[26] Also, the Guidelines confirm that the transferor and transferee shall not discharge their employees just because of the division of corporation.[27]

Another issue is the scope of working conditions to which the transferee is supposed to succeed. So long as the conditions have become the contents of the employment contract through an explicit document, such as the work rules, or an implied agreement under Article 92 of the Civil Code, there are few problems about succession. This is also the case with fringe benefits that employees are entitled to receive under the employment contract. Meanwhile, difficulty arises with respect to benefits, the conditions of which are provided

---

25.   Section 2(4)(i-i) of Part 2 of the Guidelines.
26.   *See infra* notes 55–56 and accompanying text.
27.   Section 2(4)(i-ha) of Part 2 of the Guidelines.

under social security legislation. Basically, the treatment of such benefits is determined under each statute.[28]

3.2.3. Succession of collective bargaining agreements and related matters

(1) Succession of collective bargaining agreements

With respect to collective labour relations, an important issue concerns the effect of the division of corporation on a collective bargaining agreement. Here again, a number of problems will arise if there is no special legislation other than the amended Commercial Code. Among other things, if the division plan or contract provides that the employment contracts of trade union members shall be assigned to the transferee, but that their collective bargaining agreement shall not, the union members will not enjoy protection under the collective agreement regarding working conditions.[29]

Thus, there is a need for legislation to provide for the succession to a collective bargaining agreement. However, if such legislation provides merely for the automatic transfer of a collective agreement, employees who remain with the transferor will be excluded from its coverage and lose its protection. Therefore, the Labour Contract Succession Law provides that when the employment contracts of the members of a trade union are taken over by the transferee, it shall be deemed that a collective bargaining agreement which has the same contents is concluded between the transferee and the trade union (Article 6(3)). Due to such a provision, trade union members can enjoy the normative effect of collective agreements under Article 16 of the Trade Union Law, whether they remain with the transferor or are assigned to the transferee.

As a result of this regulation, there may be cases where the transferee has two or more collective bargaining agreements with different trade unions so that members of each union are subject to different working conditions. However, similar situations will occur in the event of merger: the unification of working conditions may be achieved through the conclusion of new collective agreements or the unilateral revision of work rules under the reasonableness doctrine.[30]

(2) Partial transfer

Another question is whether it is possible to divide the contents of a collective bargaining agreement and transfer a portion of its contents. Although it is doubtful or at least not clearly possible to do so under the amended Commercial Code, there are situations where such partial transfer is appropriate. For example, suppose a collective agreement provides that the trade union has the right to use two company rooms for union activities, and

---

28.   Section 2(4)(ha) of Part 2 of the Guidelines.
29.   According to Article 16 of the Trade Union Law, an individual employment contract shall not violate the provisions of a collective bargaining agreement.
30.   See infra notes 55–56 and accompanying text.

these rooms are located in two buildings, which turn out to belong to the transferor and transferee respectively. In such a case, it would be a better arrangement that the transferor and the transferee respectively owe a duty to rent out the room located in the building that they each own.

For these reasons, the Labour Contract Succession Law provides that a division plan or agreement may include stipulations regarding the transfer of a part of a collective bargaining agreement (other than clauses providing for working conditions), and that in such a case the transferee succeeds to the agreement according to the division plan or contract (Article 6(2)).

(3)   Advance notice to trade unions

Trade unions that have a collective bargaining agreement with the transferor have a keen interest in the treatment of the collective agreement in the case of transfer, and there may be a necessity to consult the transferor with respect to the partial transfer as stated above. Thus, as in the case of employees, the Labour Contract Succession Law requires the transferor to give notice to such unions at least two weeks before the shareholders' meeting that will determine the division plan or contract regarding the treatment of collective agreements (Article 2). Although the Law itself requires such notice only with respect to unions that have a collective agreement with the transferor, the Guidelines issued by the Ministry of Labour recommend that the notice be given to all the unions the members of which are employed by the transferor.[31]

3.2.4.   Worker-management consultation in the case of division of corporation

(1)   Individual consultation

A number of issues were debated when the Diet discussed the bill for the amendment of the Commercial Code and the Labour Contract Succession Law regarding the protection of workers. Those issues included whether a worker shall have the right to file an objection when he/she is included in the subject of transfer, and whether a trade union or affected workers shall have the right to joint consultation in the course of the division of corporation.[32] As to the former issue, it was decided that, as stated above, only the workers who have ancillarily engaged in the work of the department to be split off shall have the right to file an objection to the transfer. As regards the latter issue, however, the bills were amended by the Diet to provide for two types of consultation.

First, Article 5(2) of the Supplement to the Amendment to the Commercial Code provides that the transferor-employer shall consult in advance its employees who are engaging in the work of the department to be split off. This is to give such employees an opportunity to express their view regarding their status in the event of a division. Thus, it is individual employees

---

31.   Section 1(3) of Part 2 of the Guideline.
32.   These protections were proposed in the bill submitted by the opposing parties (Democratic Party and Communist Party). See Rodo Keiyaku Shokei Ho, supra note 13, at 29–43.

that the employer shall consult, and the subject of this consultation is basically limited to the status and working conditions of such individual employees. However, a trade union may ask for a consultation if it has received requests from its members. If the transferor commits a substantial violation of this duty, a court will probably declare the division of corporation null and void, although the standing for such action is limited to shareholders, directors, auditors, and creditors (including employees, such as those who have claims for unpaid wages or severance allowances) who do not consent to the division.[33]

(2) Collective consultation

Furthermore, the Labour Contract Succession Law provides that the transferor corporation should endeavour to obtain the understanding and cooperation of its employees (Article 7). Although the text of this provision is ambiguous, the Enforcement Ordinance of the Labour Contract Succession Law clarifies the duties of the transferor. According to the Ordinance the transferor should endeavour to obtain the understanding and cooperation of its employees, through consultation with a trade union that organises the majority of the employees in each workplace, or a person representing the majority of the employees if no such union exists, or by measures that are equivalent to such consultation (Article 4).

Unlike the consultation under the amended Commercial Code, this consultation is collective in nature, since the purpose of this provision is to encourage the transferor to hear the voice of workers regarding the implementation of the division of corporation. Thus, the scope of this consultation is wider than that of the individual consultation. For example, this consultation may cover such matters as the background and reasons for the division of corporation, the criteria for deciding whether the transferor's employees are engaging in the work of the department to be split off mainly or only ancillarily, the treatment of collective bargaining agreements, and so on. Also, according to the Guidelines of the Ministry of Labour, this collective consultation should begin before the individual consultation, and may be held afterwards if necessity arises.[34] Still, since this duty to consult is merely a "duty to endeavour," no legal effect is directly given to its violation.

3.2.5. Future prospects

The amended Commercial Code and the Labour Contract Succession Law took effect on 1 April 2001. A research company reported that the number of divisions of corporation that had been carried out during the period from 1 April 2001 to 30 March 2002 amounted to 617.[35] In order to implement the

---

33.   Koji Harada, *Kaisha Bunkatsu Hosei no Sosetsu ni Tsuite (Chu)* (Establishment of Legal Schemes for Division of Corporation (2)), 1565 Shoji Homu 10 (2000).
34.   Section 4(2)(ro) of Part 2 of the Guidelines.
35.   ⟨http://www.tsr-net.co.jp/topics/kaiseki/2002/0301.html⟩ (a survey conducted by Tokyo Shoko Research, K.K. based on the notification in the Official Gazette (Kanpo)) ⟨last visited 30 April 2002⟩.

division of corporation smoothly, the treatment of labour relations, whether individual or collective, is quite important. Thus, it is necessary for companies not only to be familiar with the contents of the Labour Contract Succession Law as well as the related Ordinance and Guidelines, but also to conduct consultations in good faith with their employees or trade unions.

4. ECONOMIC DISMISSAL

4.1. Case law regarding economic dismissal

Although neither the Civil Code nor the Labour Standards Law has a general provision that limits the grounds for dismissal of employees, courts have established a case-law principle that employers cannot discharge employees without showing a reasonable cause that is sufficient to justify the discharge. The Supreme Court states that "even when an employer exercises its right of dismissal, the dismissal will be void as an abuse of the right if it is not based on objectively reasonable grounds and cannot receive social approval as a proper act.[36] Thus, even when an employee has made a mistake, the courts examine every factor in favour of the employee in determining whether the dismissal is so harsh that it would constitute an abuse of the right of dismissal.[37]

As a corollary to the doctrine of abusive dismissal, Japanese courts have developed the case law that an employer must fulfill four "requirements" in order to carry out economic dismissals: (1) necessity for reduction-in-force, (2) a good faith effort to avoid dismissals, such as transfer, farming-out (as explained below), and voluntary retirement, (3) reasonableness in selecting workers to be dismissed, and (4) explanation and persuasion to obtain employees' under-standing, e.g. consultation with the majority union. This so-called "four-requirement test" was established several years after the first Oil Crisis in 1973.[38] Some scholars point out that the contents of this case law were influenced by the experience of large Japanese companies that made considerable efforts to maintain employment security during this recession period.[39]

In the past few years, however, the Tokyo District Court has made several decisions that appear to relax such restrictions. The tendency may be due to the criticisms by business circles that the restriction on dismissal is unneccesarily strong and that such restriction constitutes an obstacle to the reform of the Japanese economy. The decision in the Westminster Bank case,[40] one of the most notable in 2000, held that these "requirements" are merely "factors" for determining whether the dismissal is an abuse of right, and that

---

36. *Ichikawa v Nihon Shokuen Seizou K.K.*, 29 MINSHU 456 (Sup. Ct. 25 April 1975).
37. See SUGENO, *supra* note 2, at 403 (footnote).
38. E.g. *Toyo Sanso K.K.* v *Shimazaki*, 30 Rodo Kankei Minji Saiban Reishu 1002 (Tokyo High Ct., 29 October 1979).
39. E.g. Kazuo Sugeno, Koyo Shakai No Ho (The Law of Employment Society) 53 (1996).
40. *Yasuda v National Westminster Bank, Ltd.*, 782 Rodo Hanrei 23 (Tokyo Dist. Ct., 21 January 2000)(3rd decision in the preliminary injunction procedure).

the four-requirement test should be abandoned. A number of labour law scholars have criticised such views of the Tokyo District Court.[41]

Nevertheless, it appears that the basic framework regarding economic dismissal has remained largely intact. To be sure, most of the recent decisions that were published after the aforementioned cases generally agree that the "requirements" are "factors" in the strict sense.[42] However, most of these decisions examine the validity of economic dismissal in the light of the four "factors." In one case, the Tokyo District Court held that an economic dismissal that did not satisfy the element of reasonableness in selecting workers to be dismissed constituted an abusive dismissal in itself.[43] In this sense, the substance of the framework has not been changed after all.

In retrospect, it appears that recent Tokyo District Court decisions were influenced by the factual circumstances of each case. More specifically, some of these cases involve the employer's business judgment regarding the restructuring of the organisation. For example, in the Westminster Bank case, the employer decided to close its trade finance department because of the bleak prospects of this department in the future, and discharged the plaintiff, who had been working in this department as a specialist. Because the judgment whether the employer should close the department is a management prerogative, such a decision should generally be free from judicial scrutiny. If so, even under the traditional four-requirement test, the outcome of the case would be the same, since the first requirement, i.e. the necessity for reduction-in-force, would easily be satisfied in such a situation. In this sense, it is possible for courts to apply the four-requirement test in a flexible manner based on the type of the case.

Apart from the restriction on economic dismissal under case law, the recent amendment to the Employment Measures Law (Article 24) requires an employer who is planning to carry out reduction-in-force that will result in the loss of jobs for a large number of workers (30 or more per month) to draw up a plan to assist such workers in the search for reemployment. In drawing up the plan, the employer should consult with the majority union at the workplace, or the representative of the majority of the workers if no such union exists, and submit the plan to the Public Employment Office for approval. This amendment was passed by the Diet only last April, and took effect last October. It remains to be seen how effective this new regulation proves to be. In any event, this regulation bears certain similarities to the requirement of the Social Plan in some European countries.

---

41.   For the analysis of recent cases, *see* Shinya Ouchi, *Change in Japanese Employment Security*, Japan Labour Bulletin, Vol. 41, no.1, at 7–11 (2002).
42.   E.g. *Tazaki* v *Varig, S.A.*, 817 Rodo Hanrei 5 (Tokyo Dist. Ct., 19 December 2001).
43.   *Arahata* v *Rodo Daigaku*, 814 Rodo Hanrei 132 (Tokyo Dist. Ct., 17 May 2001) (2nd decision in the preliminary injunction procedure).

4.2. Economic dismissal in the context of business reorganisation

The validity of economic dismissal in the context of business reorganisation is determined under the case-law doctrine as described above. Courts should take into account the characteristics of the reorganisation measures in each case. For example, as mentioned previously, when a company decides to close down one of its departments, courts should generally defer to such business judgment. This is true even if the company as a whole has a good performance and decides to close down a less profitable department as a long-term business strategy. In such a case, however, courts should examine, more closely than in usual economic dismissal cases, the efforts to avoid dismissals through other means, such as the transfer or farming-out of redundant employees to other departments or companies. If such transfer is difficult, one of the possible measures is to assist redundant employees to look for other employment opportunities by providing outplacement services as well as paying additional severance allowances.[44]

In the case of the transfer of business undertakings, economic dismissals take place in two types of situations. First, workers may become redundant shortly after being transferred to other companies as a part of the undertaking, especially when the transferred undertaking's performance is poor. In this case, however, such workers have the right to refuse to be included in the subject of the transfer. Thus, as long as sufficient information is given to the workers, the reduction-in-force may be the result of their choice to a certain extent. Of course, dismissals by the new employer (transferee) are subject to judicial review under the case-law doctrine as described above.

Second, workers who have been excluded from the transfer of business undertakings may face economic dismissals, especially when the remaining operations of the transferor are suffering from poor performance. In this case, such workers' situation appears to be serious since they do not have the right to be included in the subject of transfer. However, a similar situation may take place when a company closes down its major department and workers who belong to the other remaining departments become redundant. Also, as stated before, the exclusion of such workers from the subject of transfer may be illegal and void if it is discriminatory or against public policy.[45]

On the other hand, economic dismissals are less likely to happen in the case of division of corporation. As stated before, the transferor and transferee are required to demonstrate that both corporations are financially competent to perform the obligations they will assume after the division.[46] As a result, neither the transferor nor transferee may be in a state of insolvency at the time of the division. Of course, the business of such companies may decline over time. However, since economic dismissals in such a case are little different from economic dismissals in a normal context, there is no need for a special rule with respect to such dismissals.

---

44.   *See Yasuda* v *National Westminster Bank, Ltd.*, 782 Rodo Hanrei, at 33–34.
45.   *See supra* note 11 and accompanying text.
46.   *See supra* note 19 and accompanying text.

Theoretically, there may be redundancy when an unexpected number of workers exercise the right to object to the inclusion in or exclusion from the subject of the transfer. In such a case, there may be redundancy in one of the companies, and requirement of the necessity for reduction-in-force may be satisfied. Still, with respect to the requirement of reasonableness in the selection of workers to be dismissed, it must be noted that the employer may not dismiss workers by reason of the fact that they have exercised the right to object, since that right would be practically meaningless if such a criterion is allowed.

5.   CHANGES IN WORKING CONDITIONS

5.1.   Transfers and farming-outs

Regarding the transfer of workers as a means of employment management, case law has established that the employer has the right to transfer an employee to a new workplace or position within a company, unless such employee's workplace or job is restricted to certain specific locations or positions under the employment contract, work rules, or collective bargaining agreement.[47] In fact, most work rules contain a provision to the effect that the employer has the right to transfer whenever there is a business necessity. Moreover, courts have rarely found contractual restrictions on the workplace or job contents.

The exception to this rule is based on the abuse of right doctrine: the transfer order may be void as an abusive exercise of employer's right when the employee's disadvantages resulting from the transfer are serious vis-à-vis the business necessity. Here again, however, courts are generally reluctant to rely on this doctrine. The Supreme Court upheld the transfer order even when the employee, if he followed the order, was forced to leave his family members behind because his wife had a job in the city where they were currently living.[48] Still, lower courts have invalidated transfer orders to distant locations when it is hard for the employee to leave the current workplace because of the necessity to take care of frail or disabled family members.[49]

Thus, transfers within a company take place quite often and perform various functions, such as career development through rotational assignment, more effective utilisation of an employee's ability through re-allocation, and adjustment of the workforce in the case of a business slowdown. In the context of business reorganisation, the employer can utilise this broad right to transfer employees. For example, when a company decides to close one of its branches, it usually transfers redundant employees in that branch to other branches to avoid dismissals. As stated above, such transfer is even required as a means of avoiding dismissals.

---

47.   *See generally* Ryuichi Yamakawa, *The Role of Employment Contract in Japan, in* The Employment Contract in Transforming Labour Relations 110 (Lammy Betten ed. 1995).

48.   *Toa Paint K.K.* v *Yoshida,* 1198 HANREI JIHO 149 (Sup. Ct. 14 July 1986).

49.   E.g. *Mouri* v *Hokkaido Coca-Cola Bottling K.K.,* 723 RODO HANREI 62 (Sapporo Dist. Ct., 23 July 1997).

Moreover, employers have the right to order their employees to work for another firm under certain conditions. This employment practice, called "Shukko", or farming-out, is unique in that the employee retains employment relationship with the original employer while working under the direction of the new employer.[50] Usually such an employee is supposed to return to the original employer, and the original employer retains the right to discharge him/her. Thus, according to the interpretation of the Ministry of Health, Labour and Welfare, during the Shukko period the employee has a dual employment relationship with both the original employer and the new employer.[51]

Courts have taken a slightly more restrictive position on the employer's right to order farming-outs than in the case of transfers within a company, since the employee, once farmed out, must work under the direction of an employer with whom he/she did not originally conclude an employment contract.[52] However, when farming-out is an established practice in the company and the employer has made sufficient efforts to minimise the detrimental effect on the employee's working conditions (e.g. wages and severance pay), the farming-out order is often held to be binding on the employee.[53]

Like transfer within a company, farming-out fulfills a number of roles. Sometimes it is carried out as a means of controlling subsidiaries or related companies. Furthermore, farming-out is one of the most important methods for adjustment of workforce at the time of a recession. In addition, farming-out may be a useful means to transfer employees in the context of business reorganisation. Unlike the procedure for the succession of employment contract under the Labour Contract Succession Law, employees to be farmed out to the transferee do not have the right to object, since such employees continue to have employment contracts with the transferor.

5.2. Unilateral change of work rules

With respect to other elements of employment contract, such as wages and working time, employers in Japan are not free to change working conditions established as contractual terms. More importantly, since workers under an employment contract without a fixed term are protected from unjust dismissals under the doctrine of abusive dismissal, employers may not freely discharge workers who do not accept the change of working conditions. If employers successfully conclude a collective bargaining agreement with trade unions, provisions under the agreement shall be binding on union members unless there are extraordinary circumstances.[54] Still, difficulties remain when

---

50. *See generally* Kazuo Sugeno, *Shukko (Transfers to Related Firms): An Aspect of the Changing Labour Market in Japan*, Japan Labour Bulletin, Vol. 28, no. 4 (1989).
51. Circular (Kihatsu) No. 333, 6 June 1981.
52. *See generally* SUGENO, *supra* note 2, at 376.
53. *Ibid.* at 377.
54. *Ishido v Asahi Kasai Kaijo, K.K.*, 713 RODO HANREI 27 (Sup. Ct., 27 March 1997).

members of other unions object to the change of working conditions, or when it is difficult to reach an agreement.

However, Japanese employers have a certain amount of latitude in changing working conditions. Case law has established that workers are bound by provisions in the work rules that are unilaterally revised by their employer regardless of their acceptance, if such revised work rules are "reasonable."[55] The reasonableness of such revised work rules are determined in light of such factors as (1) the necessity to change working conditions, (2) the degree of disadvantage to the workers resulting from the revision, including the measures to compensate for such disadvantage, (3) the standards of the new working conditions in comparison with those of other employers, and (4) whether the employer has made a good faith effort to obtain the consent of the majority union or the majority of workers.[56] Although it is strongly argued that the consent of the majority union should be important under this doctrine,[57] a recent decision of the Supreme Court, in which minority workers (not union members) suffered from serious disadvantages resulting from the change of work rules,[58] casts a doubt on such a view.

How, then, does this doctrine apply to cases involving business reorganisation? For example, such unilateral changes become necessary when the new company (transferee) needs to unify the working conditions of those employees who come from the transferor and those who are originally its employees. In the case of the transfer of employment contract, the working conditions of the employees of the transferor may often be maintained regardless the change of employer. Under the scheme of the division of corporation, it is impossible to change working conditions unilaterally at the time of the division. This is also the case with merger. Thus, there may be many cases where two groups of employees are working under different working conditions within the new company. In such cases, the employer may need to unify working conditions. If the employer cannot conclude a collective bargaining agreement that can cover all relevant employees, the unilateral change of work rules is a practical option.

In applying the four-factor criteria under the reasonableness doctrine as described above, the necessity to change working conditions may be easily fulfilled where it is necessary for the employer to unify working conditions, since it would create numerous problems if employees work under different working conditions in the same department or in the same job. In fact, the Supreme Court has once held that the unilateral change in work rules regarding severance allowances is reasonable in the case of merger and acquisition.[59] However, it is not clear whether there are differences between mergers and other types of business reorganisation.

---

55.   *See*, e.g., *Sato v Daishi Ginko, K.K.*, 710 RODO HANREI 12 (Sup. Ct., 28 February 1997).
56.   *Ibid.*
57.   KAZUO SUGENO, RODO HO (LABOUR LAW) 119 (5th suppl. ed., 2000).
58.   *Murose v Michinoku Ginko, K.K.*, 787 Rodo Hanrei 6 (Sup. Ct., 7 September 2000).
59.   *Ohmagari Shi Nogyo Kyodo Kumiai v Ando*, 42 Minshu 60 (Sup. Ct., 16 February 1988).

6. CONCLUSIONS

With respect to business reorganisation, Japanese law has two significant schemes: the transfer of business undertakings and the division of corporation. Although from a theoretical viewpoint these two schemes are quite different from one another, they have similar functions to the extent that the rights and duties of one corporation are inherited by the other. Still, there is an interesting contrast between these two schemes with respect to the protection of workers under labour law. In the case of business transfer, workers have the right to refuse to be included in the subject of transfer, while they may be excluded from the transfer under the agreement by the transferor and transferee. Unlike the acquired rights directive in the European Union, the succession of employment relationship is not necessarily required.

In contrast, workers who are included in the subject of the division of corporation do not have the right to object when they have been engaging mainly in the work of the department to be split off. On the other hand, workers have the right to object under certain circumstances, such as when they are excluded from the division of corporation when they have been engaging mainly in the work of the department to be split off. Also, the scheme of the division of corporation is different from the transfer of business undertakings in that consultation with workers or majority unions is necessary in carrying out the division. Furthermore, the division of corporation cannot be utilised to discard unprofitable departments, since the parties to the division are required to show that they are financially competent to perform their obligations.

It remains to be seen whether such differences will be reconciled, or whether they will continue to exist and influence the employer's choice of method for business reorganisation. As stated above, a study group established by the Ministry of Health, Labour and Welfare is conducting research to determine whether new legislation is necessary regarding transfer of business undertakings.[60] The policy question here is how the law should strike a balance between employment security within a company and promotion of the transfer of business undertakings, which may create employment in the labour market as a whole.

As regards economic dismissals and changes in working conditions in the context of business reorganisation, the doctrine of abusive dismissal and the "reasonableness" doctrine regarding the unilateral change of work rules may provide for a framework to adjust the interests of workers and employers. In this sense, Japanese labour law provides employers with internal flexibility against the background of employment security.[61] However, it is not necessarily clear how these doctrines are applied to cases involving the transfer

---

60.   *See supra* note 12 and accompanying text.
61.   Takashi Araki, *Accomodating Terms and Conditions of Employment to Changing Circumstances: A Comparative Analysis of Quantitative and Qualitative Flexibility in the United States, Germany and Japan, in* Labour Law and Industrial Relations at the Turn of the Century, Liber Amicorum in honor of Prof. Roger Blanpain 510, 531 (Chris Engels and Manfred Weiss ed. 1998).

of business undertakings and the division of corporation. It is up to courts and scholars to establish more concrete and reliable rules in such cases.

Another issue is the role of trade unions or workers' representatives in the context of business reorganisation. Statutory regulation is scarce in this respect except for the requirement of consultation under the Labour Contract Succession Law and the Employment Measures Law.[62] Otherwise, it is only under case law that the involvement of trade unions must be considered. For example, consultation with, or consent of, trade unions may be an important factor in determining the procedural fairness in economic dismissals or the reasonableness regarding the change of work rules. However, it is not necessarily clear from judicial decisions how much weight should be given to the role of the unions.

Thus, it may be worth considering the introduction of statutory provisions regarding the role of trade unions or workers' representatives in the process of economic dismissals and in the case of changes of working conditions. This may also be the case with the transfer of business undertakings. It should be noted, however, that such an effort may face difficulty in view of the modern workplace, where the interests of workers are quite diversified.

---

62.   As regards the insolvency procedure, trade unions have the right to express their opinions with respect to certain aspects of its administration. For example, the Company Reorganisation Law (Article 195) and the Civil Rehabilitation Law (Article 168) provides that the majority union, or majority of workers if no such union exists, has the right to submit its opinion about the reorganisation (rehabilitation) plan.

6. Korea

Young Hee Lee

1. INTRODUCTION

Corporate restructuring has been one of the most important issues attracting national attention during the last 10 years in Korea. This issue brought about much controversy for two administrations during that period.

First, it was put on the national agenda with the start of the democratic government in 1992. President Kim Young Sam stressed the necessity of structural reform of the Korean economy and business, in order to develop its competitive edge in the light of the globalisation of the world economy.

Second, Korea has faced an urgent need for corporate restructuring, at least in order to get out of the financial crisis that occurred at the end of YS Kim's regime. A new government led by Kim Dae Jung, launched in February of 1998, tried an overall social and economic reform, as well as business restructuring, not only in order to fulfill a promise to the IMF in return for its relief assistance, but also for the new phase of national development in the 21st century.

But the attempts at national reforms by both regimes have not been successful. Nevertheless, economic reform and business restructuring has been one of the major policy agenda issues in Korea during the last decade.

Corporate restructuring, however, should not be imposed by the government, no matter how desirable it may be from the national point of view. In principle, it should be promoted by the enterprise itself under the free operation of the market economy.

But the financial crisis has made it unavoidable that enterprises must reform themselves for their survival, and has also allowed the government actively to compel enterprises to carry out restructuring. Besides, the government has had to take the initiative in other economic and social reforms in order to overcome the financial crisis as soon as possible. It has driven forward the so-called *4 Major Reform Plan*, which applies to the fields of enterprises, banking, the public sector, and industrial relations.[1]

Restructuring of enterprises and the economy has consequently demanded industrial relations reform too. Of course, Korean labour law has not fulfilled its role in the protection of workers' interests under authoritarian

---

1.   http://www.mofe.go.kr/mofe/kor/econo_issues/ec_tol/liabrary/ej2001100402.hwp.

R. Blanpain (ed.),
Corporate Restructuring and the Role of Labour Law, 123–136.
© 2003 *Kluwer Law International. Printed in Great Britain.*

regimes in the past few decades. But many oppressive elements have been removed from the law in the process of democratisation in recent years.

Since democratisation, however, strong criticisms have come from business circles that labour law has been too much on the side of the workers, and that it was the main cause of the weakening of competitive power of business abroad. Government could no longer ignore the increasing demands from business, and admitted the necessity of rational readjustment of labour law in a new democratic situation.

Y.S. Kim's government carried out an overall amendment of labour law in 1997. This time, however, workers were indignant about the fact that the law was changed in a way that was too unfavourable to them, and made a strong protest, particularly against the introduction of the redundancy discharge system. The government had to change the law again after a few weeks, and postponed the enforcement of the redundancy discharge system for two years.

D.J. Kim's government, however, which took power with support of the dissatisfied workers, had ironically to enforce immediately the redundancy discharge system, to which they and the workers had objected strongly, when they were in the opposition party.

On the whole, Korean labour law had to adapt itself to the national task of economic reform and business restructuring. That is, labour law had to seek it's a balance between the protection of workers and the change of the employment system, which allows business restructuring a minimum of labour unrest.

But there were also strong voices against the change of labour law. They criticised the fact that business restructuring was inspired by the anti-labour philosophy of neo-liberalism and that the change of labour law meant the submission of the working class to business's offensive demands.

2. CORPORATE RESTRUCTURING AND LAWS CONCERNED

Corporate Restructuring in Korea has included many concrete tasks such as merging small banks into large banks, privatizing the public enterprises, unifying or closing down some enterprises by *big deal*, reforming the business structure under a plutocratic despotism, restructuring insolvent enterprises, and boosting promising venture enterprises etc. In particular, government created and revised 13 statutes related to the banking industry for the purpose of promoting its reform.[2]

But corporate restructuring is usually carried out according to the methods prescribed in business law, such as merger, division, transfer, and dissolution of enterprises.[3]

---

2.   In-Jae Kim, "Problems of Labour Law related with Corporate Restructuring", 2000, p. 1.
3.   Commercial law has provisions on the transfer of business in the Articles 41–45, 257, 374, on merger of business in the Articles 174, 175, 233–238, 522–530, about the division of business in the Articles 530.1–530.12, on the change of organisation in the Articles 204, 242, 604–607, and on the dissolution of business in the Articles 227, 517–521.2 etc.

These regulations on enterprise restructuring presumably have no major differences with those of foreign laws, because the business law, like other laws in Korea, was modelled on those of advanced western countries.[4]

On the other hand, restructuring of the inside of business, such as unification or dissolution of operational departments, can be carried out by the way of changing the company rules, which are under the managers' authority. It does not legally come under collective bargaining or consultation with labour unions or workers' representative. In practice, however, restructuring which has an important impact on the working conditions, such as changes of production lines or discontinuance of certain operations, is difficult to carry out by management unilaterally without consultation with labour unions.

There are no particular legal obstacles in Korea that make it difficult to perform corporate restructuring. Also, government has made significant efforts to produce the legal environment to stimulate it. But labour law has been frequently identified as an important factor preventing the adjustment of human resources in business or enhancing flexible management. Important arguments are as follows:

First of all, it was pointed out that labour law, which denies the employer's right of free discharge and prohibits discharge without justifiable cause, makes it difficult for enterprises to carry out the adjustment of human resources.

Second, labour law is equally applied to all workers with no distinction in terms of their employment types, that is, without regarding whether they are regular employees, temporary workers, or part-timers. It was claimed that this made it harder of employers to reduce employment cost, which would decrease the company's financial burden.

Third, the underdeveloped social security system, such as the unemployment insurance, has also been identified as an important factor that makes the employment structure in Korea inflexible. It means that the imperfect labour legislation prevents employers from active reallocation of the human resources in business.

Fourth, it was also indicated that an employer can not reschedule working hours efficiently, owing to the inflexible regulations on daily or weekly limits of working hours, as well as the high extra-allowance for overtime work.[5]

Fifth, a strong complaint has been that the improper interference in management affairs, as well as too many, frequently illegal, industrial actions by labour unions, hampers greatly the normal business activities.

The government resolutely carried out the revision of labour law in 1997, in response to these requests from employers. It was a change in the labour law intended to create a more favourable environment for business activities and restructuring.

---

4.   Changes of business mentioned above can basically be carried out by decision of all members of the company or by the agreement at the general meeting of stockholders. But commercial law has no provisions on matters of employees in changes of business.

5.   According to Article 55 of the Labour Standard Act, the employer should pay an additional allowance of more than fifty percentage of normal remuneration for extended work.

The government enacted a new law regulating dispatched workers, which allows more active utilisation of manpower without the use of permanent contracts. The government strengthened the Employment Insurance Act, which provides eligible workers with unemployment allowance for a maximum of 12 months.[6] The revised Labour Standard Act introduced *Flexible Working Hour System*[7] and recognised dismissal for managerial reasons, such as redundancy, as justifiable dismissal. The government even removed the two-year postponement of its enforcement in 1998.

It can now be said that restrictions from labour law against corporate restructuring have almost disappeared. Of course, this means a decrease in the level of protection for workers. The change in labour law also represented the first serious defeat and frustration of the Korean labour movement, which had expanded vigorously after the collapse of military rule in 1987.

3. CORPORATE RESTRUCTURING AND SUCCESSION OF EMPLOYMENT CONTRACTS

Any change in a enterprise, such as merger, division, transfer, or acquisition of undertaking, consigned management, or closing down of an operation, brings about corresponding changes in the status of employees concerned.

A few questions from the point of view of labour law are raised, as follows. First, can employers make the changes of management policy affecting the working conditions or the status of employees without any consultation with employees? Second, how should the problems be settled, if the change in working conditions is unavoidable due to the change of management or to the restructuring of the undertaking? Third, can the employer unilaterally decide to restructure the business if it does not have a direct impact on the existing conditions of employees?

First of all, there are no regulations which impose on an employer any obligation to seek the opinion of employees before he makes a decision on the change of his business. Furthermore, there are no provisions referring to how the problems of employees should be handled, for example, in the case of business transfer, in Korea.

---

6.   *Art. 39(1) The job-seeking benefit, unless otherwise provided in this Act, shall be provided for prescribed benefit payment days pursuant to Art. 41(1), within 12 months from the next day following a date of separation related to the qualification for benefits of the job-seeking benefits.*

7.   According to the Flexible Working Hour System, an employer can have a worker work for a specific week in excess of 44 working hours, but not over 48 hours, or for a specific day in excess of 8 working hours, on condition that the average working hours per week in a certain period within two weeks do not exceed those working hours in accordance with rules of employment (Art. 50(1)).

       When an employer reaches a written agreement with the workers' representative, he can have a worker work for a specific week in excess of 44 working hours, but not over 56 hours, and for a specific day in excess of 8 working hours, but not over 12 hours, on condition that average working hours per week in a certain period within one month do not exceed 44 working hours (Art. 50(2)).

It seems to be a mistake in the legislation that labour law has not prepared itself for these cases. On the other hand, it means that problems relating to the change of employment relations caused by corporate restructuring have not been important and pressing issues in Korea up to the present.[8]

Labour law merely has few regulations which can be applied to these cases by analogy. For example, a regulation on employment contract declares that working conditions should be freely decided on an equal basis between employer and employee.[9]

And a clause on employment rules prescribes that an employer should obtain consent from the majority of employees in the case of a change that is unfavourable to them. Otherwise, the employer may modify the rules only after listening to employees' opinions.[10]

And a regulation on the labour-management council stipulates that general rules of employment adjustment, such as relocation, retraining, and dismissal for managerial or technical reasons, should be the subject of consultation at a meeting of the council.[11] But those are neither compulsory nor matters for co-determination.

Furthermore, civil law has an article which states that an employer may not transfer his right in employment to a third person without the agreement of employee concerned.[12] In practice, however, the approval of an individual employee has no meaning at all in business transfer, because the employee has no other choice but to accept the change in his employment relationship, if he does not want to lose his job.

The majority legal opinion was that the employment relationship with the employer, in spite of the regulation in the civil code, should be succeeded to the transferee as it is, regardless of the approval or disapproval of the employees in the case of business transfer. This was also the principle

---

8. But labour law has a regulation protecting the wage credits of workers in cases such as insolvency of the employer. Article 37 says that (1) Wages, severance pay, accident compensation, and other claims arising from employment shall be paid in preference to taxes, public levies, or other claims except for certain claims by pledges or mortgages as to the total property of an employer, however, this shall not be applied to taxes or public levies which take precedence over pledges or mortgages. (2) Notwithstanding the provisions of paragraph (1), the claims which fall under the following subparagraphs shall be paid in preference to any obligation, taxes, public levies and other claims secured by pledges or mortgages as to the total property of an employer. 1. Wages of final three months 2. Severance pay of the final three years, and 3. Accident compensations.

9. Labour Standard Act, Article 3. The conditions of employment shall be determined based on the mutual agreement between employer and workers, on equal footing.

10. Labour Standard Act, Article 97(1) An employer shall seek the opinion of a trade union, if there is a trade union composed of the majority of the workers in the workplace concerned, or the opinions of the majority of workers if there is no trade union composed of the majority of workers, with regard to the preparation of and amendment to the rules of employment. Provided, however, that the rules of employment are modified unfavourably to workers, the employer shall obtain workers' consent.

11. It is prescribed at Article 19(1) No. 7 of Act Concerning the Promotion of Worker Participation and Cooperation.

12. Article 657(1) of the civil law.

established by decisions in the Korean court, much influenced by labour legislation and legal theories of European countries, particularly Germany.

The labour law prohibiting wrongful discharge[13] has played an important role for the succession of employment relations in the case of business transfer. According to the law, an employer cannot dismiss his employees on the pretext of the business transfer, nor can he refuse to hand them over to the new employer. Nor can the new employer expel workers only for the reason that he did not take over employment relations from the former employer or that he has no intention to do it.

Therefore, workers can maintain the same employment status as before, even though their work place is transferred to the new undertaking. In this case, employees do not have to conclude a new employment contract with the new employer, because legally they do not enter into a new employment relation with him. Their employment relations continue intact as before notwithstanding the change of employers. For example, the duration of service in the previous employment should be included in calculating the length of continuous service for deciding severance pay, if an employee resigns from his transferred workplace in the future.

But the new labour law allowed dismissal due to an urgent managerial need. Moreover, it added the provision that transfer, acquisition, and merger of business in order to avoid business difficulties will be regarded as an urgent managerial need.

An employer may now discharge employees on the grounds of business transfer without too many difficulties. He can do it, not only before he hands over his business to the transferee, but also after he takes over from the transferor.

Of course, dismissal is permissible only if its aim is to avoid a worsening business situation. But the meaning of *avoiding worsening business situation* is too wide and too easily abused by employer. The provision does not include the case of division of business. But it seems clear that it has not been intentionally dropped.

In short, workers are no longer guaranteed succession of employment relations in the case of business transfer. It is doubtful whether their status can be automatically succeeded, as was the case previously. Workers may be unable to refuse the request of the new employer for a new employment contract different from the previous one on the condition of continuous employment.

But the situation becomes different when workers are organised into a labour union, because the union can bargain with the employer about working conditions, including reemployment for its members. Of course, matters of business management are not considered to be subjects for negotiation or interference by labour unions. However, there are no established principles or standards on what belongs to the managerial prerogative in concrete terms.

---

13.   Labour Standard Act Art. 30(1) An employer shall not dismiss, lay-off, suspend, transfer a worker, or reduce wage, or take other punitive measures against a worker without justifiable reason.

This problem may finally be settled through decisions of the court or Labour Relations Commission, when an employer claims damages caused by the labour union through strikes in opposition to a unilateral restructuring of business, or when a labour union demands redress for an employer's punishment of its members who have participated in strikes.

But the legal precedent on this problem has not yet been established. Court decisions in Korea are neither unanimous nor consistent.[14] Nor does the new labour law demonstrate any such explicit principle.

Industrial action by labour unions intervening in business management has in general been treated as illegal. But nevertheless, in practice disputes by workers are not stopped. It is impossible to accuse all of them of a violation of the law. Repeated illegal activities that have no legal sanction also tend to open up the possibility that those activities are not regarded as being illegal in subsequent industrial relations activities. In such case, workers are also prone to consider the dispute action as their last resort.

4. CORPORATE RESTRUCTURING AND ECONOMIC DISMISSAL

According to labour law, an employer can not discharge employees without justifiable reason,[15] and the employer who violates this will have to suffer the punishment.[16] This provision was originally aimed at unjustifiable disciplinary dismissal. But it has become a general clause to be applied to all kinds of dismissal.

This clause has displayed an important function not only as a protective apparatus preventing wrongful discharge, but also as a legal tool securing *de facto* life employment in Korea. The normal type of employment contract has no fixed term, because labour law does not allow employment contracts with terms exceeding one year except when this is required for completion of a certain project.[17]

The provision prohibiting unjust discharge has in fact changed the nature of employment without fixed term, not into employment-at-will, but into employment guaranteed until retirement age, unless the employee commits wrongdoing which can be the subject of disciplinary discharge, or unless a situation occurs which makes the continuation of employment difficult.

However, though an employer's right to discharge was restricted by law, the matter of what in practice was a justifiable discharge had been always controversial. In the meantime, the court itself has already recognized dismissal

---

14.   Examples of affirmative decision; Chuncheon D.C., 98, no. 1147, 7 October 1999; Cheongju D.C., 99, no. 534, 9 June 2000; Examples of negative decision; Daejeon D.C., 98, no. 2805, 13 August 1999; Pusan A.C., 99, no. 34, 23 May 1999; Daejeon D.C., 33, kodan 251, 31 March 1999.
15.   See the preceding foot-note on Article 30(1) of Labour Standard Act.
16.   According to Art. 110 of Labour Standard Act, a person who has violated the provision of Article 30(1) or 30(2) should be punished by imprisonment for less than five years or by a fine not exceeding thirty million won.
17.   Article 23 of Labour Standard Act.

in the case of *urgent managerial difficulties* as a justifiable discharge through its decisions.

But the court has restricted the urgent managerial cause to a situation in which a business faces bankruptcy or a similar crisis. Furthemore, the court has deemed a discharge to be just, only if the employer has made every effort to avoid dismissal, has selected the dismissed employees according to reasonable criteria if unavoidable, and has had prior consultation with the labour union or the representative of employees.[18]

But the court has gradually softened the requirements for discharge for managerial reasons.[19]

By introducing a new provision allowing discharge for managerial reasons, the revised law elevated its requirements above the standards that used to be applied in court decisions. Article 31 of the Labour Standard Act prescribes as follows;

1. *If an employer wants to dismiss a worker for managerial reasons, there shall be urgent managerial needs. In such cases as transfer, acquisition and merger of business which are aimed at avoiding financial difficulties, it shall be deemed that there is an urgent managerial need.*

2. *In the case of paragraph (1), an employer shall make every effort to avoid dismissal of workers and shall select workers to be dismissed by establishing rational and fair standards of dismissal. In such cases, there shall be no discrimination on the ground of gender.*

3. *With regard to the possible methods for avoiding dismissal and the criteria for dismissal as referred to in paragraph (2), an employer shall give a notice 60 days prior to the dismissal day to a trade union which is formed by the consent of the majority of all workers in the business or workplace concerned (or a person representing the majority of all workers if such trade union does not exist, hereafter referred to as a "workers" representative) and carry out genuine consultation.*

4. *When an employer intends to dismiss more than a certain number of workers which is defined by Presidential Decree under conditions as referred to in paragraph (1), he/she shall report it to the Minister of Labor as determined by Presidential Decree.*

5. *In cases where an employer has dismissed workers in accordance with the requirements as stipulated in paragraph (1) to (3), it shall be deemed that the dismissal concerned is made based on justifiable reasons in accordance with paragraph (1) of Article 30.*[20]

An employer is now able to dismiss workers when he has an urgent managerial need, even it is not a need to hand over, take over, divide, or annex his business. A court decision made clear that a claim for urgent managerial need could be admissible, even if no urgent situation exists at the present

---

18. Supreme Court 87daka2132 (23 May 1989); 88daka34094 (12 January 1990); 89daka24445 (13 March 1990).

19. Supreme Court 91da647 (10 December 1991); 90nu9421 (12 May 1992), 92nu3076 (26 January 1993).

20. http://www.molab.go.kr/English/English.html.

moment, saying" "Discharge on the grounds of urgent managerial need is not only allowed in the case of discharge to avoid a bankruptcy. It could also be regarded as an urgent managerial need if the managerial decision to reduce workers in business is judged to be rational from an objective point of view."[21]

The employer should give a notice to the workers' representative 60 days ahead of the dismissal and should carry out consultation with them on the methods of avoiding the dismissals and the criteria for selecting the workers to be dismissed. But this is not a procedure intended to obtain the workers' opinion as to whether there is indeed an urgent managerial need or not, but a formal procedure aimed at making the dismissal process smooth.

Though the employer should genuinely consult with the workers' representative, he does not have to obtain their consent. Neither does the employer have to accept any counter-proposal from the workers' representative aimed at avoiding or reducing a massive dismissal. And he can carry out the dismissal by himself, if he considers that he had had sufficient talks with them.

The employer should report to the Minister of Labour if he intends to dismiss a large number of workers, for example, more than 10% of the workforce in an establishment with 100 to 999 workers. But the minister has no power to suspend the dismissal, or to reduce or limit the number of dismissed workers.[22]

An employer is now relatively free to carry out discharge for managerial reasons. However, it would not be approved by the court if an employer abused his right to discharge.[23] He should not discharge an excessive number of workers, or select the workers to be discharged arbitrarily on the pretext of managerial reasons, though the revised law somewhat mitigated its requirements.

On the other hand, workers regard dismissal as a serious problem threatening their economic survival. Besides, they are not ready to accept the managerial discharge. They are likely to think that the economic difficulties necessitating the discharge have been brought about by the mistakes or the incompetence of the employer. They think it is not the workers but the employer who should be held responsible for the mismanagement. Therefore, workers do not hesitate to go on strike in protest at managerial discharge, even if the employer tries to enforce it through the lawful procedure.

Most employers actually make efforts to persuade workers, not by simply holding talks with workers in the consultation process, if they are unable to avoid massive dismissal. Economic dismissal is still one of the toughest tasks for an employer in the process of corporate restructuring.

---

21. Supreme Court 92nu3076 (26 January 1993).
22. Article 9–2(1) of Presidential Decree of Labour Standard Act.
23. Past decisions in the court; Supreme Court 94nu15783 (5 December 1995); Seoul A.C., 95nu19784 (9 May 1996).

5. CORPORATE RESTRUCTURING AND CHANGE OF EMPLOYMENT CONDITIONS

Korean employers themselves have in the past invented some devices to make the employment structure more flexible, in order to curtail labour costs. The preferred methods were to reduce the portion of regular employment, for example, to increase the number of temporary workers on fixed-term contracts under one year, or to use the dispatched workers, or to move to outsourcing.

The increase in atypical employment in Korea has been encouraged by the actions of employers to curtail labour cost and to make adjustment of employment much easier. These changes in employment structure have been much influenced by the anti-union wishes of employers to keep workers from becoming organised or to weaken union power. Labour unions are mainly organised at the level of enterprises in Korea, and union membership is usually restricted to regular employees.

In any case, labour law was unable to ignore or neglect the differences of working conditions varying from different types of employment. Finally, it gave restricted protections to workers in atypical employment, while accepting their inferior working conditions compared with those of regular workers.

The law permitted an employer to make a separate employment rule which would be applied only to the workers employed for temporary work or for very short hours of work in a day or a week.[24]

An employer can use dispatched workers for a maximum of two years without directly employing them. The law now allows dispatched workers to be used in 26 kinds of work.[25]

One of the biggest tasks for corporate restructuring since the financial crisis of 1997 was to dismiss redundant workers. A preferred device was so-called *retirement in honour*, which induced older workers to leave work voluntarily before the predetermined retirement age, with more severance benefits than usual. Of course, it could also be applied to younger workers.

One of the characteristics of the wage structure in Korea is that the wage of workers with longer service is relatively high owing to the seniority wage system.

Retirement in honour has functioned as *de facto* compulsory retirement. So it can be considered age discrimination. But age discrimination has never been dealt with as a serious problem violating the equal-treatment principle of labour law. Besides, female workers were also a preferred subject of discharge compared with the male workers.

Labour law demands that an employer must obtain approval from the workers" representative when he wants to change the employment rules unfavourably to workers.

But the court has presented an opinion that the change of employment rules which could be admitted as *reasonable* in view of the commonly accepted

---

24. Article 9(1) No. 5 ka of Presidential Decree of Labour Standard Act.
25. Article 5(1), 6(1) of Statute of Protection for Dispatched Workers, and Article 2(1) of presidential decree of that statute.

social norms was not an unfavourable change, even if it was actually unfavourable to workers.[26]

According to the court opinion, an employer is able to change the rule unfavourably to workers in spite of their opposition, if it looks socially reasonable.

Collective agreements are assumed to be concluded through equal negotiations between employers and unions. Therefore, it is also possible for a labour union to lose the working conditions secured already through the previous negotiation, if its bargaining power becomes weak, or if the company falls into financial difficulties. In fact, it has been a useful instrument for the readjustment of the existing working conditions. Important changes in working conditions, such as the abolition of progressive retirement allowance, curtailment of bonuses, reductions in working hours, and enforcement of rotational lay-off, could be attained through collective agreements.

6. CORPORATE RESTRUCTURING AND THE STATUS OF LABOUR UNIONS

There has been little discussion of what effect the transfer of business has on labour unions. What will be the future of labour unions, if the affiliated workers are moved to a new employer owing to a business transfer?

A labour union is originally not an organisation under the control of employer. Its existence does not depend on the recognition of employer. Moreover, it does not matter whether the labour union is organised at the outside of business or at the level of trans-enterprise.

Accordingly, the labour union basically has nothing to do with transfer of the business. But in practice, it is difficult, especially for the labour union organised at enterprise level, to escape from the impact brought about by the change of business.

In the case of a transfer of business, the problem for the labour union is what the future of a collective agreement between the previous employer and the union will be. Should it properly be succeeded to the new employer following the succession of employment relations? Or, does only *the normative part* of a collective agreement transfer to the new employer, the part which has been automatically incorporated into the employment contract? Or, must the employer obtain the union's consent in advance about the transfer of a collective agreement, in order to make the new employer take over the agreement? Or, doesn't he have to get union's consent at all, if the new employer agrees to take it over?

Regretfully, Korean labour law has not made any provision to address these questions. A court decision directly answering this problem has not been yet made. Legal theories on this matter are currently being developed.

---

26.   Supreme Court 92 da 39778 (15 January 1993).

As long as workers want to retain their present membership of the labour union, the new employer who takes them over through a transfer of business can probably neither ignore their representative organisation nor refuse collective bargaining with it, since such attitudes or activities of an employer would fall under *unfair labour practices*.

However, the employer taking over the business has no obligation to take over the existing collective agreement between the former employer and labour union. In other words, the transferor has no right to compel the transferee to take over his collective agreement with the labour union, or to hand over his collective agreement to the transferee unilaterally without the consent of the labour union.

In short, *the obligatory part* of the collective agreement does not automatically transfer to the new employer. This also means that the collective agreement does not belong to the concept of business or its assets that can be transferred at the employer's will.

In principle, the existing collective agreement loses its effect after the transfer of business if the new employer does not want to take it over. In such a case, the labour union should perhaps try to conclude a new agreement with the new employer, in which the clauses on union security, such as union office, union shop, check off, and so on would be included as matter of course.[27]

In the case of a division of business, the labour union does not have to divide itself. But it would be natural to be split into two unions, if the union itself wants to be organised at each enterprise level. In such cases, it is also possible for workers to organise a new union, after they withdraw from the existing union, without taking measures for its division.

In the case of a merger of business, a problem will arise if the labour union is organised separately at each company. Since plural unionism is still not allowed in Korea,[28] they should be unified to a single union after the merger. But if workers remain in the same, but separate, workplace as in the past even after merger of business, and if two unions have no problems with their separate activities within the same jurisdiction, they would not have to be consolidated unconditionally.

CONCLUSION

What kind of role does labour law play in corporate restructuring? What would be the ideal role for labour law in such cases? Labour law in Korea has

---

27.   There are also opinions insisting on succession of the collective agreement in case of business transfer for the reason that the labour union, otherwise, would be unjustly deprived of the established interests. See Kyuong-Ho Ha, "Corporate Restructuring and Validity of Collective Agreement, Labour Agreement, and Employment Rule", p. 162 in Kyoung-Ho Ha & Jong-Hee Park (ed.), *Restructuring of Business and Task of Labor Law*, 1998.

28.   According to Article 5(1) of Addenda of Trade Union and Labour Relations Adjustment Act, in cases where a trade union exists in a business or workplace, a new trade union which has the same organisational jurisdiction as existing trade unions may not be formed by 31 December, 2006.

changed to the extent that an employer has no difficulties in implementing his business restructuring. It has made the legal structure of employment relations so flexible that an employer can manage his business efficiently and strengthen its competitive edge. The labour law is functioning well so far in this regard.

On the other hand, however, labour law does not protect the workers" interests, which was its original aim. But this seems to be the fate of labour law in a globalising economy, and Korean labour law no exception.

Meanwhile, the economic difficulties of 1997 in Korea made an important contribution to moderating the militant labour movement. Labour unions came to realise that they had no alternative but to endure corporate restructuring for the survival of the majority of workers, and they put their best efforts into reducing any excessive sacrifice of workers.

The unemployment insurance system has not yet displayed any meaningful role as an effective social safety net. Labour unions have continued to press the government to expand the system so as to provide unemployed workers with more substantial protection, but progress is still far from being satisfactory.

REFERENCES

Suk-Ho Seonwoo, *M&A: Merge, Acquisition, and Restructuring of business*, bupmunsa, Seoul, 2001.

Jong-Hee Park & So-Young Kim, *Problems and Task of Labor Law on Change of Business*, Korean Labor Institute, Seoul, 2000.

Hoon Kim & Jun-Sik Park, *Restructuring and New Industrial Relations*, Korean Labor Institute, Seoul, 2000.

Kyoung-Hyo Ha & Jong-Hee Park(ed.), *Restructuring of Business and Task of Labor Law*, Korean Labor Institute, Seoul, 1998.

In-Jae Kim, "Problems of Labor Law related with Corprorate Restructuring", *Journal of Labour Law (J.L.L)*, Vol. 12 (June 2000), Korean Society of Labour Law (K.S.S.L), pp. 1–27.

Jong-Hee Park, "Interpreting and Implementing the Provision of Restriction on Dismissal for Managerial Reasons in the Labor Standard Act Revised on Feb. 20, 1998", *J.L.L*, Vol. 8 (Dec. 1998), K.S.S.L, pp. 97–130.

Sung-Wook Lee, "Legitimacy of Lay-off based on Business Transfer", *J.L.L*, Vol. 8 (Dec. 1998), K.S.L.L, pp. 403–442.

Ki-Kap Hong, "Employment Adjustment", *J.L.L*, Vol. 8 (Dec. 1998), K.S.L.L, pp. 443–462.

Seoung-Hwan Kim, "The Korean Law of Redundancy: Collective Consultation", *J.L.L*, Vol. 8 (Dec. 1998), K.S.L.L, pp. 581–599.

Sang-Duck Lee, "Transfer of Undertaking and Succession of Employment", *J.L.L*, Vol. 7 (Dec. 1997), K.S.L.L, pp. 235–238.

Kyo-Sook Kim, "A Proposal for Improvement of Redundancy Law", *J.L.L*, Vol. 7 (Dec. 1997), K.S.L.L, pp. 259–288.

7. Taiwan

Chih-Poung Liou

1. INTRODUCTION

The recent shift of the Taiwanese economy towards foreign trade has had a major impact on the development of Taiwanese industry. The effects of both the pressures of the international economic environment and the necessity to compete on a global scale has greatly reduced the competitive advantage held by the "Asian Tiger" economies in the labour-intensive industries. This has forced many of Taiwan's traditional labour-intensive industries to move offshore, or else restructure into a technologically based industry in order to reduce costs. The major indictor of this trend has been observed in the pattern of employment during the period 1988 to 1996. The composition of the type of labour employed in both manufacturing and service industries has shifted, with the employment of lowly skilled workers on the decline, whilst the employment of highly skilled workers has been steadily increasing.[1]

In order to raise global competitiveness, corporations have been aggressively pushing for restructuring and reorganisation. The government, keen to promote these trends, has recently made major amendments to Corporate Law, Act on Mergers and Acquisition of Financial Institutes and Financial Holding Company Act. Implemented last year, these amendments have helped to facilitate structural reform by removing the obstacles that existed in the previous legislation, and have streamlined the procedures of mergers and acquisition, thereby increasing procedural efficiency.

The downside of corporate reorganisation is the labour problems it causes, such as mass dismissals, which have become a major social issue in recent years due to the downturn in the economy. The government has endeavoured to address these issues by not only changing the regulations in the Corporate Mergers and Acquisition Act but also proposing a bill for the Protection of Labour Against Mass Dismissals Act, due to be enacted in spring 2002. Thus, the focus of this paper will be the effect of reorganisation on labour, and its relationship to Taiwanese Labour Laws.

---

1. Chang, Ching Yun, "*The Structural Change of Global and Taiwanese Labour Employment Patterns*", Economic Planning and Development Council, Executive Yuan; Yang, Jia Yen, "*A Study on Global Trends and its Influence on the Developmental Policies of Taiwanese Indusries*" (APEC Review, December 2001) at p. 35.

R. Blanpain (ed.),
Corporate Restructuring and the Role of Labour Law, 137–152.
© 2003 *Kluwer Law International. Printed in Great Britain.*

2. GOVERNMENTAL REGULATIONS ON CORPORATE RESTRUCTURING

2.1. Summary of current laws and regulations

According the data released by the Fair Trading Commission of the Executive Yuan, the number of cases of corporate mergers or acquisitions has increased dramatically, from only 314 cases in 1996 to 1,020 in the year 2000, with an annual average of over 700 cases a year. Interestingly, this trend of corporate reorganisation has not been observed across all industries. Instead, the majority of merger and acquisition cases have been limited to the retail and finance industries, whilst the motoring, steel, petroleum, semiconductor and other technological-based industries have remained largely unchanged. In 1999, the government implemented several schemes designed to promote corporate reorganisation in these industries. Not only do these schemes assist with the process of mergers and acquisition through simplification of merger procedures and the removal of the administrative restrictions that plague the current legislation, they also provide tax-breaks as incentives.[2]

As part of the schemes to promote corporate reorganisation, the government has made some important changes to Corporate Law in the area of mergers. Enacted in October 2001, these changes:
(a) Reduced the number of shareholders required in order to establish a company limited by shares. Under the previous legislation, there were required to be at least seven shareholders in order to establish a company limited by shares. The new legislation allows the formation of a company limited by shares with usually only two shareholders, and where the shareholder is the government or a legal entity, with only one shareholder.
(b) Filled gaps within Corporate Mergers Procedures. For example, in order to simplify the merger regulations of a parent company and its subsidiaries, it now states: if the controlling company owns over 90% of the merged company, the mergers can be passed at a special meeting between both boards of directors. This legislation also provides tax incentives for mergers.
(c) Created regulations with regards to division of companies.

At the same time, the government also enacted the Corporate Mergers and Acquisitions Act, which is aimed at assisting management reorganisation and efficiency (Article 1). It states the following:
i.   Scope of Legislation: The scope of this legislation is limited to companies limited by shares.
ii.   Mergers and Acquisitions: This terminology relates to all company restructuring process; it includes mergers, acquisitions and the division of companies. Acquisition and division of companies are new legal concepts.

---

2.   Financial Research Department of Economic Planning and Development Council, Executive Yuan, "*Domestic and Foreign Developmental Trends of Corporate Mergers and Acquisition*", 17 January 2001.

The concept of acquisition applies where the present law, Corporate Law, Securities Exchange Act, Act on Mergers and Acquisition of Financial Institute and Financial Holding Company Act has been utilised to purchase other companies' shares, operations or assets in exchange for your own company shares, cash or assets.

The concept of division of companies applies where present laws or other regulations mentioned above are utilised to take a part of or the whole operations of an independent entity in order to establish a new company or companies in exchange for new shares in the new company or old company.

2.2. Corporate restructuring and labour contracts

Article 20 of the Labour Standard Law 1984 states: Where a enterprise transfers undertakings or undergoes reorganisation, except for the workers retained by through negotiations between the previous and current employers, the rest shall be given advanced notice of termination of labour contract as according to the regulations in Article 16 of this Act, and be legally entitled to statutory separation pay (more commonly known as redundancy payments) as according to Article 17 of this Act. The new employer shall recognise the seniority of the service of the retained workers.

Accordingly, the following principles apply when an enterprise transfers undertakings or undergoes reorganisation:

i.   Both new and old employers have the power to determine which employees to retain. In other words, the workers have no right to ask the new employer to retain them.

ii.   For the workers chosen to be retained by either the previous or the current employer, the new employer shall recognise the seniority of the service of retained workers.

iii. For workers not retained by the new employer, the old employer is responsible for giving advance notices of termination and paying the redundancy payment due to them as required under Labour Standard Law.

Problems arise in the situation if a worker chosen to be retained by the new employer rejects the offer of employment. Whether the worker has the right to reject or demand redundancy payment from the new and old employers is a contentious issue, and one that is not address under Article 20 of the Labour Standard law. As a result of this, many disputes occur.[3]

In order to address these issues, Article 16 of Corporate Mergers and Acquisitions Act states: The company remaining after merger or acquisition, the newly established company or the receiving company shall have 30 days

---

3.   Chan, Wen Kai, "Corporate Mergers and Its Effect on Labour Contracts", *Journal of Labour Banking Unions Alliance*, 5 October 2001; Lelong, Sophia H., "Corporate Mergers and Acquisition and the Stability of the Workforce", *Formosan Brothers Law Journal*, July 2000.

prior to the Mergers and Acquisition Standard Date, to issue written notice to workers who the company intends to retain. The notified workers then shall have 10 days to accept or reject the offer of employment. The notified workers that do not reply are deemed to have accepted this offer. The seniority of the service accumulated by the retained workers whilst the company is undergoing reorganisation shall be recognised by the company remaining after merger or acquisition, the newly established company or the receiving company. The employer pre-reorganisation shall be responsible for issuing advance notice of termination (according to the regulations of Article 16 of LSL) to workers not retained by the company, or workers whom rejected the offer of employer according to Article 16 of the Corporate Mergers and Acquisition Act. The employer pre-reorganisation shall also be responsible for redundancy payment to which the dismissed workers are entitled. (Article 17 of LSL)

When the three articles, Article 16 of the Corporate Mergers and Acquisition Act, and Article 17 and 20 of Labour Standard Law, are evaluated against one another, it can be seen that:

i.   The scope of the Corporate Mergers and Acquisition Act includes the corporate reorganisation process of merger, acquisition and division of companies, whilst the scope of Labour Standard Law includes the area of corporate reorganisation and transfer. Evidently, there is significant overlap in scope between these two legislations.

ii.   Both Corporate Mergers and Acquisition Act and Labour Standard Law give the old and new employers the right to determine which workers are to be retained, but do not give workers any right to request retention.

       Furthermore, on what contractual terms should new employers employ the retained workers? Do new employers need to negotiate a new employment contract with retained workers? The legislation is silent on these two issues.

iii.   With regard to the workers not retained, the employer(s) only have to follow the employment termination procedure prescribed under Labour Standard Law and pay workers' redundancy payments.

iv.   The new employer has no obligation to negotiate with the union established under the pre-merged or acquired company.

       Accordingly, the new employer is under no obligation to consider the opinions of the union with regard to matters such as the identity, number and employment terms of the workers to be retained.

In order to resolve the potential problems arising from disputes between employers and all workers employed under old management, the Corporate Mergers and Acquisition Act and Labour Standard Law give more power to the new and old employers with respect to the determination of workers to be retained. The issue of whether the rights of workers employed by the old employer are adequately protected is one that is not fully considered.

3.   CORPORATE REORGANISATION AND ECONOMIC DISMISSALS

3.1.   Current labour market conditions

Due to a significant economic downturn in Taiwan's economy during the latter half of 2001, the Taiwanese labour market is presently in a very unhealthy state. According to the data released by the Council for Economic Planning and Development of Executive Yuan, the size of the Taiwanese workforce stands at 9.919 million people, with 524 thousand unemployed.

Thus, presently, the Taiwanese unemployment rate stands at around 5.2%, with the contraction or closing down of businesses being the main contributor to such high unemployment rate.[4] A comparison between the statistics for May 2000 and May 2001 indicates that surplus workers are evident and on the increase in many industries. During this time, the number of surplus workers in the heavy and service industries increased by a massive 7.62% from the May 2000 total of 17.5%. Among these figures, heavy industries' surplus workers represent 24.1%, and due to many of the traditional manufacturing industries moving offshore, the figure for manufacturing industries' surplus workers stands at around 25.19%. Investigations into the reasons for the increase in surplus workers demonstrate that a slump in operations is the main cause, while corporate reorganisation and rationalisation of the workforce are also contributors. Surveys of businesses in heavy and manufacturing industries indicate that 60% of the businesses prefer to retain surplus workers, whilst 40% prefer to reduce the workforce. Of the methods considered by the businesses which chose to retained surplus workers, a reduction in working hours is the most popular at 62.20%, with a reduction in salary next at 58.61%, and encouraging workers to take a vacation at 53.78%. Of the methods considered by business seeking to retrench or reduce their workforce, 76.17% prefer paying redundancy payments, 50.74% prefer to encourage workers to take early retirement and 36.78% choose to encourage the workers to change companies.[5]

3.2.   Regulations relating to economic dismissals

Article 488.2 of Civil Law states: In a labour contract where the length of time has not been set or else cannot be determined from the nature or target of employment, both parties have the right to terminate the labour contract at any time.

However, since the enactment of the Labour Standard Law (LSL), employers must now follow the regulations and procedures prescribed in the

---

4.   Manpower Planning Department of Economic Planning and Development Council, Executive Yuan, *"The Unemployment Statistics Monthly in the Taiwan Area of the Republic of China"*, (January 2002).

5.   Directorate General of Budget Accounting and Statistics of Executive Yuan, *"Survey into the Employment Conditions Yearly in the Taiwan Area of the Republic of China"*, November 2001 at p. 8.

Labour Standard Law, which states, employers can only terminate a labour contract with reasonable cause. What is considered reasonable can be separated into two broad categories:

i.   Economic Dismissals: An employment contract may be terminated on the grounds of economic causes, such as operating losses, contraction, closing down or transfer of business. However, in order to terminate a labour contact in this way, an employer must meet the advance notice requirements and pay statutory separation pay (redundancy payment). In principle, a worker terminated shall be entitled to a redundancy payment equal to one month of their average wage for each year of service (Article 16 and 17 of LSL). Also, according to Article 34 of Employment Service Act, employers have a duty to notify the competent local authorities and the public employment institution, seven days before the worker(s) leaves the job. After receiving the notification, the public employment institution can, according to the aspirations and ability of the worker(s), assist in the re-employment process. (Article 34 of Employment Service Act).

ii. Punitive Dismissals: Where an employee, without reasonable excuse, did not appear for work for more then three consecutive days, or where the actions of the employee violate a major term of the labour contract or rules of the workplace, the employer is entitled to terminate the labour contract immediately, and is not obligated to give any redundancy payments. (Article 11 of LSL).

Conditions that allow for economic dismissals, as set out in Article 11 of the Labour Standard Law, are explained below:

i.   Suspension or Transfer of Business (Article 11.1)
     The term "suspension of business" refers to the permanent shutting-down of a business, and this includes a business that is either dissolved, liquidated or going thorough the process of bankruptcy.[6] The term "transfer of business" refers to the transfer of all assets and equipment which results in the destruction of the legal entity, or a change in the identity of the management in charge, whether it be a sole proprietor or a partnership.

ii. Business Contraction or Suffering Operating Losses (Article 11.2)
     The term "business suffering operating losses" does not include business suffering temporary or short-term losses. Instead, it refers to continuous, long-term operating losses. In this situation, only if business is in fact suffering from operating losses, and not in the position of employ, can employers choose to retrench workers.[7]
     The term "business contraction" refers to the situation where a business is experiencing a period of slump in sales or yield, resulting in the contraction of business. However, where only one sector of the business is experiencing a slump, with other sectors within normal or expanding

---

6.   Huang, Cherng Kuan, "*Labour Law*", February 2002 at p. 484.
7.   Taiwan Shihlin District Court, 11th Labour Law Judgment of 1999.

working capacity, employers cannot claim business contraction as a reason for termination of employment. In another words, employers can only terminate labour contracts by reason of contraction in business, if the business as a whole is undergoing contraction, and if as a result of these circumstances employers can no longer employ the workers.[8]

iii. Business Suspension due to Force Majeure (Article 11.3)

Circumstances beyond the control of the management (such as natural disasters or wars and other human acts) which prevent the business from operating for more then a month, give the employer right to terminate a contract with notice.

iv. Reduction in Workforce is necessitated by the Change in Nature of Business and the Terminated Employees cannot be assigned to Other Positions. (Article 11.4)

"Change in nature of business" mainly refers to the change in substance or elements of the business. An example of this is where a business originally focussed mainly on the area of manufacturing, due to a shift in business operating policy, changes to focus mainly on retailing, thus resulting in the necessary adjustment and reduction in worker numbers in the manufacturing department. A more contentious example would be one where employers, in order to increase efficiency, modify the method of production or production technologies. Can this be considered a change in the nature of business? Many academics agree with this definition,[9] although up to now there has been no judicial confirmation from the courts. Employers seeking to use this as a reason for termination must satisfy the two requirements. Firstly, the reduction in employees must be a necessity, and secondly, there must be no other positions or work assignable to the worker(s).

According to the regulations in Labour Standard Law, as long as the employer satisfies one of the four requirements set out above, he/she would have just cause to terminate a labour contract. However, LSL still does not address the following issues:

i. In the situation where employers terminate labour contracts on the grounds of economic difficulties, the legislation imposes no duty on the employer(s) to explain or negotiate this situation with either workers or unions.

ii. Similarly, how do employers, in the situation of economic dismissals, determine which worker is to be dismissed? The legislation has not indicated the standard or methodology by which a worker is chosen.

iii. In the situation where employers terminate on the basis of change in the nature of business and where terminated employees cannot be assigned to other positions, the legislation imposes a duty on employers to avoid dismissal of employees. However, in the situation where there is a

---

8. Supreme Court of Taiwan, 2456th Judgment of 1986; Supreme Court of Taiwan, 2767th Judgment of 1994.

9. Yang, Tong Shiuan, *"A Discussion on Labour Laws and Change in Nature of Business under the Information Age"* (Taiwan Bar Journal, May 2000) at p. 20.

suspension/contraction of business or where business is suffering from operating losses, the legislation does not impose the same duty on the employers to avoid dismissal. This represents a level of inconsistency in the law.[10]

3.3. Problems of mass dismissals and measures undertaken

i.   "Guidelines on Protection for Labour Against Mass Dismissal"
      In recent times, there has being a growing trend towards mass dismissals observed in Taiwan. Factors such as economic downturns, factory closures due to industries moving offshore, corporations undergoing reorganisation and simplification of management structure have all been major contributors to this trend. In 1999, the government responded to this problem by announcing an administrative order known as the "Guidelines on Protection for Labour Against Mass Dismissal". Designed to work in conjunction with the Protection of Labour Dismissal Regulations already set out in Article 11 of the Labour Standard Law and through coordination between various government agencies, the Guidelines aim to reduce the damages caused by mass dismissals. The following is a summary of the main points in the Guidelines:
      1.   Definition of Mass Dismissal
           In the case where an enterprise employs more then 200 workers, mass dismissal is defined as the continuous retrenchment of over a third of its original workforce during a 6-month period, or the retrenchment of over 30 workers at one time.
           In the case where an enterprise employs less then 200 workers, mass dismissal is defined as the continuous retrenchment of over a third of its original workforce during a 6-month period, or the retrenchment of over 20 workers at one time.
      2.   Measures Undertaken
           (a) Operations of the Advance Notification Procedures
                The inquiry committee set up by the Labour Commission of the Executive Yuan, after receiving the advance notification with respect to proposed mass dismissal from the specific corporation, must undertake preliminary investigations to determine whether there is a real necessity for mass dismissal. The inquiry committee is also responsible not only for facilitating the discussions between the employer, employees or union, but also for utilising measures designed to prevent disputes from occurring.
           (b) Employer's Duty to Notify and Negotiate
                An enterprise has the duty to notify the union or labour representatives when there is an intention to retrench large

---

10.   Huang, Cherng Kuan, "*Labour Law*", February 2002 at p. 486.

number of workers for management reasons. They would also have a duty to summon a negotiation conference, at which they must put forward a dismissal plan. They also need to send a copy of the dismissal plan to the relevant local authority, for reference. The content of the dismissal plan must address the following issues: reason for dismissal, department, time, number of workers, selection standard for workers to be dismissed, calculation of redundancy payments and plans of assistance for transfer into another company.

(c)   Selection of Retained or Retrenched Workers

Where an enterprise unit wishes to implement mass dismissals, they must observe the following principles with regard to the negotiation with the union or labour representative:

- The selection of workers to be dismissed must be based not only on the reality of the circumstances at hand, but on an objective and reasonable standard. Accordingly the selection mechanism must not contravene Article 5 of the Employment Service Act and be subjectively biased towards workers with higher salaries or those with disabilities, and must not consider whether they need to support a family.
- The changes to the allocation of workers must be based on need and efficiency, and must not abuse rights.
- In order to protect labour rights, the enterprise must preserve the union(s)' or representative(s)' right to negotiate and not discriminate against those undertaking duties of the union.

The above measures are designed to fill the existing gaps in the Labour Standard Law. At present, the Labour Standard Law still imposes no duty on enterprise undergoing mass dismissals to negotiate with workers or unions.

ii.   Draft of "The Protection for Labour Against Mass Dismissal Act"

Under the continuous pressures of the economic downturn of the past few years, workers collectively agree to the necessity for legislation to regulate labour problems arising from mass dismissals. As the "Guidelines on Protection for Labour Against Mass Dismissal" discussed earlier constitute only an administrative order, parliament is now currently debating the "Protection for Labour Against Mass Dismissal Act", which could be enacted as early as spring 2002. The following is a summary of the main points in the proposed Act:

1.   Scope

This definition of mass dismissal is limited to the situation in which an employer is suffering the economic problems set out in Article 11 of the Labour Standard Law, or undergoing a merger or reorganisation process, and in which the following situation with respect to retrenchment occurs:

(a) In the situation where an enterprise or one of its factories employs more than 200 workers, mass dismissal is defined as the continuous retrenchment of over a third of its original workforce during a 60-day period, or the retrenchment of over 50 workers in one day. Where the number of workers employed is over 30 but under 200, mass dismissal is defined as continuous retrenchment of over a third of its original workforce during a 60-day period, or the retrenchment of over 20 workers in one day.

(b) Where an enterprise employs more then 500 workers, mass dismissal is defined as the continuous retrenchment of over one fifth of its workforce during a 60-day period.

2. Announcement of Dismissal Plan

The enterprise should announce their dismissal plan 50 days before the planned dismissal to unions and workers. They also need to notify and deliver the dismissal plan to the relevant authorities. The content of the dismissal plan must address the following issues: reason for dismissal, the affected department, time of dismissal, number of workers, the selection standard for workers to be dismissed, calculation of redundancy payments and plans for assistance for transfer to another company. Enterprises which do not announce their proposal 50 days before the planned dismissal to unions, workers or relevant authorities are liable to a fine of at least $NT100,000 and up to $NT500,000.

3. Negotiation

Ten days after the announcement of the dismissal plan, the union and the employer must commence a negotiation conference. Where an agreement cannot be reached, the relevant authorities must establish a negotiation committee within 10 days of notification. The committee will be composed of between 3 and 9 members, with a representative assigned by the relevant authority and the representative(s) chosen by employers and workers separately. Enterprises which refuse to negotiation may be liable to a fine of at least $NT30,000 and up to $NT150,000.

4. Agreement

If the negotiation conference is successfully concluded, an agreement must be produced. The relevant authorities would then have 7 days to deliver the agreement to a court of applicable jurisdiction for examination. After examination, the agreement can be enforced by the court.

5. Establishment of Precautionary Measures

In an enterprise unit that employs more then 30 workers, in situations of merger, or suspension of the whole or part of the operating departments, if the enterprise unit fails to pay wages to a certain level, the workers or unions have a duty to notify relevant authorities.

6. Prevention of Responsible Member(s) of the Enterprise from Leaving the Country
    Where the accumulation of debts such as legal retirement benefit, redundancy or salary payments totals over the legally set amount (for example, if in a business which employs more then 30 but less then 100 workers, the accumulated debts with respect to workers retrenched totals $NT 5 million), and the enterprise is undergoing mass dismissal, the competent authority shall set definite dates by which the workers must be paid. If the enterprise fails to pay by the set date, the authority concerned must summon a major wage negotiation conference and notify the immigration authorities to prevent the responsible persons of the enterprise unit from leaving the country.

According to the regulations set in the Labour Standard Law and Corporate Mergers and Acquisition Act, when businesses undergo the process of merger or acquisition, the management have no duty to negotiate with trade unions or workers on the arrangements with respect to labour contracts or terms of employment. In contrast, the Protection for Labour against Mass Dismissals Act imposes a duty on businesses undergoing merger or simplification of operating structures to prepare dismissal proposals and to negotiate with workers or unions. In this sense, the Protection for Labour against Mass Dismissal Act greatly preserved the workers' right. However, as regulations in these Acts present an inherent conflict, it is uncertain how the matters would be resolved if the Protection of Labour from Mass Dismissal Act is enacted; this will have to be subjected to further discussions.

4. UNFAVOURABLE CHANGES TO TERMS AND CONDITIONS OF EMPLOYMENT

Article 70 of the Labour Standard Law states: In the situation where an enterprise unit employs more than 30 workers, employers must set the work rules. After examination by the relevant authority, the work rules are to be published and enforced. The content of work rules should include: working hours, wage, allowance, bonus, rules to be observed in the workplace and other important employment conditions. However, according to the LSL, the process of determination of work rules can be quite unilateral, as the legislation imposes no duty on the employers to take into account the opinions of the workers or union. Furthermore, given the relatively weak position that Taiwanese unions are currently in, they have no power to force employers to bargain with the workers collectively.[11] Thus, for both sides, the terms of work

---

11. According to statistics released by the Council of Labour Affairs of Executive Yuan, up to September 2001, there are 1,081 industrial unions (the majority of which are enterprise-wide unions), and 2,688 occupational unions. Of these, only 304 unions have signed collective agreements.

rules become the most important means of determining the standards of employment conditions.

Subsequently, problems can arise in circumstances where the employers face unfavourable economic conditions. In order to raise competitiveness, the employers may change and implement a new set of labour conditions and regulations which are disadvantageous to workers. In this case, are the employers entitled to change labour conditions without the consultation of the workers or union? As the legislation is not clear, the issue is often a topic of major dispute.

In 1991, the Council of Labour Affairs of the Executive Yuan released the following statement with regard to this issue: "The employment conditions should be determined by negotiation between employers and employees. Even in the situation where employers wish to lower work rule standards, while still keeping them better then the minimum employment conditions set out in the Labour Standard Law, the conditions should still be negotiated between both parties."[12] This statement is unhelpful in the circumstance where both parties cannot reach an agreement. It does not suggest any mechanisms by which the dispute can be resolved.

Three years after the 1984 enactment of the Labour Standard Law, the Taipei District Court adjudicated in a case that relates to this issue. The facts of the case are as follows. Before the plaintiff started working at the defendant's company, both parties negotiated and agreed to a labour and employment contract. Furthermore, according to the defendant company's Human Relations Management Regulations, after an employee fulfils a set period of service, they are entitled to certain retirement benefits. The defendant company sought to change the regulations, which would then become more unfavourable to the workers. The court held that The regulations had become part of the terms of employment, and thus, where there is an unfavourable change in the regulations that results in the plaintiff suffering losses, the plaintiff has the right to dispute the change. Where the plaintiff has not yet agreed to the change, the operating contract would still be the one that both parties agreed to in 1976, that is the one that both parties negotiated and agreed on when the plaintiff joined the company.[13] According to this ruling, work rules become part of the labour contract after its enforcement. Consequently, if employers change the work rules unfavourably towards the workers, in essence, it becomes an alteration in the labour contract. Such alterations must have the approval of the employees, otherwise the alteration cannot be forced upon the employees.

In 1995, the Taipei District Court stated: "This court believes that both the protection of employee's rights and the necessary actions taken as part of the employer's management strategy need to be preserved. Where employers seek to change work rules unfavourably towards workers, on principle they must seek the employee's consent and must not restrain workers opposing the

---

12. The council of Labour Affairs of Executive Yuan, 23 October 1991. Tai (80) Employment Law Explanation, No. 27545.
13. Taipei District Court (1987) 6299th Judgment.

change. However, where the change is based on reasonable cause, an exception to the principle can be made, and workers opposing this adjustment can be restrained."[14] It is apparent from this decision that Taipei District Court has changed their opinion on the 1984 decision.

In 1998, the Taipei District Court announced the following judgment: "The defendant, in dealing with managers' salaries, made unfavourable changes resulting in losses to the plaintiff. The extent of economic loss suffered by the plaintiff range from $NT4,100 to the tune of a couple of tens of thousands. Despite the severity of these changes, the defendant offered no compensation in terms of other more favourable changes to employment conditions. ... In essence, salary conditions can be said to be the most significant component of employment conditions, thus any unfavourable adjustments to work rules which affect the salary conditions must be based on reasons of absolute necessity. On inquiry, it is discovered that the defendant only implemented these changes to increase profit margins, and thoughtlessly adjusted the salary structure for the reasons of convenience. There was no evidence of deteriorating financial or management position such that business would be inoperable without undertaking these measures. It is difficult to see, from the evidence provided by the defendant, how such unfavourable adjustments such as these can be justified as actions of absolute necessity."[15] This judgment is an extension of the 1995 decision. However, when determining whether employers had reasonable cause for unfavourable adjustment to employment conditions, employers' provisions of other types of compensation should be an element for consideration.

Finally in 1999 the Supreme Court of Taiwan made the most definitive judgment to date: "In the present labour and management relations, both the size of the corporations and number of employees are constantly on the increase. In order to increase the efficiency in administrating human resource management, many of the rules about work environment and content, along with other important issues such as employee's duties, retirement, assistance, redundancy payments and other regulations, are commonly set up within a general operating standard, and after these standards have been set up as work rules, they must be obeyed by the workers. The employment conditions and work rules set out between the employers and employees have a restraining effect on both parties. Regardless of whether workers understand, agree to, or have knowledge of the content of work rules, except in the situation where the work rules contravene mandatory or prohibitive provisions of laws, regulations or collective agreements, work rules are considered to be part of their labour contracts. On the other hand, employers seeking to change work rules unfavourably towards workers, on principle must seek employees' consent and must not restrain workers opposing the change. However, in the situation where the change is based on reasonable cause, an exception to the principle can be made, and workers opposing the change can be restricted and

14. Taipei District Court (1995) 38th Labour Law Judgment for Appeal.
15. Taipei District Court (1998) 30th Labour Law Judgment.

sanctioned."[16] On these grounds, employers with reasonable cause can change the work rules unfavourably, without the consent of the workers, and can enforce the change upon them.

In a more recent example, a national airline sought to reform the corporation, and altered and implemented a new wage structure, which resulted in a reduction of wages and salaries. The High Court of Taiwan gave the following reasons for their judgment: "The Appellants, in order to implement their plans of corporate reform, sought to adjust the salary structure of airline personnel on all flights, with the aim of achieving not only a reasonable and simple salary structure but also a fair and systematic method of personnel management. On further inquiry, it is discovered that the employer implemented this change by adjusting work regulations without consultation with employees, which resulted in an unfavourable change to employment conditions. Questions arise in relation to whether the employer has a right to restrain or restrict employees who oppose these changes, or alternatively, in what circumstances do employers have a right to restrain workers who oppose? Academically, these issues are still in dispute. However, in general, an adjustment to work rules is similar to an exploitation of workers' vested rights, and imposition of unfavourable employment conditions on the workers in principle should not be allowed. Employers can only restrain or restrict workers who oppose in the situation where there is reasonable and necessary cause for this course of action. Especially in the case of wages, retirement benefits and other important rights, the changes to employment conditions must be based on a "high degree of necessity." In that case, the whole situation, such as deterioration of operating conditions and the degree of necessity for wage reform, the degree of impact on workers' economic situation after the reform, and whether other changes to work rules have undergone collective negotiations with other workers, are all issues that need to be considered. In the present case, the Pilot Personnel Management Measures publicized by the Appellant on 1 October 1998, implemented by adjusting work rules, resulted in a change in a salary structure and unfavourable employment conditions. Although the employers argued that the changes were implemented to establish a reasonable and simple salary structure, along with a fair and systematic scheme for personnel management, they have not provided solid evidence demonstrating the high degree of necessity required for the legal implementation of this change. Thus these adjustments cannot be enforced."[17]

From this decision, it is evident that in deciding reasonableness of the work rule changes sought by employers, whether or not the employer has undergone negotiation with employees collectively prior to the change is a major factor.

Following the train of developments in court decisions, it is clear that the Taiwanese courts are developing a new principle of law. Whilst the courts recognise the management challenges which employers face by allowing for employers' need for flexibility and space for work rule adjustments, they also

---

16. Supreme Court of Taiwan (1999) 1696th Judgment.
17. High Court of Taiwan (2000) 17th Labour Law Judgment.

have to ensure that these adjustments will not significantly compromise the workers in relation to employment conditions. In a country where unions have very little power, the courts thus have a very important task in establishing this balance.

5. CONCLUSION

Taiwanese corporations have been facing major challenges in the past few years. The government has responded to these difficult periods by facilitating measures designed to assist in corporate reorganisation with the aim of increasing efficiency and competitiveness. Other than making major amendments to the preexisting Corporate Law, it also enacted the Corporate Mergers and Acquisition Act, which set out clearly the procedures and regulations relating to the issues of mergers, acquisition and division of companies. These reforms are not limited to the process of corporate reorganisation, but also address the employment issues and gaps that exist in the Labour Standard Law. In addition, in dealing with the issue of unfavourable change to employment conditions during economic downturn, the legislation gave both parties in a labour dispute the right to collectively negotiate the terms of employment. However, due to the current weak positions of the Taiwanese labour unions, instances of collective negotiation have been rare. Employers are more likely to change employment conditions through altering work terms and conditions. The legality of this method, through 10 years of judicial reform, has finally been simplified into this judicial rule: Generally, where employers seek to change labour conditions unfavourably with respect to the worker, on principle they need to seek permission and agreement from employees. However, where the change is a reasonable management response to unfavourable economic conditions, the employer can implement these changes without employees' consent. The result of this judicial interpretation is that now employers have the opportunity to adjust work conditions, according to the changes in the operating environment.

BIBLIOGRAPHY

REFERENCE MATERIALS

Chan, Wen Kai "*Corporate Mergers and Its Effect on Labour Contracts*" (Journal of Labour Banking Unions Alliance) October 5th, 2001.

Chang, Ching Yun "*The Structural Change of Global and Taiwanese Labour Employment Patterns*," Economic Planning and Development Council, Executive Yuan.

Directorate General of Budget Accounting and Statistics of Executive Yuan, *Survey into the Employment Conditions Yearly in the Taiwan Area of the Republic of China* (November 2001) at p. 8.

Huang, Cherng Kuan *Labour Law* (February 2002) at p. 484.

Financial Research Department of Economic Planning and Development Council, Executive Yuan, *"Domestic and Foreign Developmental Trends of Corporate Mergers and Acquisition"* January 17, 2001.

Council of Labour Affairs of Executive Yuan, 23rd of October, 1991. (80) Employment Law Explanation, No. 27545.

Lelong, Sophia H. *"Corporate Mergers and Acquisition and the Stability of the Workforce"* (Formosan Brothers Law Journal) July 2000.

Manpower Planning Department of Economic Planning and Development Council, Executive Yuan, *The Unemployment Statistics Monthly in the Taiwan Area of the Republic of China*, (January 2002).

Yang, Jia Yen *"A Study on Global Trends and its Influence on the Developmental Policies of Taiwanese Industries"* (APEC Review, December 2001) at p. 35.

Yang, Tong Shiuan, *"A Discussion on Labour Laws and Change in Nature of Business under the Information Age"* (Taiwan Bar Journal, May 2000) at p. 20.

CASE LAW

High Court of Taiwan (2000) 17th Labour Law Judgment.

Supreme Court of Taiwan (1999) 1696th Judgment.

Supreme Court of Taiwan, 2456th Judgment of 1986; Supreme Court of Taiwan, 2767th Judgment of 1994.

Taipei District Court (1987) 6299th Judgment.

Taipei District Court (1995) 38th Labour Law Judgment for Appeal.

Taipei District Court (1998) 30th Labour Law Judgment.

Taiwan Shihlin District Court, 11th Labour Judgment of 1999.

8.   The United Kingdom

Catherine Barnard

1.   INTRODUCTION

The characteristic feature of the law in this area is not restraint on the employer's ability to restructure but an examination of who bears the costs of that restructuring. Once restructuring is on the cards, the law ceases to focus on the bilateral relationship between the employer and employee and becomes, instead, multilateral, taking account of a number of other parties – third party purchasers, creditors in the case of an insolvent company and the state who picks up certain liabilities. How the law allocates responsibility and risk is a recurring theme throughout this paper.

2.   LEGAL FRAMEWORK GOVERNING CORPORATE RESTRUCTURING

In this section I briefly examine the corporate rules on restructuring and the employment implications of these rules, and the labour law provisions, in particular the common law remedy of wrongful dismissal, and the statutory claims of unfair dismissal and redundancy (although the details of the redundancy claim are considered in detail in Section 4.1 below). I also outline the provision relating to transfer of undertakings.

2.1.   Corporate law

Companies in financial difficulties can take a variety of steps. One possibility is to carry on trading in the hope that the financial difficulties will pass.[1] If this does not satisfy the creditors of the company then the company can apply to the court for a *voluntary arrangement* with creditors either with the approval of the court under s. 425 Companies Act 1985 or with the approval of the majority of the creditors under the Insolvency Act 1986.

The Insolvency Act and the Insolvency Rules also govern administration and liquidation. Both procedures involve the appointment of a qualified

---

1.   The following section is drawn from Birds, Boyle, Ferran and Villiers, *Boyle & Birds' Company Law* (Jordans, 4th ed., 2000), 637–638.

R. Blanpain (ed.),
Corporate Restructuring and the Role of Labour Law, 153–176.
© 2003 *Kluwer Law International. Printed in Great Britain.*

insolvency practitioner to a company, displacing the existing board of directors from their management function. *Liquidation* (or winding up) can occur either by a resolution of the company or by a court order on an application by the creditors. The purpose of liquidation is to terminate the company's business, realise its assets, pay its debts and liabilities and then distribute any remaining assets to the members of the company. At the end of the procedure the company ceases to exist. An *administration* order can be made on an application by the company itself and also its creditors. The purpose of this procedure is intended to rescue the company either in whole or in part. If that is not possible, the administration procedure is also available to secure a more advantageous realisation of the company's assets than would be possible on a winding-up; and administration can also be used to bolster a voluntary arrangement between a company and its creditors. The Insolvency Act also regulates some aspects of the receivership process. Receivers are appointed by secured creditors to realise their security.

Employees of a company which has entered insolvency proceedings (administration, liquidation, receivership or the approval of a company voluntary arrangement) can claim against the National Insurance Fund for upto 8 weeks unpaid wages as well as payments in lieu of notice, any basic award of compensation under and any protective award, subject to a statutory ceiling.[2] In addition, employees rank as preferential creditors in claims for unpaid wages and holiday pay up to a maximum of £800 where the sums have accrued in the four months prior to the proceedings.[3] This preferential status also applies to receivership[4] but not to administration.

Finally, it should be noted that it is a well established principle of English corporate law that directors owe a duty to the company and the company alone. That position has now been enshrined in statute.[5] However, s. 309(1) provides that:

> The matters to which the directors of a company are to have regard in the performance of their functions include the interests of the company's employees in general, as well as the interests of its members.

Since the directors' duties are owed to the company this means that the duty to consider the interests of the employees is not owed and not enforceable by the employees themselves. The duty to consider the interests of the employees therefore forms part of the general duty owed by the directors to the company and so can only be enforced by the company. In reality, the interests of employees

---

2.   SS 182, 184, 186 ERA 1996. The Secretary of State is then subrogated to the employee's claim against the insolvent employer.

3.   Ss 175 and 386 Insolvency Act 1986 and Reg 4 Insolvency Proceedings (Monetary Limits) Order 1986 (SI 1986/1996).

4.   S. 40 IA 1986.

5.   S. 309(2) Companies Act 1985.

have been given little attention in British company law.[6] In the case of insolvency (and possibly in other circumstances),[7] it is the creditors' interests which intrude.[8]

2.2. Labour law

At common law an employer is able to dismiss its employees on an indefinite contract at will without having to show a good reason:[9] all that is required is notice. Statutory regulation of minimum notice periods is now provided for by ss. 86–91 ERA 1996 which take effect as implied terms. The contract itself may specify longer periods of notice. In the event of a dismissal without notice, the employee has available the common law action for damages for breach of contract (also known as an action for *wrongful dismissal*), unless the employer pays wages in lieu of notice (PILN) or gives some other benefit which is permitted by s. 86(3).[10] However, no notice needs to be given in the case of gross misconduct by the employee which leads to summary dismissal (see Figure 8.1).[11]

However, even if the dismissal is justifiable at common law (because notice or equivalent has been given) it is not necessarily fair under statute (see Figure 8.1). The statutory provisions (ss95–134A ERA 1996) concern the claim of *unfair dismissal*. They apply to *employees* with one year's service (except in the case of automatic unfair dismissal where no service requirement is applied) who have been dismissed (see Figure 8.2). According to ERA s. 95(1), there are three categories of dismissal:

(a) where the contract of employment is terminated by the employer, by notice or otherwise. It also covers the situation where the employer unilaterally imposes radically different terms of employment.[12]

(b) where, if the contract of employment is a contract for a fixed term, the term expires without being renewed.

(c) where the employee terminates the contract, by notice or otherwise, "in circumstances such that he is entitled to terminate it without notice by reason of the employer's conduct", i.e. constructive dismissal. The question is whether the employer has committed a repudiatory breach of contract. In terms of corporate restructuring this would include unilateral variation of the terms of the contract.[13]

---

6. Bercusson B., "Workers, corporate enterprise and the law" in R. Lewis (ed) *Labour Law in Britain* (Oxford, Blackwell, 1986) and Lord Wedderburn, "Companies and employees: common law or social dimension" (1993) 109 LQR 220.
7. *Lonrho* v *Shell Petroleum* [1980] 1 WLR 627.
8. *West Mercia Safetywear Ltd* v *Dodd* [1988] BCLC 250.
9. *McClory* v *Post Office* [1992] ICR 758.
10. *Baldwin* v *British Coal Corporation* [1995] IRLR 139.
11. *Pepper* v *Webb* [1969] 1 WLR 514; *Wilson* v *Racher* [1974] ICR 428; *Neary* v *Dean of Westminster* [1999] IRLR 288.
12. *Hogg* v *Dover College* [1990] ICR 39; *Alcan Extrusions* v *Yates* [1996] IRLR 327.
13. E.g. *Coleman* v *Baldwin* [1977] IRLR 342 (permanent removal of the employee's most interesting and enjoyable duties) and *Millbrook Furnishings* v *McIntosh* [1981] IRLR 309 (transfer from highly skilled to unskilled work); *Courtaulds* v *Sibson* [1988] IRLR 305 (forced change in place of work may be constructive unfair dismissal depending on circumstances).

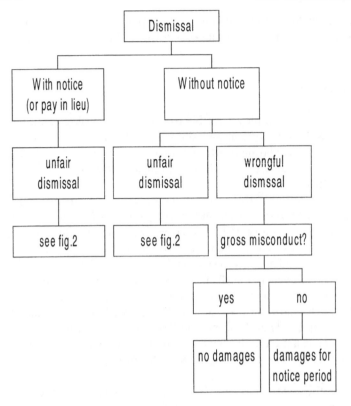

Figure 8.1: Wrongful and unfair dismissal

The burden of proof rests for these matters rests with the employee.

Unless one of the automatically unfair reasons is alleged (e.g. dismissal on the grounds of trade union membership), the burden shifts to the employer to show a potentially fair reason for dismissal. According to s. 98(2) ERA 1996 the grounds are:

(a)   capability or qualifications of employee for work of the kind he employed to do

(b)   conduct of employee

(c)   redundancy

(d)   contravention of statutory prohibition (illegality).

To this, s. 98(1)(b) adds: "some other substantial reason of a kind such as to justify the dismissal of an employee holding the position which that employee held" (SOSR).

For our purposes, redundancy and SOSR are the most important headings. If the dismissal is on the grounds of *redundancy* then there is no successful unfair dismissal claim but a redundancy payment will be made under the s. 135 (see below). However, if the dismissal for redundancy is carried out in an unfair manner (e.g. unfair system of selection, including the criteria by

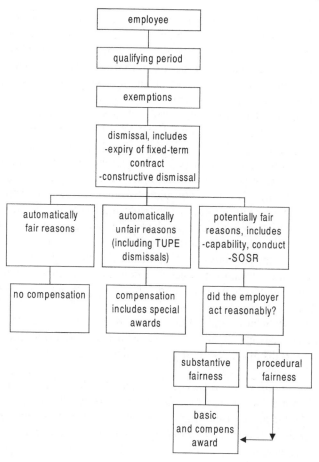

Figure 8.2: Unfair dismissal

which the individual is selected, and lack of consultation or unfairness in the manner in which the system is applied) there will also be a claim for unfair dismissal. *SOSR* covers, *inter alia*, the situation of quasi-redundancies and unilateral variation of terms. As we have seen, a unilateral variation of the employee's terms and conditions could constitute grounds for constructive dismissal. If the employee adopts this course, it is open to the employer to argue SOSR as a potentially fair reason. This can be seen in *RS Components Ltd* v *Irwin*.[14] The employers, who manufactured electrical components, faced a serious problem from members of their staff leaving and setting up in competition and soliciting former customers. So they sought to impose a restrictive covenant on sales staff to prevent them from soliciting customers for up to 12 months. When Irwin refused to accept the new term he was dismissed. His dismissal was found to be fair: the employer was dismissing for a

---

14.   [1973] IRLR 239.

substantial reason and was acting reasonably. Brightman J in the EAT said it is not difficult to imagine a case where it would be essential for employers embarking on a new technological process to invite existing employees to agree to some reasonable restriction on the use of that knowledge. It would therefore be essential to terminate the contract of an employee who refused to agree to that without infringing the employment legislation.

Thus, for SOSR to apply, the employer need only put forward a "sound, good business reason",[15] an onus which is not difficult to discharge,[16] and the courts are reluctant to get involved in assessing the commercial and economic reasons put forward by the employer.[17] This can be seen in *Catamaran Cruises* v *Williams*.[18] The case concerned a failing river boat business was taken over by another company. The new company wanted to improve the safety and efficiency of the company and, in consultation with the trade union, put forward new contracts which many of the employees agreed to. However, seven employees did not and were dismissed as a result. In considering the SOSR justification and the reasonableness of the dismissals, the EAT said that the tribunal should have taken into account, *inter alia*, the fact that many of the employees accepted the terms and that the employees' trade union recommended the changes.

In the case of potentially fair reasons the final question is whether the employer acted reasonably in the circumstances in treating the reasons as sufficient for the dismissal. S. 98(4)(a) provides:

> *the determination of the question whether the dismissal was fair or unfair, having regard to the reasons shown by the employer:*
> (a) *shall depend on whether in the circumstances (including the size and administrative resources of the employer's undertaking) the employer acted reasonably or unreasonably in treating it as a sufficient reason for dismissing the employee; and*
> (b) *[that question] shall be determined in accordance with equity and the substantial merits of the case.*

There are two components to any assessment of the reasonableness of the employer's decision:
- the reasonableness of the actual decision (substantive fairness),
- and the fairness of the procedure by which that decision was actually reached.

Of general relevance is the idea that the employer is protected as long as he acts in a "band of reasonableness". As Browne-Wilkinson J explained in *Iceland Frozen Foods* v *Jones*:[19]

---

15. *Hollister* v *NFU* [1979] ICR 542, 551.
16. *Banerjee* v *City and Est London AHA* [1979] IRLR 147, 150.
17. *James Cook* v *Tipper* [1990] IRLR 386.
18. [1994] IRLR 386.
19. *Iceland Frozen Foods* v *Jones* [1982] IRLR 439, 442.

"in judging the reasonableness of the employer's conduct an industrial tribunal must not substitute its decision as to what the right course to adopt for that of the employer ... in many, though not all, cases there is a band of reasonable responses to the employee's conduct within which one employer might reasonably take one view, another might quite easily take another; .. the function of an industrial tribunal, as an industrial jury, is to determine whether in the particular circumstances of each case the decision to dismiss the employee fell within the band of reasonable responses which a reasonable employer might have adopted".

Although serious doubt was cast on this test by Morrison J in the EAT in *Haddon* v *Van den Bergh Foods*,[20] the status quo has been restored.[21]

Not only must the dismissal be substantively fair, but it must also be procedurally fair. The courts have read principles akin to those of natural justice into the statute to achieve a broad standard of reasonableness. In doing so they have received much guidance from the ACAS Code of Practice on Disciplinary and Grievance Procedures.[22] Failure to comply with this procedure is likely to render the dismissal unfair.[23]

The remedy for unfair dismissal reinstatement or reengagement under ss. 114 and 115 (awarded in only about 3% of all cases) or, in the absence of such an order compensation under ss. 118–127. This includes a basic award intended to reflect the loss of accrued continuity of employment. It is calculated on the same basis as a redundancy payment (age, length of service and normal weekly pay) subject to a maximum of £7,200.[24] In addition the tribunal can make a compensatory award under s. 123 of "such an amount as the tribunal considers just and equitable". Awards under this head are subject to a statutory maximum of approximately £52,000.

2.3. Special legislation concerning transfer of undertakings

The Transfer of Undertakings Directive 2001/23[25] uses three means to achieve the objective of safeguarding acquired rights:

1. automatic transfer of the employment relationship from the transferor to the transferee, (Art. 3): automatic novation unless the employee objects),[26] including all rights and liabilities;

---

20.   [1999] IRLR 672.
21.   *Madden* v *HSBC* [2000] IRLR 288; *Beedell* v *West Ferry Printers* [2000] IRLR 650.
22.   This Code must be taken into account by the tribunal where it appears relevant (s. 207 TULR(C)A 1992).
23.   *Polkey* v *Dayton Services* [1987] IRLR 503.
24.   It is reduced by the amount of any statutory redundancy pay actually received.
25.   Codifying and repealing Directive 77/187 as amended by Directive 98/50.
26.   Reg 5(4A), (4B).

2. protection of employees against dismissal due exclusively to a transfer of the undertaking (Art. 4) unless there is an economic, technical or other organisational reason (ETOR);
3. information and consultation with the representatives of employees in the transferor and transferee undertakings (Art. 7).

The basic aim of the Directive and the British implementing legislation TUPE[27] was to ensure that whatever level of employment protection employees enjoyed before the transfer of an undertaking those rights would continue to be enjoyed after the transfer.

When considering the three strands of protection conferred by the Regulations and the Directive, Deakin and Armour describe employment protection law and TUPE in particular as providing "contingent control rights to employees which are triggered by a significant change in the form of the enterprise threatening their firm-specific human capital. They argue that this right can be said to be in the nature of a property right when employees' existing or acquired rights arising from employment automatically bind third parties such as the transferee. They also argue that employment law operates to collectivise the employees' divergent interests in such a way as to overcome the governance costs of renegotiating the terms of employment contracts, by vesting these negotiation rights in the designated employee representatives who have monopoly representation rights.[28]

The Directive applies to transfer of an "undertaking, business or part of a business to another employer as a result of a legal transfer or merger" excluding sea-going vessels.[29] Regulation 2(1) of TUPE says that "undertaking" includes "any trade or business", and TUPE applies "whether the transfer is effected by sale or by some other disposition or by operation of law".[30] The transfer may be effected by a series of two or more transactions, and may take place whether or not property is transferred.[31] However, TUPE (like the Directive) does not apply to a transfer by the sale of shares in the acquired company, since there is no change of employer.[32] This principle is unreal: "the transferee company, instead of acquiring the undertaking, might have bought the whole of the shares, changed the management, adopted new articles, amended the objects and other clauses in the memorandum, changed the nature of the business, increased the capital, and with the consent of the Department of Trade, even have adopted a new name. All this could have been done and the servant still would have been bound to serve the 'master' who, in theory, but not in fact certainly remained the same."[33]

---

27. Transfers of Undertakings (Protection of Employment) Regulations 1981, SI 1981/1794.
28. Armour J. & Deakin, S. "Insolvency, Employment Protection and Corporate Restructuring: the Effects of TUPE", paper presented at a conference held at the University of Cambridge, *Corporate Governance: Reassessing Ownership and Control*, 19 May 2001.
29. Art. 1(3), TUPE reg. 2(2).
30. Reg. 3(2).
31. Reg. 3(3)
32. *Brookes* v *Borough Care Services* [1998] IRLR 636, EAT.
33. *Gower's Modern Company Law.*

Initially the public sector was excluded from the scope of TUPE until the UK was condemned before the European Court of Justice.[34] The real problems in this area have been the application of the Directive and thus of the Regulations to contracting out. This has come to the fore due to the policy of Compulsory Competitive Tendering (CCT). According to CCT, public authorities especially the NHS and local authorities, subject the supply of services to bids from in-house and outside service providers. It is now clear from the Court's case law and form the revisions to Directive 77/187 that contracting-out is potentially covered by the Directive.[35] The difficulty lies with the decision in *Süzen*.[36] In that case the ECJ held that Art. 1(1) of the Directive did not apply if "there was no concomitant transfer from one undertaking to another of significant tangible or intangible assets or the taking over by the new employer of a major part of the workforce, in terms of their numbers and skilled, assigned by his [sic] predecessor to the performance of the contract". In other words, in place of the approach which gave weight to all relevant factors, the Court laid down two pre-conditions to the finding of a transfer: either significant assets had to be transferred, or a major part of the workforce had to be taken over by the transferee. The judgment has been strongly criticised[37] for undermining the employment protection objectives of the ARD. This has left the law in a confused state, but it was followed by the Court of Appeal in *Betts* v *Brintel Helicopters Ltd*.[38] However, it was distinguished in *ECM (Vehicle Delivery Services) Ltd* v *Cox*.[39] where the Court of Appeal refused to interpret *Süzen* as deciding that transfers in which the new employer did not take on any of the pre-existing employees necessarily fell outside the Directive and the Regulations.[40] In *Lightways (Contractors) Ltd* v *Associated Holdings Ltd*[41] the Court of Session ruled that the tribunal could examine the motive of the transferee in refusing to take on the employees with a view to checking that whether a particular transaction was deliberately structured with a view to avoiding TUPE altogether.

34.　The new Article 1(1)(c) of the Directive now provides that: "This Directive shall apply to public and private undertakings engaged in economic activities whether or not they are operating for gain. An administrative reorganisation of public administrative authorities, or the transfer of administrative functions between public administrative authorities, is not a transfer within the meaning of this Directive."

35.　Art. 1(1)(b): "*There is a transfer within the meaning of this Directive where there is a transfer of an economic entity which retains its identity, meaning an organised grouping of resources which has the objective of pursuing an economic activity, whether or not that activity is central or ancillary.*"

36.　Case C-13/95 *Süzen* [1997] IRLR 255.

37.　Davies (1997) 27 ILJ 193–97.

38.　[1997] IRLR 361 (no relevant transfer when contract to transport contractors to an from North Sea rigs transferred from one contractor to another because insufficient assets transferred).

39.　[1999] IRLR 559.

40.　See also *RCO Support Services Ltd and Aintree Hospital Trust* v *UNISON* [2000] IRLR 624.

41.　[2000] IRLR 247 although cf *Whitewater Leisure Management Ltd* v *Barnes* [2000] IRLR 456.

If there is a transfer of an undertaking this provides the gateway to the protection outlined above. The three strands of this protection are considered below.

3. CORPORATE RESTRUCTURING AND SUCCESSION OF EMPLOYMENT CONTRACTS

3.1. Transfer of undertakings

Where the identity of the employer changes the common law gives the individual worker the negative freedom not to consent to a change of employer.[42] However, more usually the workers want to have the right to work for the new employer. In a transfer situation Regulations 5(2) says that the effect of a transfer is to assign to the transferee all of the transferor's rights, powers, duties and liabilities under or in connection with the contract of employment. Thus, the transferee must maintain the pre-transfer terms and conditions.

However, often the transferee wants to change the transferor's employees terms and conditions to bring them into line with those if its existing staff. If the transferee is offering other benefits, or if the employees think that these changes might safeguard their jobs in the longer term the employees may want to accept the changed terms. However, the ECJ's decision in *Daddy's Dance Hall*[43] suggests that this would not be possible. The Court said:

> employees are not entitled to waive the rights conferred on them by the Directive and ... those rights cannot be restricted even with their consent. This interpretation is not affected by the fact that ... the employee obtains new benefits in compensation for the disadvantages resulting from an amendment to his contract of employment so that, taking the matter as a whole, he is not placed in a worse position than before.

This view underpins the House of Lords' decision in *Baxendale* and *Wilson*.[44] In *Baxendale* the House of Lords had to consider the case of employees who were made redundant, received non-statutory redundancy pay and were then reengaged by the transferee on different terms and conditions. In *Wilson* a nursing home was transferred from Lancashire CC to St. Helens BC due to funding difficulties. Prior to the takeover the union had been involved in negotiations with the transferor and it was agreed that staff would be reduced

---

42. *Nokes v Doncaster Amalgamated Collieries* [1940] A.C. 1014, HL, esp. per Lord Atkin at 1026 ("the right to choose for himself whom he would serve constituted the main difference between a servant and a serf"). See also the Court of Justice's decision to that effect in Joined Cases C-132, 138 and 139/91 *Katsikas* [1992] ECR I-6577 and the UK's implementation in Reg. 5(4A) and (4B) of the TUPE Regulations 1981.
43. Case 324/86 [1988] IRLR 315.
44. [1998] 4 All ER 609.

and those kept on had their contracts terminated by reason of redundancy and then they were reemployed at lower rate of pay. They argued that they were entitled to the same terms and conditions as before. The House of Lords held that although on a transfer the employee's rights against the former employer were enforceable against the transferee and could not be amended by reason of the transfer itself, there could be a variation of the contract for reasons which were not due to the transfer, either on or after the transfer of undertaking. However, the House of Lords offered little guidance as to how to decide whether a purported variation was due to the transfer (and so invalid) or was due to some other cause (and so valid). Lord Slynn said that it might be difficult to decide whether the variation is due to a transfer or attributable to some separate cause but there may come a time when the link with the transfer is broken or can be treated as no longer effective. Among the relevant factors may be the proximity in time of the variation to the transfer, and whether the employees have received compensation for giving up their old rights.[45] The implication is that such a variation is void even if overall the employee is better off as a result of the variation. This is despite the fact that empirical research has also shown that TUPE protection is "bad news for employees because it makes businesses harder to sell and therefore jobs hard to rescue ... At the margins I'm sure there are cases where the businesses didn't sell because of the burdens that the purchaser would have had to take on".[46]

3.2. Transfer of undertakings, insolvency and related proceedings

As we have seen, there is a potential conflict between the acquired rights of employees and those of other creditors upon insolvency. If the purchaser of an insolvent business has to take over the employees and past liabilities to them, it will pay less to the receiver/liquidator, and hence the pool of assets against which the creditors of the insolvent business can claim will be reduced. Hence there is an argument that protecting the legal rights of employees will actually reduce the prospects of selling the business as a going concern and will reduce the overall number of jobs.

The 1977 Directive allowed Member States the choice whether to apply the Directive to all insolvency proceedings, and this has been done in the UK, where TUPE draws no distinction between insolvency, semi-insolvency and non-insolvency situations. However, Regulation 4 of TUPE does permit the practice of "hiving-down" by receivers and liquidators where the receiver transfers the business of an insolvent company to a newly created subsidiary while retaining the employees working for the parent company. The parent then lends the employees to the subsidiary. Since *Litster*[47] there has been no

---

45.   In *Credit Suisse First Boston (Europe) Ltd* v *Lister*, CA, [1998] IRLR 706, (decided before the HL in *Meade and Wilson*) acceptance by the transferring employee of a new restrictive covenant was held to be void because this was by reason of the transfer.
46.   Armour and Deakin, above n.X, 21.
47.   See below. See also *In the matter of Maxwell Fleet and Facilities Management Ltd* [2000] IRLR 368.

advantage in "hiving down" with the result that Regulation 4 (which may be invalid anyway) is no longer used in practice.

In the absence of express provisions in the Transfer of Undertakings Directive 77/187 and the uncertainty of the impact of the Directive on the labour market, the ECJ in *Abels* and *D'Urso*,[48] held that the Directive did not apply to transfers taking place in the context of insolvency proceedings instituted with a view to the liquidation of the assets of the transferor under the supervision of the competent judicial authority. However, it did apply where the business is transferred in the course of semi-insolvency ("rescue") proceedings such as judicially sanctioned suspension of payments as opposed to full liquidation proceedings.[49]

Reflecting the case law of the Court of Justice, the 1998 revisions of the Directive provided that Member States could exclude the Directive where the transferor was the subject of insolvency proceedings with a view to the liquidation of the assets of the transferor under the supervision of a competent authority.[50] Where the Directive does apply the Member State may (a) provide that the transferor's debts arising from any contract of employment before the opening of insolvency proceedings shall not be transferred to the transferee, provided that the employees are protected under the Insolvency Directive 80/987/EEC (below); and/or (b) provide that the transferor/ insolvency practitioner may negotiate changes in terms of employment with employee representatives designed to safeguard employment opportunities by ensuring the survival of the business. Provision (b) may be applied only where there has been declared under national law to be a situation of serious economic crisis. Member States must provide measures to prevent the misuse of insolvency proceedings in such a way as to deprive employees of their rights under the Directive.

In its consultation paper,[51] the UK government notes that the underlying aim of these options is to allow Member States to promote the sale of insolvent businesses as going concerns. It says that this is in line with the "rescue culture" which the Government wishes to promote. The government therefore proposes to take advantage of this derogation and says that where insolvency proceedings have been opened in respect of a transferor, any outstanding debts toward employees either:

- fall to be met from the National Insurance Fund, if they are within the categories and statutory upper limits on amounts guaranteed under the insolvency payments provisions of the Employment Rights Act 1996; or
- pass to the transferee, as at present, if they are not.

The Government also proposes to take up the second option and provide that where insolvency proceedings falling within the new derogation have been opened in respect of a transferor, changes by reason of the transfer itself (i.e. changes for which there is no ETO reason that would render them

---

48.   Case 135/83 *Abels* [1985] ECR 469 and Case 362/89 *D'Urso* [1992] IRLR 136.
49.   See e.g. Case C-319/94 *Jules Dethier Equipment SA* v *Dassy* [1998] IRLR 266.
50.   Now Art. 5 of directive 2001/23/EC.
51.   *http://www.dti.gov.uk/er/tupe/consult.htm*

potentially valid in any event) may be lawfully made to the terms and conditions of employment of affected employees if:

- they are agreed between either the transferor or the transferee and appropriate representatives of those employees;
- they are designed to safeguard employment opportunities by ensuring the survival of the undertaking or business or part of the undertaking or business; and
- they are not otherwise contrary to UK law (e.g. the National Minimum Wage Act).

The Government continues that in the light of case law developments, and of its proposal to take advantage of the new derogations in the Directive, "the existing provision in Regulation 4 of TUPE relating to 'hiving down' no longer serves any useful purpose." It therefore proposes to remove that provision.

4. ECONOMIC DISMISSALS BEFORE AND AFTER CORPORATE RESTRUCTURING

In this section I consider the rules on redundancies and redundancy consultation and the provisions in TUPE in respect of dismissals.

4.1. Redundancy

According to s. 135(1) ERA 1996 an employer must pay a redundancy payment to any employee not excluded from payment if the employee is dismissed by the employer by reason of redundancy. The redundancy payment is calculated on the same basis as the basic award for unfair dismissal. Redundancies are defined in s. 139(1) ERA. It provides that:

> *For the purposes of this Act an employee who is dismissed shall be taken to be dismissed by reason of redundancy if the dismissal is wholly or mainly attributable to –*
> (a) *the fact that his employer has ceased or intends to cease –*
>   i.   *to carry on the business for the purposes of which the employee was employed by him, or*
>   ii. *to carry on that business in the place where the employee was so employed, or*
>
> (b) *the fact that requirements of that business –*
>   i.   *for employees to carry out work of a particular kind,*
>   ii. *for employees to carry out work of a particular kind in the place where the employee was employed by the employer*
>
> *has ceased or diminished or are expected to cease or diminish.*

This embraces three ideas:

- the business disappears permanently or temporarily (s. 139(1)(a)(i))
- the workplace disappears (s. 139(1)(a)(ii))
- the job disappears (s. 139(b)).

The first two categories are perhaps the most straightforward. The only problems that have arisen here concern those employees with mobility clauses in their contracts. The courts have vacillated between a geographic test looking at the place where the employee was actually required to work, and the "contractual test" looking at the place where the employee was required to work under his contract of employment,[52] including any contractual mobility clause. Therefore, under the contractual test, if the employee was required expressly or impliedly by contract to work elsewhere, the employee must work in the new location. If he refuses and is dismissed the dismissal is on the grounds of misconduct and not redundancy. The courts have now reverted to the geographic test. As the EAT said in *Bass Leisure Ltd* v *Thomas*,[53] the place of employment is "to be established by a factual enquiry, taking into account the employee's fixed or changing place or places of work and any contractual terms which go to evidence or define the place of employment and its extent, but not those (if any) which make provision for the employee to be transferred to another".

More difficult is the situation of the disappearing job. Once again the courts have attempted to develop various tests to establish whether this has occurred. The *function test* focused on the need of the employers for the particular work: an employee was not redundant if the essential tasks remained the same, even though other terms and conditions might change. An early example of this can be found in *Vaux and Associated Breweries* v *Ward*.[54] The employers decided to revamp their business by employing young "bunny girls" in place of the older waitresses and dismissed the middle-aged waitresses. The older-women's claim for redundancy was defeated because the work done by the bunny girls was not so different from that done by the older women, even though the type of person required to do it was different. This was not a redundancy situation. The Court of Appeal adopted a similar approach in *Chapman* v *Goonvean and Rostowrack China Clay Ltd*.[55] The employers provided 7 employees with a bus to take them to work. When this became uneconomic and the bus service was cut, the employees claimed that they had been constructively dismissed for the purposes of redundancy. The Court of Appeal disagreed: it said that there was no diminution of the requirements of employees doing work of that particular kind. The requirements of the business for the work of the seven men continued just as before. This outcome coincided with Lord Denning's notion of public policy: "it is very desirable in the interests of efficiency that employers should be able to propose changes in the terms of a man's employment for such reasons these to get rid of restrictive

---

52.   *UK Atomic Energy Authority* v *Claydon* [1974] ICR 128.
53.   [1994] IRLR 104. See also *High Table* v *Horst* [1997] IRLR 513 (Court of Appeal).
54.   (1968) 3 ITR 385.
55.   [1973] 1 WLR 678.

practices, or to induce higher output by piece work or to cease providing transport at excessive cost". Finally, in *Johnson v Notts Combined Police Authority*[56] the police authority introduced a new shift system from 8 am to 3 pm and 1 am to 8 am instead of 9.30–5.30. When the employees refused to do these shifts they were dismissed. The Court of Appeal said they were not dismissed for reason of redundancy since the clerical work had not ceased or diminished. If there was a change in the terms and conditions it was for the employer to prove that it was done for efficiency and not so as to meet a redundancy situation.[57] Since the change was introduced to meet the needs of the business it was likely to constitute an SOSR for the purposes of an unfair dismissal claim.

The approach adopted in these cases reinforces managerial prerogative: it enables the employer to reorganise its business without that falling within the definition of redundancy. In other words if the job is not less (i.e. the quantum of work is not less) but the method of doing is different or the terms are different this is not a redundancy situation and so the individual receives no redundancy pay. Furthermore, as we have already seen, work reorganisation can fall within the heading of SOSR. Any dismissal could therefore be potentially fair. This would result in the employee receiving neither redundancy pay nor unfair dismissal compensation.[58]

In *Haden v Cowen*[59] the Court of Appeal rejected the function test in favour of the *contract test* which focused on the work the employee could be required to do by contract. Only if all that worked diminished was there a redundancy. However, in *Safeway v Burrell*[60] the EAT dismissed both tests. It rejected the function test on the grounds that it focused on a diminution of the *work* to be done rather than on a diminution in the requirements for employees to do that work. It also said that the contract test was wrong: the terms of the employee's contract were wholly irrelevant. The correct approach was to ask whether the employer's requirements for *employees* to do work of a particular kind had ceased or diminished. The case concerned the downgrading of a post. Burrell was the manager of a petrol station. As a result of management reorganisation Burrell's post disappeared and was replaced by a lower-grade, lower paid post of petrol filling station controller. B did not want the new post and was dismissed. The wing members applied the function test and said there was no redundancy. The chairman applied the contract test and said that since the manager's post was more responsible that job had disappeared and there was a redundancy. The EAT said both approaches were flawed and that the correct question was whether the business needed fewer *employees* to do the work of a particular kind. This was for the IT to decide.

56.   [1974] IRLR 20.
57.   See also *Lesney Products* v *Nolan* [1977] IRLR 77.
58.   See also *Johnson* v *Notts Combined Police Authority* [1974] IRLR 20; *Lesney Products* v *Nolan* [1977] IRLR 77.
59.   [1982] IRLR 314.
60.   [1997] IRLR 200.

Safeway v *Burrell* still leaves the question open: what work? The statute says "work of a particular kind". This was at issue in *Murray* v *Foyle Meats.*[61] The applicants were employed as meat plant operatives. They normally worked in the slaughter hall but their contracts of employment required them to work elsewhere in the factory and they had done so occasionally. When business declined the applicants were made redundant as the employer needed fewer slaughters. They claimed that their dismissal was unfair. The employers argued this was a redundancy situation: diminution in the employer's requirements for employees to carry out work of a particular kind. According to Lord Irvine of Lairg, the language of "para. (b) is in my view simplicity itself. It asks two questions of fact. The first is whether one or other of various states of economic affairs exists. In this case, the relevant one is whether the requirements of the business for employees to carry out work of a particular kind have diminished. The second question is whether the dismissal is attributable wholly or mainly, to that state of affairs. This is a question of causation".

Since the tribunal had found that the requirements of the business for employees to work in the slaughterhouse had diminished and that that state of affairs had led to the appellants being dismissed, there was a redundancy situation. Thus, the Lord Chancellor adopted a broad-brush approach to redundancy but in so doing effectively removes the works "work of a particular kind" from the face of the statute.

4.2. Redundancy consultation

I have already referred to the need for employers to consult with *individual* employees and trade unions for the purpose of avoiding an unfair dismissal claim. In *Williams* v *Compair Maxim*[62] the EAT laid down some guidelines as to what constituted good industrial practice in redundancies and these were developed in *Mugford* v *Midland Bank*[63] in respect of consultation. Clark J in the EAT said:

---

61.   [1999] IRLR 562.
62.   [1982] IRLR 83:
- the employer will seek to give as much warning as possible of impending redundancies so as to enable the union and employees who may be affected to take early steps to inform themselves of the relevant facts, consider possible alternative solutions and, if necessary, find alternative employment in the undertaking or elsewhere;
- the employer will consult with the union as to the best means by which the desired management result can be achieved fairly and with as little hardship to the employees as possible. In particular the employer will seek to agree with the union the criteria to be applied in selecting the employees to be made redundant;
- Whether or not an agreement as to the criteria to be adopted has been agreed with the union the employer will seek to establish the criteria for selection which so far as possible do not depend solely upon the opinion of the person making the selection but can be objectively checked against such things as attendance record, efficiency at the job, experience or length of service;
- The employer will seek to ensure that the selection is made fairly in accordance with these criteria and will consider any representations the union may make as to such selection.
63.   [1997] IRLR 208.

"(1) Where no consultation about redundancy has taken place with either the trade union or the employee the dismissal will normally be unfair, unless the tribunal finds that a reasonable employer would have concluded that consultation would be an utterly futile exercise in the particular circumstances of the case.[64]

In the case of large-scale *collective* redundancies (the dismissal of 20 or more workers), there are additional duties to consult with worker representatives as a result of EC Directives 75/129 as amended by 92/56. These two Directives have now been repealed and replaced by Directive 98/59.[65] The definition of redundancy for the purposes of consultation is contained in s. 195 TULR(C)A 1992:

> *In this chapter references to dismissal as redundant are references to a dismissal for a reason not related to the individual concerned or for a number of reasons all of which are not so related.*

This definition is broader than the definition of redundancy in s. 139 for the purposes of a redundancy payment.[66]

Under British law it used to be the case that the employer was obliged to consult with an authorised representative of a recognised trade union. However, if the employer did not recognise a trade union or had de-recognised a trade union, it could avoid the obligation to consult. As a result the European Court of Justice ruled[67] that this was an incorrect implementation of the Directive. This led to the enactment of SI 1995/2587[68] by the Conservative government extending the definition of those who must be consulted to "employee representatives elected by them" and giving the employer the choice which group to consult in the event of there being both a recognised trade union and worker-representatives in a particular workplace. This has now been

---

64.   It also said:
       (2) consultation with the trade union over selection criteria does not of itself release the employer form considering with the employee individually his being identified for redundancy;
       (3) it will be a question of fact and degree for the tribunal to consider whether consultation with the individual and/or his union was so inadequate as to render the dismissal unfair. A lack of consultation in any particular respect will not automatically lead to that result. The overall picture must be viewed by the tribunal up to the date of termination to ascertain whether the employer has or has not acted reasonably in dismissing the employee on grounds of redundancy".
65.   OJ 1998 L225/16.
66.   See *GMB* v *Man Truck & Bus UK* [2000] IRLR 636 where the EAT emphasised the breadth of this definition. It said that s.195 definition did not merely apply to lost jobs or workers. Therefore, on the facts, the employer was obliged to consult with employee representatives where following a merger the employer sought to harmonise terms and conditions of employment of the two groups of employees by terminating the employees' contracts of employment and offering fresh employment on new terms.
67.   Case C-383/92 *Commission* v *UK* [1994] IRLR 412.
68.   The Collective Redundancies and Transfer of Undertakings (Protection of Employment) (Amendment) Regulations 1995.

changed by SI 1999/1925[69] and the employer can only consult elected worker representatives in the absence of a recognised trade union.

Thus, according to s. 188 TULR(C)A 1992 – the overriding duty on an employer when proposing to dismissal an employee for reasons of redundancy is to begin consultation in good time and, in any event

- if the employer is proposing to dismiss 20–99 employees at the same at establishment over period of 90 days then consultation must begin at least 30 days in advance of first dismissal.
- if the employer is proposing to dismiss 100 + redundancies at same establishment within 90 days then employer must begin consulting at least 90 days in advance.

Failure to consult leads not to the dismissals being declared a nullity as in some Continental countries but to the payment of a Protective award on the application of the trade unions or elected worker representatives,[70] unless the employer can prove that there were special circumstances.[71] This award effectively requires the employer to pay the employee's salary again during the protected period for up to a maximum of 90 days. While the different approaches adopted on the Continent and in the UK appear significant, as Deakin and Armour point out, by doubling the salaries of the workforce for a period of weeks the sum owed by the employer soon mounts up thereby undermining the viability of a particular managerial strategy for restructuring. They therefore conclude that the difference between the protective award and nullification is one of degree.

The consultation provisions provide at best an opportunity for the worker's representatives to have their say and at worst they represent a financial hurdle to be negotiated around. They do not interfere with the essential managerial prerogative to decide to make employees redundant. However, the rights in respect of redundancy go further than the City Code on Mergers and Takeovers and the terms of the draft Thirteenth Directive on Takeover bids where the duty is simply to provide information: identifying in the offer document the plans the company has to alter the terms and conditions of employment and other existing rights of employees. In the event of failure to comply there is no effective sanction for the employees.[72]

4.3. Dismissal on the transfer of an undertaking

Regulation 8(1) TUPE makes the dismissal for a reason connected with the transfer automatically unfair for purposes of ERA 1996 Part X.[73] TUPE Reg.

---

69. The Collective Redundancies and Transfer of Undertakings (Protection of Employment) (Amendment) Regulations 1999.
70. S. 189(3) and (4).
71. S. 188(7) and 189(6).
72. Deakin and Slinger, "Hostile Takeovers, Corporate Law and the Theory of the Firm" (1997) 24 JLS 124.
73. ARD, Art. 4(1) (the transfer "shall not in itself constitute grounds for dismissal by the transferor or the transferee").

8(5), inserted by 1995 Regulations, means that only an employee eligible to complain of unfair dismissal (e.g. one years' service) is protected. There is, however, an important exception: Regulation 8(2) provides that "where an economic, technical or organisational reason [ETOR] entailing changes in the workforce of either the transferor or the transferee before or after a relevant transfer is the reason or principal reason for dismissing an employee", then the dismissal is potentially fair [under ERA 1996, s. 98(1)(b)] as a "for a substantial reason of a kind such as to justify the dismissal". The normal test of fairness under ERA 1996, s. 98(4),[74] then applies (Figure 8.3). However, ETOR is wider than SOSR in that it embraces redundancy and so the employer is liable to make a redundancy payment. On the other hand, it is narrower than SOSR because reasons of flexibility and cost-cutting (which would fall under SOSR) are not ETORs because they do not "entail changes in the workforce".[75] ETOR also does not include the situation where the purchaser of the business puts pressure on the vendor to dismiss employees as a precondition of the sale going ahead.[76]

The Regulation 8(1) protection applies only if the employee was employed immediately before the transfer. In *Litster*[77] the transferee, who did not want to employ the transferor's employees since it had its own employees who would work for less, tried to avoid the Regulation 8(1) problem by persuading the transferor to dismiss the workforce one hour before the transfer. The transferor, being in receivership, could not meet any of the liabilities (holiday pay, unfair dismissal and wrongful dismissal) owed to its former workforce. Consequently, they sued the transferee which refused to pay since the employees were not employed "immediately before the transfer". The House of Lords said that a dismissal occurring before the transfer and just because of the transfer was prohibited and, for the purposes of considering Article 3(1) of the Directive and Regulation 5, was ineffective. Thus Regulation 5(3) should be read as applying not only to those who were employed immediately before the transfer but also to those who would have been so employed if they had not been unfairly dismissed in the circumstances described in Regulation 8. Thus the liabilities for a dismissal which took place prior to the transfer and was automatically unfair under Regulation 8(1) were transferred to the transferee.

This case indicates that if the transferor dismisses the employee for a transfer-related reason before the transfer, or the transferee itself dismisses the employee for such a reason after the transfer, then the transferee is liable for all secondary statutory and contractual obligations (i.e. the right to complain any outstanding breach of contract and the right to complain of unfair dismissal), but the employee cannot enforce the primary obligation to continued employment. This view was confirmed in *British Fuels Ltd* v *Baxendale*;

---

74.   See above at Section 2.2.
75.   *Berriman* v *Delabole Slate Ltd* [1985] ICR 546.
76.   *Wheeler* v *Patel* [1987] IRLR 211, EAT.
77.   *Litster* v *Forth Dry Dock & Engineering Co. Ltd* [1990] 1 AC 546.

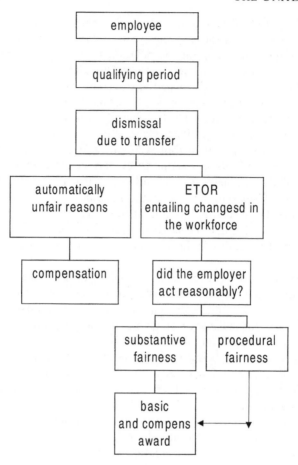

Figure 8.3: TUPE dismissals

Wilson v *St Helens Borough Council*[78] where Lord Slynn said that a dismissal for a reason connected with the transfer of an undertaking was legally effective and not a nullity as the Court of Appeal had argued. A dismissed employee could not compel the transferee to employ him. He said that if the transferee did not take the employee because the employee has been dismissed by the transferor or because the transferee has dismissed the employee then the transferee had to meet all the transferor's contractual and statutory obligations unless (a) the employee objects to being employed by the transferee and (b) the reason or principal reason for the dismissal is ETOR.

---

78.   [1998] 4 All ER 609.

4.4. Consultation in the event of a TUPE transfer

Regulation 10 of TUPE requires both the transferor and the transferee to consult trade unions or elected worker representatives of employees who may be affected by the transfer. The UK faced similar problems to those outlined above for collective redundancies in respect of consultation of worker representation in the event of a TUPE transfer and resolved them in much the same way. Failure to comply with the consultation requirements leads to an award of compensation not exceeding 13 weeks pay.[79]

The need to consult with trade unions in the event of a complex transfer and collective redundancies can provide a useful bargaining tool. This can be seen in the case of the proposed sale of Rover by BMW to Alchemy, a group of venture capitalists unpopular with the trade unions due to their declared intention to make large scale redundancies.[80] Since no consultation had occurred under either the collective redundancies or the transfers provisions, the trade unions initiated 28,000 claims for protective awards on behalf of the Rover workforce. They also brought started claims for breach of contract. Together the potential value of these claims amounted to over £300 million which would have to be borne by the transferee. Since Alchemy refused to indemnify BMW against these claims, the deal collapsed. This opened the door to the Phoenix consortium's bid led by John Towers, a former chief executive of Rover who was committee to retaining Longbridge for volume car production. Rover was sold to Phoenix for £10 with BMW putting in £575 million to help meet short-term running costs. As Armour and Deakin then point out, the Phoenix management pressed the unions to agree to a waiver of the claims arising out of the failure of BMW to begin consultation at the time when the sale to Alchemy was announced. While refusing to waive the claims, the unions did agree that consultation had begun at an earlier date. In return, Phoenix agreed to insert enhanced redundancy terms into the contracts of employment of Longbridge employees. This saved £100 million and a further £200 million was saved by Phoenix's decision to dismiss fewer than 1,000 workers at Longbridge, thereby avoiding large-scale redundancy claims.

5. CHANGES IN TERMS AND CONDITIONS OF EMPLOYMENT

5.1. Changes in terms and conditions

An employer can vary the terms and conditions of employment in four ways. First, an employer can do so with the agreement of the individual employee, usually on giving some consideration. Secondly, and a variation on the first, if the employer recognises a trade union for the purposes of collective bargaining

---

79.   Regulation 11(11).
80.   Armour and Deakin, "The Rover Case (2) – Bargaining in the Shadow of TUPE" (2000) 29 ILJ 395. See also Villiers, "The Rover Case (1) The Sale of Rover Cars by BMW – the Role of the Works Council" (2000) 29 ILJ 386.

and there is an express or implied bridging term in the individual contract of employment then any revisions in the collective agreement – both for better[81] *and* for worse[82] – will be incorporated into the individual contract provided that the terms are suitable for individuation. A third possibility is for the employer to vary the terms of the contract unilaterally. The employee then has a choice: either to accept the changes without protest and eventually be deemed to waive his or her rights, or to protest about the changes. If he protests he can either treat the contract as terminated and sue for constructive unfair dismissal provided that he satisfies the conditions outlined in Section 2.2 above or bring a claim for damages. He may lose his claim for constructive unfair dismissal if, as in *Catamaran Cruises*,[83] the employer points to a potentially fair reason and the dismissal is procedurally fair. The fourth possibility is for the employer to dismiss the employees and reengage them on new terms. Once again this leaves the employer exposed to potential wrongful and unfair dismissal claims or possibly redundancy. However, as we have seen, the employer could avoid these claims by giving proper notice, raising the SOSR defence and arguing that this does not constitute a redundancy situation as defined by s. 139 ERA. However, it might still constitute redundancy for the purposes of collective redundancies.

Increasingly employers have tried to avoid these problems by incorporating flexibility clauses into the contracts themselves. Thus, for example, in research conducted by Brown et al. for the DTI the researchers found that broad flexibility clauses of the following kind were common:[84]

> During your employment with the Company, you will be required to co-operate in the development of new working arrangements as necessary, including participating in training in order to improve both individual skills and the profitability of the Company. This will include being flexible in regard to the duties undertaken and mobile within the Company's establishment in which you are employed.

Another agreement stated:

> The Company may make reasonable changes to the terms and conditions of your employment. Such changes will be confirmed in writing.

---

81.   *Robertson* v *British Gas Corporation* [1983] ICR 351 employee's terms and conditions are such as "laid down from time to time".
82.   *Lee* v *GEC Plessey Communications* [1993] IRLR 383.
83.   See above n.X.
84.   For a brief discussion, see Deakin, "Organisational Change, Labour Flexibility and the Contract of Employment in Great Britain" in Deery S. and Mitchell R., *Employment Relations. Individualisation and Union Exclusion.* (The Federation press, 1999).

While the legality of these clauses have not been tested, some have suggested that they might breach the implied duty of mutual trust and confidence[85] or the employer's duty to protect the employee's health and safety.[86]

Even in the absence of such clauses the courts have recognised an implied duty to cooperate with the employer. In *Cresswell* v *Board of Inland Revenue*[87] Walton J said that the employees were in breach of this duty by refusing to cooperate with the introduction of new, computer-based technology. He said: "an employee is expected to adapt himself to new methods and techniques introduced in the course of his employment". This is subject only to the obligation on the part of the employer to offer training where "esoteric skills" were involved.

5.2. Transfers of undertakings

What about variations of contractual terms on the transfer of an undertaking? Can employees validly agree with the new employer to less favourable terms (perhaps because they know there will be no work for them if they refuse)? TUPE reg. 12 prohibits attempts to contract-out of the Regulations, a principle stated by the ECJ in *Daddy's Dance Hall* (above) to be inherent in the Directive. In addition, Regulation 5(5) provides that an employee can terminate his contract without notice if a "susbstantial change is made in his working conditions to his detriment". The Regulation continues that "no such right shall arise by reason only that ... the identity of his employer changes unless the employee shows that, in all circumstances, the change is a significant change to his detriment". The issue of changing terms and conditions of employment was also raised in *Baxendale* and *Wilson*, as we have already seen where the House of Lords adopted the rather unhappy distinction between changes connected and unconnected with the transfer. Part of the British problem is caused by the fact that the UK has not taken advantage of a provision permitting Member States to allow collective agreements to vary the terms and conditions of employment of the transferred employees a year after the transfer. In the light of the uncertainty created the Government now proposes that the Regulations do not preclude transfer-related changes to terms and conditions that are made for an ETO reason.

CONCLUSIONS

The striking feature of the law in this area is that it reinforces managerial prerogative – the right for the employer to manage its business, with little interference from employees who have no property right in their employment. In return, the law provides for (limited) compensation when the employee loses

---

85.   *Malik* v *BCCI* [1997] IRLR 462.
86.   *Johnstone* v *Bloomesbury Health* [1992] QB 333.
87.   [1984] IRLR 190.

their job and imposes certain procedural hurdles over which the employer must jump in order to ease the employee out of their employment. If these hurdles are ignored, then the costs for the employer mount. As we saw in the rover case, law becomes an instrument and possibly a barrier in the whole process of restructuring. However, if used strategically by well advised trade unions negotiating in the shadow of the law, it can become an effective vehicle for securing their own objectives.

9.   The United States

Stewart J. Schwab

1.   INTRODUCTION

Compared to most other industrialised countries, the United States has little legal protection for workers during corporate restructuring. The lack of protection reflects (and probably helps shape) a culture that prides mobility and expects turnover and change.

Let me briefly recount some labour-market statistics that show the extent of turnover and the generally bright prospects for workers losing their jobs. According to official Bureau of Labour Statistics data, about 4.2 million workers were "displaced" in 1997–1998.[1] About half had been with their employer less than three years, and their displacement rate – the proportion of all such workers who lost or left their job – was 5%. Often these displacements occur because of a bad job match; turnover to get a better match is good for the worker and economy. But 1.9 million displaced workers had been with their employer at least 3 years. Job loss by these long-tenured workers is potentially more serious. In 1997–1998, however, their displacement rate was only 2.5%. Half of these long-tenured workers lost their job because their plant or company closed or moved, one-third because their position was abolished, and one-fifth because of insufficient work. For long-tenured displaced workers, the median period between jobs was 5.3 weeks, and about 43% received unemployment-insurance benefits (18% exhausted their UI benefits). Displaced workers finding jobs suffered almost no loss in median weekly earnings. Nearly half found a new job in a different major industry and 40% were in a different occupation. Nine percent of long-tenured displaced workers moved to another area to find work, and 91% of those were re-employed. Overall, 78% of long-tenured displaced workers were re-employed within two years, 5.6% remained unemployed, and 16.5% were out of the labour force (with 40% of displaced workers over age 55 being out of the workforce). In the United States, most workers rely on employer-provided health insurance plans, and job loss puts

---

1.   See Ryan T. Helwig, Worker Displacement in a Strong Labour Market, Monthly Labour Review 13–28 (June 2001). The two-year period 1997–1998 is the latest available. In more recent periods with a weaker economy, the statistics will be less favourable. Displacement data come from a supplement to the February 2000 Current Population Survey. A displaced worker is one who answers yes to survey questions asking whether you lost or left a job because a plant or company closed down or moved; or because the plant or company remained operating but had insufficient work, the position or shift was abolished, or a seasonal job was completed; or because a self-operated business failed.

R. Blanpain (ed.),
Corporate Restructuring and the Role of Labour Law, 177–196.
© 2003 *Kluwer Law International. Printed in Great Britain.*

them at risk of losing benefits. Nevertheless, after displacement, 83% were covered by some health plan.[2] In summary, these numbers suggest that a high number of long-tenured American workers lose their jobs due to plant closings or other reasons. Most displaced workers, however, suffer relatively short periods of unemployment and find jobs with equal salaries, often in another industry or occupation.

2. OUTLINE OF REGULATIONS OF CORPORATE RESTRUCTURING

Perhaps because of the relatively benign effects of job loss to most workers, American laws do not provide extensive protections against job loss from plant closings or other corporate restructuring. This section of the paper will focus first on the limited protections of workers during corporate restructuring provided by corporate law. Second, the paper then turns to labour law issues involving successor employers. Third, the paper will discuss various employment laws.

2.1. Corporate law protections of workers

2.1.1. General views of american corporate managers

Most American corporate managers strongly believe that they should only serve shareholders. Shareholders usually benefit when their corporation's workers are motivated and productive (unless the costs of motivation outweigh the gains), and so managers often act to benefit workers. But when there is a conflict, as often occurs during corporate restructuring, most American corporate managers believe they should focus solely on the interests of shareholders and not other stakeholders.

A recent comparative survey confirms the striking differences in attitudes between American and other corporate managers on protecting workers.[3] The survey asked senior managers whether "shareholders' interest should be given first priority," or whether "a company exists for the interest of all stakeholders." In America, 76% of managers declared that shareholders' interest have top priority, compared to 71% in the UK, 22% in France, 17% in Germany, and 3% in Japan. Similar answers came when managers were asked whether "executives should maintain dividend payments, even if they must lay off a number of employees," or whether "executives should maintain stable

---

2.   Due to limitations in the survey questions, it is not known what fraction of displaced workers were covered by any health plan prior to displacement, but 70% participated in their own employer's health plan.

3.   The survey is from Allen F. & Gale D., Corporate Governance and Competition, ch. 2 in X. Vives (ed.), Corporate Governance: Theoretical and Empirical Perspectives (Cambridge Univ. Press 2000), and is reported in Marco Pagano & Paolo Volpin, The Political Economy of Finance, 17 Oxford Review of Economic Policy 502, 507 (2001).

employment, even if they must reduce dividends." In America (and in Britain), 89% favoured dividends over stable employment, while about 50% of French and German managers, and only 3% of Japanese managers, favoured dividends over stable employment.

2.1.2. Corporate law mechanics of mergers

In the United States, corporations receive their charter from a particular state, rather than the federal government, and so the law regulating the internal governance of the corporation varies by state. This creates some uncertainties or variability in American corporate law. Nevertheless, most state laws are similar in basic design. Another important feature of American corporate law is the primacy of the state of Delaware. For complex historical reasons, most large corporations are incorporated in Delaware, so that state's corporate law is particularly important.

Let me quickly sketch the American corporate law of corporate restructuring. First, the board of directors is legally in control of the corporation. Shareholders elect the directors to a specific term of years (sometimes individual directors hold staggered terms), but generally shareholders cannot force directors to act in specific ways during their term of office. Thus, for example, if the board of a multi-plant corporation decides to sell or close a single plant, shareholders have no legal right to interfere. Shareholders do have rights to ratify certain major changes in corporate direction. Often, shareholder rights are triggered during corporate mergers.

There are three basic ways one corporation can acquire another: statutory merger; sale of assets; or sale of stock. In a statutory merger, the boards of directors of the two companies agree on a plan of merger and the shareholders vote to approve the plan (usually by simple majority, although some states require a supermajority vote). The surviving corporation obtains all the assets and liabilities of the merged corporation, which can include the collective bargaining contract with employees. The merger plan might propose, for example, that Company A's operations be shut down and the employees dismissed. The shareholders of each corporation must approve this merger. In addition to the right to vote to approve the plan, dissenting shareholders have an "appraisal" right to demand that the corporation cash them out at a fair price set by appraisal. Finally, shareholders in a statutory merger can sue for breach of the directors' or controlling shareholders' fiduciary duty to all shareholders.

The sale of assets resembles a statutory merger in that both boards of directors must approve the sale. If a corporation sells substantially all its assets (a test not always easy to apply), its shareholders must vote to approve the sale. Some states do not provide appraisal rights. More importantly for corporate-law purposes, the buying corporation's shareholders generally have no right to veto the purchase, nor do they have appraisal rights. In general, the buying company does not necessarily obtain all liabilities of the corporation, and often (depending on how the deal is structured) will not be bound to the terms of the selling corporation's collective bargaining agreement.

Purchase of stock is the third basic method for one corporation to acquire another. The key feature here is that the transaction does not require the approval of the selling corporation's board of directors. Rather, the agreement is between the buying corporation (in a plan approved by its board of directors, if the purchase is substantial) and individual shareholders of the selling corporation. Hostile takeovers, in which incumbent managers are ousted against their will, take this basic form. Once the buying corporation has majority control of the selling corporation, it can run the selling corporation as a subsidiary or liquidate it. In general, however, it will be bound by the collective bargaining contract.

2.1.3. Corporate law regulation of fiduciary duties of managers to employees

The preceding sketch of corporate law shows that, with the exception of the hostile takeover through stock purchase, the boards of directors are the key players in corporate acquisitions. Corporate law gives employees, whether through labour unions or otherwise, no formal role in the process. In particular, with rare exceptions (such as Chrysler Corporation), no union representative is a member of the board of directors. A key question, then, is whether the directors must or may consider employee interests when planning and approving sales and acquisitions.

To whom the board of directors owes a fiduciary duty has been a major question in American corporate law. The traditional assumption is that directors owe a fiduciary duty only to their shareholders. Two intertwined issues are lurking here: First, do the corporate directors ever have a legally enforceable duty to employees or other non-shareholder stakeholders? Second, if not, may corporate directors ever consider the interests of employees or other stakeholders at the expense of shareholders consistent with their fiduciary duties?

Turning to the first intertwined issue, in general directors owe a legally enforceable fiduciary duty only to shareholders. An exception may arise, however, when the corporation approaches insolvency. In this situation, some cases suggest, directors owe a fiduciary duty to the corporation as a whole rather than simply the shareholders.[4] Once the company is insolvent, directors may owe a fiduciary duty directly to the creditors, which can include employees.[5]

The reason for requiring firms to stop focusing entirely on shareholders in this situation is that the interests of shareholders and creditors (including employees) can sharply diverge with impending insolvency. To illustrate[6] the

---

4.   *Credit Lyonnais Bank Nederland, N.V.* v *Pathe Communications Corp.*, No. CIV.A. 12150, 1991 WL 277613 (Del. Ch. 30 December 1991).
5.   *Geyer* v *Ingersoll Publications Co.*, 621 A.2d 784 (Del. Ch. 1992).
6.   The illustration is my own, but is similar in spirit to Chancellor Allen's much-discussed footnote 55 in the *Credit Lyonnais* case.

divergence, suppose a corporation teetering on insolvency has assets of $100 million, but owes employees $98 million in back wages (or perhaps more realistically in the American context, owes that money to the employee pension fund). The directors are considering a project that requires an investment of $10 million and has only a 10% chance of making $90 million. The expected value of the project, then, is negative ($10 investment with a $9 expected return). The employees want the directors to reject the project, because they gain nothing directly if it succeeds and lose substantially if it fails and the company becomes insolvent. The shareholders, however, may want the project because they were getting little without it, and the project might succeed and earn them a residual return.

Overall, however, only exceptional cases would give employees or other creditors a legal right to force directors to consider their interests when they conflict with shareholders. The basic focus of directors is on shareholder welfare. As one influential source puts it, a corporation "should have as its objective the conduct of business activities with a view to enhancing corporate profit and shareholder gain."[7]

The second intertwined issue is whether directors, even if not required, ever have discretion to consider employee or other interests at the expense of shareholders. The ALI Principles allow directors to deviate from shareholder gain in three circumstances.[8] First, corporations *must* act within the bounds set by law, even if doing so harms profits. Second, corporations *may* take into account ethical considerations "reasonably regarded as appropriate to the responsible conduct of business." Third, corporations *may* devote a reasonable amount of resources to public welfare, humanitarian, educational, and philanthropic purposes. Putting legal requirements to one side, the other two exceptions (ethical considerations and humanitarian purposes) do not provide much room for corporate directors to consider the interests of employees.

The ALI Principles gives an interesting illustration of a plant closing that tests the degree to which corporate boards can consider employee interests.[9] Suppose a multi-plant corporation with annual earnings of $13-$15 million has one plant that loses $4 million a year with no sign of ever becoming profitable. Deciding to sell the plant, the corporation receives only one bid, from a buyer who proposes to convert the plant to another use and replace all existing employees. Can the corporate directors reject the bid in order to preserve the employees' jobs? Definitely not, says the ALI Principles. Although the action is humanitarian, the expenditures are unreasonably large in relation to earnings. No ethical obligation would justify keeping open the plant, because a corporation "is not ethically obliged to continue indefinitely the operation of a business that is losing large amounts of money, equal to more

---

7.   American Law Institute, Principles of Corporate Governance: Analysis and Recommendations § 2.01(a) (1992).
8.   American Law Institute, Principles of Corporate Governance: Analysis and Recommendations § 2.01(b) (1992).
9.   See American Law Institute, Principles of Corporate Governance: Analysis and Recommendations p. 67–68, illustration 19 (1992).

than one fourth of the corporation's earnings, for the purpose of keeping workers employed."

In the 1980s, many states passed "corporate constituency" or "stakeholder" statutes. These statutes authorise directors to consider constituencies other than shareholders when making decisions, particularly decisions involving mergers, buyouts, and other transactions involving corporate control. Most of the statutes explicitly mention employees as a relevant constituency that directors may consider. Only the Connecticut statute requires directors, however, to consider other constituencies, and even this may be legally unenforceable.[10] While some scholars suggest these constituency statutes represent an important and needed shift in corporate responsibility toward workers and communities,[11] most commentators believe the statutes will be and should be narrowly construed.[12] The enforcement mechanisms are weak, and probably allow incumbent management to justify any decision – whether for or against shareholders – without fear of legal challenge.

It is important to remember that these constituency statutes were enacted during the 1980s boom in corporate takeovers, and their prime function (and hidden motivation) may be to protect incumbent management.[13] The theoretical argument against these statutes is that fiduciary duties are more valuable when they are not shared. Because shareholders are the residual claimants to a corporation, they value fiduciary duties more highly than do employees or other groups who can better protect themselves through contracting devices.[14]

---

10.   Connecticut Stock Corporation Law § 33–313 (1990) reads in part: "a director ... *shall* consider, in determining what he reasonably believes to be in the best interests of the corporation, ... the interests of the corporation's employees, customers, creditors and suppliers." [Emphasis added.]

11.   See Lawrence Mitchell, A Theoretical and Practical Framework for Enforcing Corporate Constituency Statutes, 70 Texas L. Rev. 579 (1991) (arguing that these statutes shift corporate law from a focus on shareholder wealth maximisation to social wealth maximisation by recognizing that the costs to employees and communities of corporate restructuring often outweigh the gains to shareholders); Marleen O'Connor, Restructuring the Corporation's Nexus on Contracts: Recognizing a Fiduciary Duty to Protect Displaced Workers, 69 N.C. L. Rev. 1189, 1190 (1991) (arguing that these statutes allow "judicial intervention to ameliorate the impact corporate restructuring, plant closings and layoffs have on employees").

12.   E.g., American Bar Association Committee on Corporate Laws, Report: Other Constituencies Statutes: Potential for Confusion, 45 Bus. Law. 2253 (1990).

13.   See Jonathan R. Macey & Geoffrey P. Miller, Corporate Stakeholders: A Contractual Perspective, 43 Univ. Toronto L.J. 401, 405 (1993): "the true purpose of these statutes is to benefit a single non-shareholder constituency, namely the top managers of publicly held corporations who want still another weapon in their arsenal of anti-takeover protective devices. In other words, like many other legislative initiatives, other constituency statutes do not benefit the interests or groups that they ostensibly are intended to benefit. Rather, such statutes benefit a well-organised, highly influential special-interest group, namely the top managers of large, publicly held corporations who wish to terminate the market for corporate control."

14.   See Macey & Miller, *supra.*

2.2. Labour law regulations regarding corporate restructuring

Only about 9% of the American private-sector workforce is unionized.[15] Labour law (i.e. the laws which regulate unions and collective bargaining) has developed intricate "successor employer" rules to determine whether an employer, after restructuring, must recognise the prior union or the prior collective bargaining contract.

First, let me sketch the basic process of certifying a union under American law. The key fact of American labour law is that union formation and collective bargaining is highly decentralised. Workers in an appropriate bargaining unit can petition for a union-representation election. If the union obtains a majority in the election supervised by the National Labour Relations Board, the NLRB will certify the union as the exclusive bargaining agent for all workers in the unit. Sometimes the union will represent all production workers in a plant, but often it will represent a certain craft or occupation. Usually the local union will affiliate with a national union (usually called an "international" union because it often has Canadian as well as American affiliates). But the legal focal point is the local union. The National Labour Relations Act (NLRA) requires the employer to bargain in good faith with the certified union to try to reach a collective bargaining agreement over wages, hours, and other terms and conditions of employment. The NLRA does not require agreement, however, and many newly certified unions never obtain a collective bargaining agreement.

An American collective bargaining agreement is for a definite term, usually no longer than three years. The three-year limit comes from tradition and from the contract-bar rule. During the first three years a collective bargaining agreement is in force, rival unions are barred from ousting the incumbent union. After three years, however, workers can vote for a rival union, who will not be bound by a contract, while the incumbent union that signed the contract remains bound. Thus, incumbent unions in the fourth or longer year of a contract are at a significant disadvantage in warding off challenges from rival unions, who can promise better terms that the incumbent cannot legally achieve.

At the end of the (usually three-year) collective bargaining agreement, the employer has a duty to bargain with the union for a new agreement, unless the union clearly no longer commands majority support from the workers. After the contract expires, the employer can only implement changes after it has bargained to impasse with the union about the proposed changes.

With this sketch in hand, let me turn to successorship issues when one company with a certified union and possibly a collective bargaining contract sells the bargaining unit to a successor corporation. The successorship issue has three parts: First, is there a duty to hire, or to give preference in hiring, the predecessor's employees? Second, when must the successor employer continue to recognise and bargain with the union that represented the predecessor's

---

15.   About 35% of the public sector workforce is unionized, so that the overall rate of unionisation in the United States is about 15%.

employees? Third, when is a successor employer bound by prior employer's collective bargaining agreement?

2.2.1. No duty to hire prior employees

All employers have a duty, under §8(a)(3) of the NLRA, not to discriminate on the basis of union status when hiring employees. Thus, the subsequent employer cannot refuse to hire workers because they worked for the prior, unionised employer and so might be sympathetic to the union. However, the subsequent employer is under no obligation to prefer prior workers. As discussed below, much of a successor's bargaining obligation turns on whether a majority of the new workforce comes from the prior employer. Employers wishing to avoid the union have a large incentive to hire workers mostly from the outside rather than the prior employer, if they can find qualified workers. Occasionally, the Board and courts have found discrimination when a majority of the subsequent employer's workforce is not from the prior employer.[16] Many commentators, however, feel that unions have great difficulty proving discrimination in hiring. Hiring standards are vague, and employers can tell from the application whether an applicant worked for the prior employer and be ready with a distinct reason for rejecting the application.

2.2.2. Bargaining obligations of successor employers

As mentioned above, an employer has a duty under the NLRA to recognise and bargain in good faith with a union certified by the NLRB as the exclusive bargaining representative of the bargaining unit. When a business is sold, the question often arises whether the purchaser has this duty to bargain.

In general, the key factor is the similarity in workforces. The most recent Supreme Court case on successorship is *Fall River Dyeing & Finishing Corp.* v *NLRB.*[17] In that case, a business collapsed and was liquidated. Nine months later, after acquiring much of the old company's assets, a new firm began operations at the same location. The firm gradually hired a workforce: in September, 18 of 21 employees had worked for the old firm; in January, 36 of 55 employees had worked for the old firm; and when fully operating in April, 52 of 107 employees had worked for the old firm. The local union that had represented the prior employees demanded that the new employer recognise and bargain with it. When the company refused, the NLRB concluded it committed an unfair labor practice.

---

16.   See US Marine Corp. v NLRB, 944 F.2d 1305 (7th Cir. 1991); Dasal Caring Ctrs., 280 N.L.R.B. 60, 69 (1986), enforced without opinion, 815 F.2d 711 (8th Cir. 1987) (finding a violation of §8(a)(3) when the new employer "conducted its staffing in a manner precluding the predecessor's employees from being hired as a majority of [its] overall workforce to avoid the Board's successorship doctrine").
17.   482 US 27 (1987).

The Supreme Court affirmed, establishing a two-part test for successorship: (1) there must be substantial continuity between the two enterprises; and (2) a majority of the successor's employees must have been employed by the predecessor. The Court held the Board appropriately found substantial continuity despite the nine-month hiatus in operations, describing the substantial-continuity test as "whether the business of both employers is essentially the same; whether the employees of the new company are doing the same jobs in the same working conditions under the same supervisors; and whether the new entity has the same production process, produces the same products, and basically has the same body of customers." Turning to the second part of the test, the Supreme Court held the Board appropriately found a union majority at a time (in January) when there was a "substantial and representative complement" of workers, even though when full operations resumed only a minority of workers had worked with the prior employer. Therefore the successor was ordered to recognise and bargain with the union. The Court emphasised the need of workers for union representation without unnecessary delay.

Scholars have long criticised the successorship test for being manipulable by employers, on the one hand, and often overestimating employee support for the union, on the other. If the second employer is careful not to hire a majority of workers from the predecessor firm, it will not have an obligation to recognise the union. On the other hand, the majority-from-predecessor test has been criticised for too generously presuming the union has majority support of the new workers. For example, suppose only 60% of the predecessor firm's employees in *Fall River* supported the union. (Indeed, most union elections are relatively close, so this is not an unrealistic supposition in general.) In January, when the new employer had a substantial and representative complement, a clear majority (36 of 55) of workers were from the prior employer. But perhaps only 21 or 22 of those 36 prior workers supported the union. If so, most of the successor's employees do not support the union, yet the legal test will presume majority support.

2.2.3. *Contractual obligations of "alter ego" employers*

Suppose a "new" employer takes over the operations of a predecessor before the collective bargaining agreement has expired. If the new employer is the "alter ego" of the predecessor, not only must it recognise and bargain with the union, it will be bound by the collective bargaining agreement. While the focus in successor cases is on the continuity of the workforce, the focus in alter ego cases is on the continuity of the employer. Of course, many of same the criteria apply to alter ego and to successor cases, and courts sometimes mix the two doctrines together.

As the NLRB declared in the leading case of *Crawford Door Sales Co.*, alter ego status arises "where the two enterprises have 'substantially identical' management, business purpose, operation, equipment, customers, and supervision, as well as ownership."[18] In that case, a corporation that installed garage doors was liquidated and ownership transferred to other members of the same family. Operations, equipment, customers, and management remained the same. The Board held that the second firm was the alter ego of the first and therefore bound by the collective bargaining agreement.

The Board and courts developed the alter ego doctrine to prevent owners from evading labor obligations merely by changing their corporate form. While an employer has the right to go completely out of business for anti-union reasons,[19] the employer cannot resume operations in disguised form to avoid the union. Despite the primacy of anti-union animus to the alter ego doctrine, however, it is not a necessary condition. If the other factors are present, an alter ego can be found without evidence of improper motivation. Most alter ego cases involve common ownership of the predecessor and surviving corporation. The other key factor is whether the two entities share common, centralised control of labor relations.

The difficult alter ego cases arise when the corporate transfer occurs through sale of assets. If the corporate transfer occurs through a statutory merger or stock purchase, it is generally easier to find a continuity of operations sufficient for alter ego status. Nevertheless, the courts are reluctant to draw clear lines based on the form of corporate transfer. As the Supreme Court put it: "the refusal to adopt a mode of analysis requiring the Board to distinguish among mergers, consolidations, and purchases of assets is attributable to the fact that, so long as there is a continuity in the 'employing industry,' the public policies underlying the doctrine will be served by its broad application."[20] For example, if after a statutory merger or stock sale the new employer substantially changes operations, particularly labor supervision, it may be inappropriate to call it an alter ego employer bound by the old collective bargaining agreement.

The limits of the alter ego doctrine is shown by a leading Supreme Court case that refused to enforce a predecessor's promise to arbitrate disputes onto a successor, *Howard Johnson Co. v Hotel & Restaurant Employees, Detroit Local Joint Executive Board*.[21] There, a hotel franchisee had a collective bargaining agreement that called for arbitration of disputes and purported to bind any successors to the employer. In an asset sale, the hotel chain purchased the personal property (but only leased the real property) from the former franchisee. The chain fired all the former employees and supervisors, hiring back only 9 of the 45 new employees. The union asked the chain to submit to an arbitrator the question of whether it was obliged to hire more prior employees. The Supreme Court refused to require the arbitration, holding that the promise to arbitrate disputes[22] did not carry over to the new employer.

---

18. Crawford Door Sales Co., 226 N.L.R.B. 1144 (1976).
19. *Textile Workers* v *Darlington Mfg. Co.*, 380 US 263 (1965).
20. *Golden State Bottling Co.* v *NLRB*, 414 US 168 (1973).
21. 417 US 249 (1974).
22. In so holding, the Court had to distinguish its prior decision in John Wiley & Sons v. Livingston, 376 US 543 (1964). In that case, a large corporation "swallowed up" (i.e. engaged in a statutory merger with) a smaller whose collective bargaining agreement had

2.2.4. Protections from the predecessor corporation in corporate restructuring

So far, the discussion of labor law protections has focussed on the successor employer, and whether the duty to bargain or the collective bargaining agreement attaches to the successor. Much of the protection of unionised employees against corporate restructuring, however, is done in the collective bargaining agreement itself rather than through positive law, by enforcing promises made by the predecessor firm. In other words, if the unionised workers value protection against future restructuring, they can bargain with their current employer for it.

Most collective bargaining agreements contain a successor and assigns clause that purports to make the employer's obligations binding on successor corporations. Arbitrators, the Board, and courts usually treat this boilerplate language, however, as just that – boilerplate without legal significance. Often decision makers say that the key question is whether the subsequent employer is a "successor," a question that is answered with the multi-factored analysis discussed above. Unless the subsequent employer is a successor, the "successor" language in the collective bargaining agreement will not be triggered.

Other language in the collective bargaining agreement is treated more seriously. Occasionally an employer will expressly agree in the collective bargaining agreement only to transfer operations to a buyer willing to assume the collective bargaining agreement. In interpreting such a clause, an arbitrator may enjoin the sale or award significant damages for lost wages and benefits if the sale occurs.[23]

Often, a collective bargaining agreement will contain detailed clauses describing the job protections employers will give when they restructure. A recent BNA survey suggests that over 90% of collective bargaining agreements contain provisions enhancing job security, such as "recall rights," subcontracting restrictions, or advance notice of shutdowns. For example, the 1999 four-year agreement between DaimlerChrysler and the United Automobile Workers union includes a plant closing and sale moratorium, where the company promises not to close, sell, consolidate, or otherwise dispose of any bargaining unit under the agreement. Another job protection feature in the auto industry collective bargaining agreements is the companies' promise to hire new workers whenever attrition openings are not filled for whatever reason. This provides a strong disincentive to outsource work.

In general, American unions in collective bargaining agreements try to extract promises that work will not be relocated or subcontracted, but do not

---

not expired. In the collective bargaining agreement, the employer had promised to arbitrate disputes. The Supreme Court held that the successor corporation had a duty to arbitrate so long as there existed a "substantial continuity of identity in the business enterprise."

23. See Samuel Estreicher, Successorship Obligations, in Labor Law and Business Change: Theoretical and Transactional Perspectives 68–69 (Samuel Estreicher & Daniel G. Collins (eds.), 1988).

try to prevent layoffs. There is an economic basis for unions being extremely worried about relocating work while not being concerned with layoffs. First, an efficient collective bargaining contract will consider the number of jobs as well as wages. Compared to an "on the demand curve" agreement where the union negotiates a wage and the employer then sets the number of jobs without union input, both employer and union would prefer a contract with a lower wage and more jobs.[24] Thus, keeping work in the bargaining unit, rather than allowing the employer to move work elsewhere to avoid high labor costs, is extremely important to unions.

But suppose the union has not obtained a specific clause in the collective bargaining agreement preventing the firm to relocate work during the contract term (but the company similarly has no specific clause authorising relocation). Should the default position be that the company be free to relocate, or must it stay until the contract expires? The Board has given conflicting answers to this question, but current law is that relocation is not a breach of the collective bargaining agreement or the duty to bargain unless the contract has specific language prohibiting relocation.[25]

Relocation of work is one thing, layoffs are another. American collective bargaining contracts generally give firms the right to lay off workers during business downturns, but never allow firms to reduce wages or benefits in response to business downturns. Some find it puzzling that workers would not prefer to keep their jobs at reduced pay. The asymmetry of information between the employer and employee, however, suggests that workers should agree to layoffs, but not wage cuts, when the employers says business conditions are poor. Employees cannot easily assess whether business conditions are truly bad when the employer claims they are. Even if conditions were good, the employer has an incentive to claim bad conditions and cut wages, thereby increasing its profits. If the employer's only permissible response to bad conditions is to lay off workers, however, its claim is self-monitoring. If the employer falsely claims times are bad and lays off employees, it reduces the output of the firm and lowers its own profits.[26]

2.2.5. Mandatory vs permissive subjects of bargaining with the predecessor corporation

As discussed in the section above, collective bargaining agreements can and frequently do contain provisions about plant closings, relocations, or other

---

24. For a non-technical explanation of efficient, "off the demand curve" model of bargaining, see Samuel Estreicher & Stewart J. Schwab, Foundations of Labor and Employment Law 50–54 (2000).

25. For an analysis of this issue, and in particular the argument that the Coase Theorem implies that the value the parties place on a relocation clause, rather than the initial legal presumption, determines whether the contract will contain a relocation clause, see Stewart J. Schwab, Collective Bargaining and the Coase Theorem, 72 Cornell L. Rev. 245, (1987).

26. For a formal model using this argument, see Sanford Grossman & Oliver Hart, *Implicit Contracts, Moral Hazard and Unemployment*, 71 AM. ECON. REV. 301 (1981).

restructurings. In general, however, employers are not required to bargain about such provisions.

Employers and unions have a duty to bargain in good faith over mandatory subjects, which include wages, hours, and other terms and conditions of employment. If the subject is permissive, however, the employer does not have to bargain over it, and the union cannot strike over the issue.

The mandatory/permissive line in corporate restructuring is a vexing one. Relocations of work are often a mandatory subject of bargaining, while plant closings often are not mandatory subjects. The key factor is whether the restructuring is based on labor costs, in which case it is a mandatory subject of bargaining, or whether the restructuring is based on issues of capital commitment or the scope of the enterprise, in which case it is permissive.

Two leading Supreme Court cases illustrate the positions. In *Fibreboard Paper Products Corp.* v *NLRB*,[27] the employer decided to contract out the maintenance work in the plant in order to save labor costs. The Supreme Court held that this decision was a mandatory subject of bargaining, emphasising that it involved the replacement of bargaining-unit employees with those of an independent contractor to do the same work under similar conditions, and noting that collective bargaining agreements often contained contracting-out restrictions. Justice Stewart wrote an influential concurring opinion, accepting the result of mandatory bargaining in the case but emphasising that employers had no duty to bargain over "managerial decisions, which lie at the core of entrepreneurial control. Decisions concerning the commitment of investment capital and the basic scope of the enterprise are not in themselves primarily about conditions of employment [and therefore are not mandatory subjects]."

Echoing Justice Stewart's concurrence in *Fibreboard*, the Court in *First National Maintenance Corp.* v *NLRB*[28] held that the decision of a cleaning firm to discontinue the contract with one customer was not a mandatory subject of bargaining. The Court conceded that the decision had a direct impact on employment, but emphasised, first, that employers in decisions like these needed speed, flexibility, and secrecy, and second, that employers always can voluntarily bargain with the union if labor costs are an important factor in the decision. The Court noted that collective bargaining agreements rarely called for bargaining over closings like this. The employer would be required to bargain with the union over the effects of the closing, but not the decision to close.

2.2.6. Summary of labour law protections

In sum, the successorship doctrine has taken many twists since the Supreme Court first addressed the issue in *John Wiley* nearly 40 years ago. The broad contours are clear, however. First, the successor corporation is under no affirmative obligation to hire predecessor workers, although it cannot

27.   379 US 203 (1964).
28.   452 US 666 (1981).

discriminate against them in hiring. Second, the successor corporation has a duty to bargain with the union when a majority of its workforce is from the prior employer and a substantial continuity exists between the two enterprises. Third, the collective bargaining agreement is most likely to be imposed on subsequent employers in two situations: (a) the same individuals or family owns the predecessor and successor corporations; or (b) the transfer arises from a stock sale or statutory merger rather than asset sale, although form of sale is not controlling. Finally, much job protection comes not from labor law itself but from specific provisions negotiated by the parties in collective bargaining agreements. In general, unions will try to protect workers from transfer of work out of the bargaining unit far more than they protect against the elimination of work. Tracking this practice, the law often makes the decision to out-source work a mandatory subject of bargaining, while the decision to close plants is often a permissive subject, unless it clearly turns on labor costs.

3.3. Special legislation concerning transfer of undertakings

3.3.1. Notification of plant closings (warn act)

In 1988, Congress passed the federal Worker Adjustment and Retraining Notification Act (WARN Act), which requires employers with 100 or more full-time employees to give their workers and local government officials 60 days' advance notice of plant closings or mass layoffs. The key term in the WARN Act is "employment loss," which is defined as a termination of employment (other than through discharge for cause, voluntary resignation, or retirement), a layoff for more than six months, or a greater than 50% reduction in hours over a six-month period. With this term defined, the WARN Act then requires notice for any plant closing or mass layoff, which it defines as follows:

A "plant closing" is a temporary or permanent shutdown of a single site that causes an employment loss for 50 or more employees during a 30-day period.

A "mass layoff" is a reduction in force other than a plant closing that causes an employment loss during a 30-day period for 50 employees and one-third of the workforce, or for 500 employees even if less than one-third of the workforce.

The WARN Act has two major exceptions. The first is a "faltering company exception," which applies to plant closings and not layoffs. A faltering company can give less than 60 days' notice if it had been actively seeking new financing to keep the plant open and in good faith believed that notice would jeopardise the negotiations. The second exception is for "unforeseeable business circumstances," and applies both to plant closings and mass layoffs. Such circumstances include a client's sudden and unexpected termination of a major contract, and natural disasters such as floods and earthquakes.

Violators of the WARN Act are liable for up to 60 days of backpay and benefits for each employee, as well as attorney fees, and are subject to a civil penalty of $500 per day. At least one district court has held that punitive damages are unavailable under the act. Courts are not authorised to enjoin the plant closing. The WARN Act does not preempt employees' rights under state law or union contracts. Not surprisingly, the WARN Act's requirements have led to complex regulations and disputes over such issues as part-time employees, adequate notice, and the like.

Importantly, the WARN Act is limited to loss of employment. Employers do not have to give advance notice when a major decision can foreseeably cause a loss of wages or benefits. For example, in one litigated case,[29] a company sold its business to a nonunion business. Almost all the employees continued working for the new business, but with lower wages and benefits. The union sued for a violation of the WARN Act, arguing the employees were effectively laid off without advance notice. In a 2–1 decision, the court held that the sale of the business and a reduction in wages was not a WARN event. If the buying company had laid off workers, it, rather than the selling company, would be responsible for giving the WARN notice. Judge Ferguson, dissenting, complained that the decision "eviscerates the protections against unprecipitated termination which WARN was enacted to guarantee."

In enacting the WARN Act, Congress required the General Accounting Office to assess the effectiveness of the Act. In its 1993 report, the GAO found that more than half of the employers who laid off workers were not required under the law to give notice, primarily because the layoff or plant closure did not affect enough workers. Even where layoffs met the WARN triggers, half the employers gave no notice and another 29% gave fewer than 60 days' notice. The GAO concluded that private enforcement in the courts appears not to be working, and suggested that Congress give the Department of Labor the responsibility and authority to enforce the law.

3.3.2. Bankruptcy rules regarding collective bargaining contracts and retiree health benefits

There are two types of corporate bankruptcy in the United States. In a Chapter 7 bankruptcy, the corporation liquidates by selling its assets and paying off creditors to the extent possible. In a Chapter 11 reorganisation bankruptcy, the bankrupt firm renegotiates some debts, repudiates others, and continues operations under the supervision of a Bankruptcy trustee with the hopes of regaining solvency. Under either type of bankruptcy, the Bankruptcy Code contains elaborate procedures and priorities for resolving claims of creditors. Workers' claims for wages earned after the company files for bankruptcy are considered administrative expenses and given first priority for unsecured claims

---

29. *International Alliance of Theatrical & Stage Employees* v *Compact Video Services, Inc.,* 50 F.3d 1464 (9th Cir. 1995).

in the bankruptcy proceeding.[30] Wages and vacation, severance, and sick pay earned prior to the company's filing for bankruptcy are given fourth priority for unsecured claims. This priority is limited to $4,300 per employee for compensation earned within 90 days before filing or the cessation of business, whichever occurs first.[31]

The Bankruptcy Code has special provisions regulating collective bargaining agreements. The bankruptcy court must specially approve any repudiation of the collective bargaining agreement. Approval will come only after the company has conferred with the union about proposed modifications and shown that the proposed plan is necessary for reorganisation, the union has rejected the plan without good cause, and the balance of the equities clearly favour rejection of the collective bargaining agreement. In one case, the court refused to repudiate a collective bargaining agreement when doing so would decrease operating expenses by only two percent.[32]

In balancing the equities, the bankruptcy court clearly favours unionised workers over the nonunion workforce. If management has any further ability to save costs by terminating nonunion (at-will) workers, the court will not approve repudiation of the collective bargaining agreement. For example, in *In re Allied Delivery System*,[33] the court declared that if cost savings from further cutting nonunion employees would be more than minute, this would alone be grounds for not accepting the company's proposal to change the collective bargaining agreement.

Even if the bankruptcy court approves the repudiation of the collective bargaining agreement, the bankrupt employer still has a legal duty to bargain in good faith with the union. The union retains the right to strike, even when a strike might doom the bankrupt company.

In 1988, Congress added Section 1114 of the Bankruptcy Code, which mandates special procedures before a bankrupt company can repudiate its promise to provide retirees with health-insurance benefits. The employer must bargain with a representative of the retired workers (not necessarily a union, because often the retirees will not have union representation). If no agreement is reached, the employer must apply for court approval of the repudiation in a process similar to repudiation of the collective bargaining agreement.

3.3.3. Health insurance portability for dismissed workers

Most Americans under age 65 obtain health insurance from an employer plan (either their own or their spouse or parent). Although employers are not required to provide health insurance, most large employers do so. When an employee loses his job, a major concern is the availability of health insurance.

---

30. 11 U.S.C. § 507(a)(1) (1994).
31. 11 U.S.C. § 507(a)(3) (1994).
32. In re American Provision Co., 44 Bankr. 907 (Bankr. D. Minn. 1984).
33. 49 Bankr. 700, 704 (Bankr. N.D. Ohio 1985).

Congress has twice reacted to the portability problem of health insurance. In 1986, Congress required employers who offer group health insurance to continue to provide coverage for 18 to 36 months from the time of an event (such as a death or job termination) that might otherwise result in loss of coverage. This type of coverage is called "COBRA" continuation coverage because it was initially enacted as part of the Consolidated Omnibus Budget Reconciliation Amendment Act of 1986.[34] The basic approach of COBRA is to require continued coverage with the "old" employer to give the employee (or spouse or dependent) time to find new health insurance coverage.

COBRA rights are important to workers in individual dismissal cases, because the employer and its health plan still exist. True, the terminated worker must pay the ordinary cost of the premium, even if (as is typical) the employer paid most of the premium while the worker was working. Because of the cost of premiums, the terminated worker often declines COBRA continuation coverage unless he anticipates significant health expenses for himself or his family. The option to accept or decline coverage creates a large adverse selection problem. Healthy workers will forego insurance, while workers needing insurance will sign on at the rate fixed for all employees. As a result, COBRA continuation beneficiaries receive 3.5 times more benefits than they pay in premiums.

COBRA rights are also useful in mass terminations or plant closings, but only if the employer maintains the health-insurance plan. The employer has the power to terminate the plan at any time, and some employers will terminate plans during restructuring as a cost-saving device. If so, the COBRA rights to participate in the plan vanish along with the plan.

In 1996, Congress reacted to the portability problem again, enacting the Health Insurance Portability and Accountability Act ("HIPAA").[35] While COBRA looked to the old employer as the primary source of insurance to bridge the gap during transition periods, HIPAA looks instead to new employers and the private insurance market. HIPAA limits the ability of new employers and private insurers to deny health insurance coverage to new applicants through pre-existing conditions or through waiting periods. HIPAA is especially important to dismissed workers whose old employer has terminated its health-insurance plan. If the workers can find a new job with an employer who offers health insurance, HIPAA generally requires that the worker be allowed into the health insurance plan, even if the worker (or more often, family members) have expensive pre-existing health conditions.

---

34.   COBRA is part of the Employee Retirement Income Security Act (ERISA). The COBRA
        sections are 29 U.S.C. §§ 1161–1168.
35.   HIPAA is another part of ERISA, codified in 29 U.S.C. §§ 701–702.

3.3.4. No general right to severance pay

No generally applicable statute requires employers to make severance payments to dismissed employees. Two caveats to the general rule of no-mandated-severance-pay should be made.

First, employees dismissed for corporate restructuring are generally entitled to unemployment-insurance benefits. UI benefits which typically last 26 weeks and replace one-half of prior wages up to a statutory maximum. During recessions, Congress has always enacted temporary supplemental programs for unemployed workers.

UI payroll taxes are partially experience rated, and so the employer's UI taxes may increase if it lays off workers. If the experience rating were perfect, the employer's taxes would rise by the amount of UI benefits paid to its worker, and the effect would be identical to mandatory severance pay. With imperfect experience rating, the analogy to mandatory severance pay is muted.

Second, the state of Maine requires large firms (employing 100 or more persons) who go out of business or relocate more than 100 miles away to make severance payments of one week per year of service to all workers with more than three years' tenure.[36] In an interesting opinion, the Supreme Court held that the Maine statute is not preempted by the federal ERISA regulation of employee benefits plan, because the state statute does not require employers to adopt a severance plan, merely pay benefits.[37] Nevertheless, the Maine severance-pay statute is nearly unique in the United States.

Employers often voluntarily create severance-pay plans. These plans will be governed by the federal ERISA statute, which regulates employee benefits. Several courts have held that severance plans were triggered when a plant or division was sold, even if employees were immediately hired by the successor corporation and did not miss work.[38] The rationale is that severance pay is payment for past services and becomes due when the relationship ends. Much turns on the exact wording of the severance plan, however. Most well-counseled employer can avoid paying severance pay when a business is sold (assuming workers retain their jobs) by carefully wording the plan to exclude due-on-sale payments.

4. SUCCESSION OF EMPLOYMENT CONTRACTS, ECONOMIC DISMISSALS, AND CHANGES IN TERMS AND CONDITIONS OF EMPLOYMENT

This report has so far not discussed the truly distinctive features of American labor and employment law during corporate restructuring. The distinctive part is coming now, and can be discussed quickly, largely because the distinctive quality is the non-regulation of corporate restructuring.

---

36.   Me. Rev. Stat. Ann. Tit. 26, § 625-B(2).
37.   *Fort Halifax Packing Co* v *Coyne*, 482 U.S. 1 (1987).
38.   E.g., *Blau* v *Del Monte Corp.*, 748 F.2d 1348 (9th Cir. 1984).

As mentioned above, in the United States less than 10% of the private-sector workforce is unionised. Almost all private-sector non-union workers are employed "at will," meaning the employer can dismiss workers at any time for any reason, without notice. To be sure, the past 30 years have seen significant erosions to the at-will doctrine. Most states recognise the tort of wrongful discharge in violation of public policy, classic cases being firing a worker absent for jury duty or because she refused to perjure herself when a government agency is investigating the company for wrongdoing. Third, in addition to tort erosions of the at-will doctrine,[39] courts have recognised implied contracts not to fire workers without good cause and have imposed duties for employers to act in good faith before terminating workers.[40] But these erosions on employment at will need not detain us here, because no American court would ever construe a dismissal because of internal business reorganization as a wrongful discharge in violation of public policy or inconsistent with implied-contract or good-faith obligations of the employer.

Even more important than the common law erosions of the at-will doctrine are the anti-discrimination statutes. These laws prevent employers for discriminating against workers on the basis of race, sex, national origin, religion, age, or disability. Most cases under these statutes arise from terminations, rather than refusals to hire or promote. But other than age discrimination claims, the anti-discrimination statutes are rarely at issue when companies merge or consolidate operations. Employers frequently face age discrimination claims for reductions in force if a higher proportion of older than younger workers are dismissed.

Despite these erosions, the basic at-will status of American employees creates much flexibility for employers wanting to restructure operations. Individual employment contracts do not impede a merger, transfer, or other form of corporate restructuring. If the employer and employees agree, the employees can work for the new entity under the same or different terms. But if the employer wishes, it can simply dismiss the at-will employees if it or the successor firm no longer wants their services.

Employers have complete flexibility on the number of workers they choose to dismiss or transfer to other positions. There is no regulation on transfer of workers, modification of terms and conditions of employment, or changes in duties.

Even in the unionised sector, unions play a minor role. Major corporate restructuring is almost always considered a management prerogative, unless the restructuring focusses on labor costs. Employers must bargain with the union over the effects of the corporate restructuring, but not over the decision to restructure.

---

39.   The literature on the tort erosions is long. For my own effort, see Stewart J. Schwab, Wrongful Discharge Law and the Search for Third-Party Effects, 74 Texas L. Rev. 1943 (1996).

40.   My commentary on the implied-contract and good-faith erosions of employment at will appear in Stewart J. Schwab, Life-Cycle Justice: Accommodating Just Cause and Employment At Will, 92 Michigan L. Rev. 8 (1993).

5. CONCLUSION

American legal protections of workers during corporate restructurings are fewer than most industrialised countries. This gives corporations great flexibility. Large employers must generally give 60 days notice of plant closings and mass terminations. Displaced workers receive unemployment benefits and protection on transferring health insurance benefits. In the unionised sector, successor firms may have to recognise and bargain with the union, and, depending on how the transaction is structured, may be bound for the remaining duration of the predecessor's collective bargaining contract. But 90% of the American private-sector workforce is not unionised.